The Cultural Realm of
European Integration

The Cultural Realm of European Integration

Social Representations in France, Spain, and the United Kingdom

ANTONIO V. MENÉNDEZ-ALARCÓN

Foreword by Stefan Immerfall

Contributions in Sociology, Number 140
Dan A. Chekki, Series Advisor

Westport, Connecticut
London

Library of Congress Cataloging-in-Publication Data

Menéndez Alarcón, Antonio V., 1953–
    The cultural realm of European integration : social representations in
France, Spain, and the United Kingdom / Antonio V. Menéndez-Alarcón.
        p. cm. — (Contributions in sociology ; ISSN 0084–9278 ; no. 140)
    ISBN 0–313–32034–9 (alk. paper)
    Includes bibliographical references and index.
    1. European Union. 2. Political culture—Europe. 3. Group
identity—Political aspects—Europe. 4. Regionalism—Europe.
5. European Union countries—Politics and government. 6. Europe—
Ethnic relations. I. Title. II. Series.
JN30.M453   2004
303.48′24—dc22   2003026905

British Library Cataloguing in Publication Data is available.

Library of Congress Catalog Card Number: 2003026905
ISBN: 0–313–32034–9
ISSN: 0084–9278

First published in 2004

Praeger Publishers, 88 Post Road West, Westport, CT 06881
An imprint of Greenwood Publishing Group, Inc.
www.praeger.com

Printed in the United States of America

The paper used in this book complies with the
Permanent Paper Standard issued by the National
Information Standards Organization (Z39.48–1984).

10 9 8 7 6 5 4 3 2 1

To Laura and Valeria, world citizens

Contents

Foreword

It has been said that the European Union is a federation without a people. For most of its history, European integration was an elite-driven process, rather removed from the minds and hearts of ordinary citizens. But the method of integrating Europe in spite of, or because of, prevailing indifference has run its course. For one thing, as the European Union impinges more and more on their daily lives, people start to care about "Brussels." And they don't like all they see (or that is presented to them by their national media or politicians). Moreover, while the European Union's biggest enlargement is under way to bring in countries of substantially lower economic levels and populations with historical memories not shared by the founding members of the Union, it is by no means clear that its institutions are up to the new situation.

It looks as if Europe's political leaders have lost their sense of direction. At least in the Iraq crisis, the EU's foreign policy was in total disarray, hampered by an almost complete lack of unity among its core members. The European Union is at a crossroads and no one knows for sure which way to go. It is therefore all the more important to comprehend popular perceptions of the European Union and the images its populations have for the future of the integration process.

We do have many surveys that give us a sense of people's attitudes about the EU. But simple questionnaires are not enough to fathom people's interpretation and representation of such a complex organization in the making as the European Union. Such an analysis has to take account of its description in the media, of the assertions of the elites, and, above all, the national context.

This is exactly what Menéndez accomplishes for three countries: France, Spain, and the United Kingdom. His investigation develops key questions for the future of the European Union: What is the interaction between economic and political integration and people's attachments to Europe as a common social organization? How do individual experiences and their symbolic realm connect with European orientation? In what way is national identity constructed in juxtaposition to Europe? Are Europeans, as Menéndez succinctly puts it, really ready to redefine their symbolic boundaries?

Menéndez is very sympathetic to the idea of a vital and strong European Union. He points out that only untied European countries are being heard globally and able to deal with the United States on equal terms. All the more one should heed his result, based on meticulous and broad-ranging research, that national sentiments still loom large. The lack of strong cultural attachment to the European Union does not mean that the population ignores it or does not support some form of European organization. But uniting Europeans on the basis of common cultural grounds is not yet an alternative to the lengthy building of a loyalty of the citizens to European institutions.

If a strong European Union has to be built around the objective of supersession of the nation-state, there will, at least for the time being, be no strong Union at all.

Stefan Immerfall
Schwaebisch Gmuend

Acknowledgments

The Holcomb Research Institute, Indianapolis, the West European Studies National Resource Center, Bloomington, Indiana, and the National Endowment for the Humanities Grant (FS-22884-96), Washington, D.C., funded the research that supports this book. I also benefited from the generosity of the Rockefeller Foundation, which allowed me to spend a month in the Bellagio Center in northern Italy doing Internet research and writing.

CHAPTER 1

Introduction

"L'Europe du XXIème siècle sera culturelle ou ne sera pas."

André Malraux

HISTORICAL BACKGROUND

In the history of Europe there have been several periods in which large parts of Western and Central Europe were united under the same political power. One could mention for instance the Roman Empire, Charlemagne, or the Holy Roman Empire. This unity was accomplished as a result of wars and domination by the most powerful countries and alliances of kings. The Europe that started to be developed in the twentieth century is very different. It is a Europe where each independent country decides to unite to others with a project in common, as a result of everyone's insights, and with an organization of power sharing by every member. The most well-known ideas proposing this type of European integration in the twentieth century go back to the proposals of the Comte Coudenhove-Kalergi (1922) on a society of nations (pan-Europe), and of Aristides Briand advocating a European Union in his address to the League of Nations in September 1929.[1] It is only after World War II, stirred by the ideas of Jean Monnet and Robert Schuman, that a united Europe started to be built. The horrors of the war prompted many leaders to search for a solution that would prevent future wars in Western Europe. In a speech inspired by Jean Monnet, Robert Schuman, then French Foreign Minister, proposed that Western Germany, France, and other countries that wanted to join together should organize their coal and steel resources. In the introduction to his declaration he said:

For peace to have a chance there must first be a Europe. Out of all this will come forth Europe, a solid and united Europe. A Europe in which the standard of living will rise thanks to the grouping of production and the expansion of markets, which will bring down prices. (Fontaine 2000: 3)

Indeed, the struggle over coal and steel resources was perceived, then, as the main cause of the Second World War. After the war, steel-making capacity in France, Germany, and other European countries was such that it would have created a problem of overproduction. Indeed, in the years that immediately followed the war, steel prices were falling and demand was declining; furthermore, there were indications that the producers, as they did before the war, were starting to constitute cartels in order to restrict competition. That is to say that a basic industry such as steel would have been left to speculation and organized shortages. The heightened tensions between Eastern and Western Europe by the end of the forties also stimulated to a certain extent the unity of Western Europe. Monnet pondered at the time "the merits of an international level initiative mainly designed to decompress the situation" of competition between the two big powers in Europe (the Soviet Union and the United States of America) and contribute to establishing "world peace through a real role played by a reborn, reconciled Europe" (Fontaine 2000: 4). In short, the main idea of the project was to create the conditions for a lasting peace in Europe.

The process suggested by Monnet was to incrementally exercise, together, the sovereignty over those aspects that every nation was incapable of exercising alone. In other words, the goal was to create little by little a new, federal Europe. Monnet believed that Europe could only be united by small steps. He was influenced in this project by what happened with the other two Europe-wide bodies created in the 1940s: the European Organization for Economic Cooperation set up in 1948, which had only a coordinative mission and yet had been incapable of coordinating the economic recovery at the European level, and the Council of Europe, created in 1949, which ended up having only deliberative powers. He decided that the best way to be successful was to create at first an organization with limited objectives but with clear power of decision, which would be gradually given additional responsibilities. This step-by-step strategy prompted Robert Schuman to limit the first proposal only to organizing the coal and steel industries under a common authority. Other elements that guided the construction of Europe were concrete practical achievements. This is clearly specified in the preface to the European Community of Steel and Coal Treaty (ECSC): "recognizing that Europe can be built only through practical achievements which will first of all create real solidarity" (cited in Fontaine 2000: 4).

The proposal for creating a high authority overseeing the coal and steel industries was enthusiastically received by West Germany, Belgium, Italy, Luxembourg, and the Netherlands. These countries ended up signing the treaty to establish a European Community of Coal and Steel (also called the Schuman Plan) in Paris in 1951. The six countries that participated in this first treaty were Belgium, France, West Germany, Italy, Luxembourg, and the Netherlands.

This idea of European integration was based on four basic principles, which still today constitute the basis of the European Union: the overarching role of the institutions, the independence of the community bodies, cooperation between the different institutions of the community, and equality between member states. Concrete measures were taken to ensure the application of these principles. For instance, by giving an overarching power in community aspects to the institutions of the community they wanted to assure that right prevailed over might in the community, and limit the possibility of domination and nationalism. Since then, the members of the community bodies (the Commission) have been appointed by joint agreement among the governments of the member countries; they also have financial independence and submit to the control of the European Parliament. The power of the European Parliament has been increased considerably during the 1990s. The third principle, cooperation between institutions, refers to the coordination of policies of the nation-states. The principle of equality allows for the possibility of any member country of any size to veto policies on major issues (unanimity). The specific workings of these institutions have been revised and modified through the years, but the three principles outlined above are still guiding the EU approach to integration.

The process of integration continued with the signing of a treaty in Rome in 1957 by the same six countries to create the European Economic Community (EEC). The founding countries were later joined in 1973 by the United Kingdom, Ireland, and Denmark, in 1981 by Greece, and in 1986 by Spain and Portugal. The last group of countries to join in 1995— Austria, Finland, and Sweden—brought the European Union to 15 countries.[2] The European Union of today has a population of 371 million, and an area of 3234 square meters.

The European Economic Community, in the original version ECCS, was initiated principally to ensure peace and security—"Europe was not built and we had war" said Schuman in 1950 (cited in Fontaine 2000: 3)—and to facilitate an economic flow among its member countries by creating an internal market for goods, services, and capital.[3] In the 1960s and 1970s the common market was consolidated by common policies in agriculture, trade, social affairs, cooperation with developing countries, environment policies, research, and education. In the 1980s its aims became even broader to encompass the political and social, as well as the economic sphere. The EEC came to be called the European Community (EC) to reflect that change.

A salient new impulse was given at the beginning of the 1990s with the Treaty on European Union, also called the Maastricht Treaty (signed in 1992 and ratified by all of the member states between 1992 and 1994). Comprehensive and ambitious, this treaty aimed at providing the basis to heighten the economic and political power of the EC in international affairs. The treaty proposed a single currency and political unity.[4] Following this treaty, the country members of the European Community made significant economic and institutional adjustments during the 1990s, and by the end of the century, the original aim, as stated in the Rome Treaty fifty years earlier, of creating a market without borders among its members for capital, goods, and services was finally accomplished. In 1993 the EC was renamed again and is now officially called the European Union (EU). The Treaty of Amsterdam in 1997 (also called the Consolidated Treaty) and the Treaty of Nice in 2001 amended the Treaty on European Union and the earlier treaties.[5] The latest treaty (Nice) introduced changes in the workings of the European Union institutions and prepared for its enlargement.[6] In January 2002, the monetary union became an everyday reality for most citizens of the Union, with the introduction of euro coins and notes (Denmark, Sweden, and the United Kingdom, for different reasons, choose not to adopt the common currency).[7]

Following Monnet's inspiration, the EU has followed a step-by-step strategy that has increasingly strengthened European unity, and above all, economic interdependence. The reforms carried out during the 1990s by the fifteen EU countries affected the social organization and the economy (deregulation, privatization, fiscal reforms, etc.). As a result, at the beginning of the twenty-first century numerous elements of convergence are visible at the macro level. In other words, the economies of the member countries already have largely undergone the integration process, with a common currency and free movement of goods, capital, labor, and services. And surely, much of the GNP (Gross National Product) of EU member countries results from the internal market.

There are also some similarities in other domains of social life. The model of "social citizenship state" (Esping-Andersen 1990), although considerably altered during the nineties, still prevails throughout the countries of the European Union. The variations in the welfare systems (including social security, unemployment compensation, etc.) are not very large and there are similarities in the employment structures: decline in the agricultural sector and enormous growth in the service sector (employment in which surpasses all other sectors in all member countries). There has also been reduction of differences in levels of formal education. For instance, the proportion of people in higher learning does not differ significantly from one country to another, and previous disparities in formal education levels between some of the countries of southern Europe (Spain, Portugal, and Greece) or Ireland in northern Europe and the formal education levels of the other countries have been considerably reduced. The structure of the age of the population is also approaching relatively similar characteristics. The differences in family structures are gradually disappearing (divorce rates, number of children per family, etc.).

Has this apparent commonality contributed to a more integrated Europe in the political and cultural arenas? To what extent has a European culture, or what some observers call a *cultural area* (Smith 1990, 1995), developed, and to what extent has this process reduced the impact of nationalism in the EU countries?[8] The answers are multifold and certainly problematic. This book will address these issues and attempt to explain the complicated path towards political and cultural integration in the last decade.

Until the late 1980s the European Union evolved almost with the indifference of the population. Indeed, the efforts to unify Europe from the 1950s to the earlier 1990s were largely dominated by the political and economic elites. The average citizen was rather removed from this process. As Limberg and Scheingold (1971) wrote, the interplay between European public opinion and elite action, aimed at greater integration, was characterized by a permissive consensus.

However, after the Maastricht Treaty and the latest moves toward further integration, citizens are more aware of the importance of the EU in their lives. The initiatives, policies, and actions of the EU in several areas such as economics, education, foreign policy, and the environment has produced mixed feelings among the populations of the EU's member countries. They can see that the latest developments have led to a greater level of involvement by the EU in the national governments' formulation of policies and that the EU has become an important issue in internal politics in every country of the Union. By the mid-1990s more and more citizens realized that the European integration process was affecting their everyday lives, and concerns regarding a loss of sovereignty and national identity have emerged among a considerable proportion of the population. Indeed, the voting tendencies observed in the French, Danish, Swedish, and Norwegian referenda, in surveys (Eurobarometer 44 1995, Eurobarometer 46 1996, Eurobarometer 48 1997, Eurobarometer 49 1998, Eurobarometer 50 1999, Eurobarometer 54 2000), and in the debate provoked by the acceleration of the integration process (after Maastricht), revealed that many Europeans feared that increased political and economic union might undermine their national autonomy and identity. This trend is similar to what has been observed on a worldwide scale. Indeed, as many studies of globalization have shown, two contradictory tendencies seem to predominate at the beginning of the twenty-first century:

a tendency toward a global village and economic and cultural integration, and a tendency toward cultural localism and isolationism as a means of self-reproduction and preservation.

Many books have been written on the European Union, but few have examined how the populations' interpretations of the European Union have affected integration. Yet these perceptions of the EU are fundamental for understanding the European Union process. As Connor has correctly noted, "when analyzing sociopolitical situations, what ultimately matters is not what is but what people believe" (1994a: 37). These interpretations are often connected in people's expressions with the issue of national identity and autonomy. In fact, the institutions of the European Union, and particularly the Commission and the Parliament, have recognized that cultural identification with Europe was an essential issue in the pursuit of further integration and, since the 1980s, have been producing documents that reflect this preoccupation. They started with the Genscher-Colombo plan in 1981, which reflected the political will to create a European union based on European identity, and proposed close cultural cooperation between the member countries. It was later expressed in the section on cultural cooperation issued by the European Council meeting at Stuttgart in June 1983, which indicated the intent to expand the realm of European cooperation in the cultural sphere. Cultural co-operation was to be undertaken to develop an awareness of a common cultural heritage among the member countries (Bulletin EC 1983). Likewise, the European Parliament's draft treaty establishing the European Union (1984), which was inspired largely by the federalist Altiero Spinelli, recognized the need for further cultural integration. The European Union Treaty formalized at Maastricht in 1991 specifically stated the need to enhance cultures of states and regions of the European community.[9] A new *Program Culture 2000* (succeeding the *Kaleidoscope, Ariane,* and *Raphael* programs), based on the premises laid down by the Treaty on European Union, is explicitly aimed at strengthening the feeling of belonging to the European Union, while respecting the diversity of national cultures.[10]

The importance of cultural representations in the building of the European Union was also recognized by Jean Monnet by the end of his life: "If Europe needs to be made, we should perhaps start with the culture; the Rome Treaty had made the mistake of not considering culture as one of the European construction's essential elements" (cited in Parlamento Europeo 1983: 2). Culture as defined in sociology comprises language, art, scientific knowledge, ethics, religion, political views, norms, values, and the human faculties and activities aimed at the production and consumption of goods (Williams 1981; Hall and Neitz 1993). In the context of this research I look more specifically at cultural identity and identification, and Delgado-Moreira (1997: 5) provides a definition particularly relevant for my study:

[A]ll cultural identities share a set of characteristics and functions—they provide personal identity, are ethical communities, build historical constancy, are made up by belief, tend to mark a territory, have practical purposes, are thought by their members as conferring marks that differentiate them from the others, enable patterns of behavior, beliefs and a shared language, and have a public presence. An individual can combine a number of these identities, though it is typical of cultural identities to claim monopoly of their members' behavior and thinking in certain domains of action at every moment, or even in all domains all the time.

The idea of the European Union, as it happens with the nation-state, is not something limited to concrete elements but also to abstract entities, images, and memories; that is, the symbolic experiences through which people apprehend the social world and that guide and give meaning to their behavior. Indeed, in the process of living out their lives people ritualize, codify, and transmit cultural scripts and the meanings they attach to them. In short, the social representation of the European Union is a result of the interaction between symbolic and concrete experiences. I therefore study here some of the contents of these representations and how they are produced and reproduced. Social representation is based on the definition by Jodelet (1991: 36): "a form of knowledge, socially elaborated and shared, having a practical goal and converging towards the construction of reality shared by a certain social ensemble . . . "

In sum, the book examines the social representation of the European Union in France, Spain, and the United Kingdom and how cultural identities are reproduced in connection with these representations.[11] The work attempts to reveal the connections between the European Union policies, the representations of these policies in the media, the perceptions of the European Union in the public, and to explain how these connections influence the process of European integration. Specifically, it describes and analyzes how the European union is interpreted and socially represented, as well as describing people's attachments to Europe as a common social organization. Thus, the interactions between individual experiences and their symbolic realm in connection with the process of European integration are analyzed—including the structure of opportunities offered by the EU and the role of conflicting interest in shaping national identity. Accordingly, also analyzed is the interpretation of organizational preferences for the European Union in terms of intergovernmental or supranational perspectives.[12]

In this particular context, the analysis of social representations allows us to understand the elements that shape and reflect the predominant views of the EU in the populations of the countries studied here, and their relations with other member countries. This analysis will also clarify the ways by which citizens experience the EU, and the degree to which they identify with the European union. Indeed, the identification with Europe is linked with the content of the process of integration.

Following Smith's (1991: 99) formulation, the concept of "national identity" in this work "comprises both a cultural and political identity and is located in a political community as well as a cultural one." That is to say, there is a sense of commonness with people from the same national origin and a sense of difference with regard to other communities. Indeed, "social groups tend to define themselves on the basis of a set of ideas to which members can relate positively" (Marcussen et al. 1999: 615) and these ideas can be expressed in the discourse of the members and in their ways of interacting and communicating, and in the reference to common and familiar symbols, codes, or signs. "The members thereby perceive that they have something in common" that is distinct from other social groups, "on the basis of which they form an imagined community" (Marcussen et al. 1999: 615). In addition, national identities are territorially defined and are "therefore, closely linked to ideas about sovereignty and statehood" (Risse 2000: 12). National identities, like cultural representations in general, are not fixed, and depending on a number of factors they can be reproduced or changed.[13] In the particular context of the European Union national identities are now redefined in the relationship between the nation-states and the European Union organization.

The European Union is made up of a multitude of institutional arrangements that complicates the comprehension of the process of integration. I do not claim to grasp in this book all the microcosm of European integration. I concentrate on the fundamental aspects of social representation that define Europe among political, economic, and labor union leaders and the population at large, and I analyze the European Union as experienced in everyday life by the citizens of the studied member states. In short, I try to analyze how the populations of the three studied member states subjectively comprehend the European Union.

Addressed are, in particular, the interconnections between apparent rational explanations, such as relative economic deprivation or loss of political power, and nonrational motives, such as feelings and emotions. Therefore, the analysis includes (1) ideas about cultural identity, national identity, and sovereignty; (2) "instrumental dimensions" (Cinnirella 1996) such as perceived advantages/disadvantages associated with membership in the EU, satisfaction/dissatisfaction with the EU policies, and perceived conflicting interest; and (3) ideas about what kind of organization the EU should adopt. Indeed, when a survey or a newspaper reports certain levels of support for European Union, what does that mean?[14] What type of organization are people supporting or not supporting? Are they talking about a Federal Europe as a new greater motherland, or are they talking about a Europe of Nations, or something different? Furthermore, as Díez Medrano and Gutierrez (2001) propose, one must differentiate degree of identification with the European Union from support for European integration.[15] In addition, I have examined the representations of the EU in the mass media and attempts to understand to what extent the European Union actions and policies have been catalysts of underlying conditions and sentiments that have contributed to given social representations.

The construction of the European Union is a multiple and continuously evolving process in which individuals and groups act, exist, and confront each other, and in which cognitive and normative elements mingle. For Europeans, the European Union is probably the most revealing and visible example of the globalization process at the beginning of the twenty-first century. Accordingly, I address the postnationalist theory's arguments (Bauman 1992; Camilleri 1990; Held 1992; Hobsbawm 1990; McNeill 1986; Miller 1993; Soysal 1996), which suggest the superseding of the national state by the present process of globalization, often presenting the EU as an example of this process.

The study proceeds in two distinct, but complementary directions: (1) top down, analyzing the discourse on the nation-state and the European Union offered by the political, labor union, and economic elites; and (2) bottom up, through the analysis of the general public's perceptions of the European Union. Although there is a mutual influence between the elite and the population at large, looking at both groups, as Smith suggests (1998), provides still more evidence to explain people's relation to the EU and to their nation-state rather than omitting, for instance, the perceptions of nonelite people. The perceptions the populations have of the European Union in relation to the French, Spanish, or British nation-states and national identity cannot be explained solely by the propaganda or the influence of the elite. Similarly, neither the perceptions nor the decisions that politicians make are based only on pleasing the voters. Weber (1976) suggests that national consciousness is a mass phenomenon, not an elite creation. However, as the works of several social scientists (i.e. Anderson 1983; Barker 1927; Connor 1994a; Smith 1994) show, both elements are part of the same phenomenon. Indeed, the masses do play a very important role (often neglected by historians) in the making of a nation, but it is absolutely essential that intellectuals and other opinion leaders circulate the ideas as was done, for example, through newspapers and novels in the eighteenth and nineteenth centuries. Those texts, written in the vernacular languages, allowed their readers to see that other people were sharing their ideas, tastes, and other cultural expressions.

The analysis of French, Spanish, and British attitudes towards the European Union serve as tests cases, but this study's significance is not limited to these countries and to Europe. It also contributes to the substantive sociological explanations of culture and identity. In addition, it provides some insights on the dialectical interactions between cultural integration and economic and political processes, contributing thereby to the sociological theory of integration.

Through the analysis of these cases, this book addresses issues fundamental to understanding the process of European integration but also
explores issues related to nationalist and ethnic confrontations. The European Union offers an excellent instance for analyzing the relationships
between the national state and the supranational organization. In particular, it contributes to our understanding of the issues of cultural integration in a context of multicultural expressions. It identifies the dominant
social representations that serve as reference points between nationalities
and explains how the social bonds are reproduced at the national and the
supranational level. It also provides insights to comprehend the dialectical
interactions between cultural integration and economic and political processes. This book is also relevant for topics of research such as construction
of collective identities, nationalism, agenda setting in public discourse,
and theories of power and subjectivity. The process of European union
constitutes a particular case of the tension between the contradictory process of globalization and particularization.

I hope that the analysis provided in this book will widen and deepen
understanding of the dynamics of the European integration process for
students of Europe, opinion leaders, policy makers, and the people who
are living this process.

METHODOLOGICAL APPROACH AND PROCEDURES

The study of the process of European integration has been dominated
by rational theories, relying basically on quantitative data. Neofunctionalism (Haas 1968; Mutimer 1989; Tranholm-Mikkelsen 1991), intergovernmentalism, and regime theories (Keohane 1986; Keohane and Hoffman
1991; Moravcsik 1994) multilevel governance analysis (Peterson 1999; Peterson and Bomberg 1995) historical-rational institutionalism (Amstrong
and Bulmer 1998), and even federalism (Haseler 2001; Sbragia 1992) have
tended to emphasize the rational choice that states and other actors confronted. In these approaches predominates the analysis of power and interests.[16] Other views, inspired by world system theory and critical theory
(Cox 1987; Gilpin 1992), conceived the nation-states and the European
Union mostly as the product of worldwide systems of economic or political power, exchange, and competition. All these perspectives, although
instrumental in producing very important research on the EU, have sel-
dom addressed the substantive significance of culture and its organizational presence in the European Union, particularly such aspects of culture
as symbols and social representations as well as beliefs and expressions
of concrete social relations (including feelings and emotional attachments
to particular institutional arrangements).[17] One noticeably important ex-

ception was the attempt by Inglehart (1977) to explain levels of identification with Europe. He suggested that individual levels of identification with Europe would depend on what he defined as cognitive mobilization, level of education, and postmaterialist values, classifying individuals accordingly in a continuum from parochialism (less identified with Europe) to cosmopolitanism (more identified with Europe).[18]

However, in the second half of the 1990s a range of works addressing nonrational and subjective aspects of European integration has emerged, for instance sociological institutionalism (Risse 2000) and sociopsychological analysis (Cinnirella 1996; De Rosa 1996). Also recently published are studies on the production and reproduction of national identity and the nation-state in Europe (Crawshaw 2000); on textual analysis and representation of national identity in France (Featherstone 1995); on the concept of European identity (Schlesinger 1994); on the impact of European membership on Finnish national identity (Honko 1996); and on European cultural policy (Shore 1993). These works provide a useful framework for the analysis of social representations and national identity and suggest a cultural approach that is attentive to the interaction of symbolic and tangible structures.

It is within this wide theoretical stream that my research is located. In this perspective, the nation-state and the European Union are culturally constructed and embedded, rather than unanalyzed rational actors, and social representations "contextualise, motivate, and legitimate group actions" (De Rosa 1996: 383). More specifically, the paradigm considered in this research includes the production and diffusion of social representations and elements of social identity theory as proposed by Breakwell (1993), De Rosa (1996), and Risse (2000). Culture is analyzed as substantially involved in the economic and political decision-making processes, and cultural integration is not viewed just as the result of market integration.

The methodology adopted in this research recognizes the importance of an approach free of determinism and the simultaneity and continuous linkage between individual action and structural phenomena. The concept of structuralism is inspired by Bourdieu's definition (1984), which means that within the social world there exist objective structures, historically produced and independent of the consciousness and will of agents, that are able to shepherd the daily activity of these agents as well as their social and individual representations. At the same time social reality has a specific meaning and relevant structure for human beings living, acting, and thinking within those structures.

The social representation of the European Union is embedded in a social dynamic in which individuals and groups act, exist, and confront each other, and in which the cognitive and the normative elements mingle. Between individuals, nation-states, local governments, and the European

Union lie any number of interests and groups, such as political parties, unions, and business organizations. All of these groups depend on and conflict with each other. Indeed, these agents (particularly political parties, labor unions, and businesses organizations) play a major role in the transmission of ideas and in shaping the agenda and terms of the debate concerning the European integration process.

The measure of social representations and perceptions of identity are based on the subjective criteria that the interviewees use to characterize their experiences with the EU, that is, how intensely people identify with Europe and with the nation-state, what meaning they attach to the European Union, and which boundaries people set in their idea of the European Union.

Interpreting the meaning people assign to their support or rejection of supranational structures requires the investigation of the interconnections between apparent rational explanations, such as relative economic deprivation, and nonrational motives, such as symbols and feelings. This includes examining the dynamism generated by the many divisions within the national domain itself (inconsistencies between individuals and political organizations for example), as well as the contradictions produced by the process of integration. Also important is, how the processes of social representations of Europe are formed and internalized and how these representations contribute to identification or rejection of Europe as an overarching organization. Specifically, we will be looking at the classical factors proposed in the literature on identification, such as common fate, cultural proximity, historical experiences and representations, shared threat, and so on (see for instance Lipiansky 1986; Tajfel 1981; Turner 1981; Zavalloni and Louis-Guerrin 1984). Following in particular Zavalloni and Louis-Guerrin, the "individuals should be considered in relation to the world" as being objectively situated in a social matrix. The elements of this matrix in this particular research are membership in a given society and culture, in the nation, and in the European Union. In this approach certainly identity is contextualized and allows us to understand the elements, factors, and so on that become meaningful for the people in reference to what happens in a given context, that is, in relation to the experiences and ideas they are submitted to or confronted by in the process of European integration. Differences according to gender, age group, and sector of the economy will be specified only when they are significant.

The study is based on primary and secondary data. I compiled evidence from different sources using three major techniques of research: document analysis, content analysis, and in-depth, semi-structured individual interviews. Document analysis, defined broadly here, included a detailed inspection of European Union institutions and member countries' official documents, newspapers accounts, scholarly books, and articles, and analysis of surveys related to European integration issues. The battery of questions in these surveys includes items that seek to evaluate the different dimensions of support. The most important ones related to this research will be reviewed and analyzed here, especially the questions that address the dimensions of support for European integration such as diffuse/affective and evaluative/utilitarian. The diffuse/affective dimension of support attempted to measure the vision of the *idea of Europe* without tying the answers to any specific political or economic institution. The evaluative/utilitarian measurement of support attempted to evaluate the calculated appraisal of the immediate costs and benefits of membership in the European Union as well as the measurements that attempt to quantify identification with Europe and national identity.[19] These measurements allowed interpreting the meaning people had of the complex process of European integration, with the awareness that there were manifold aspects of meaning to be discerned. We are analyzing an organization that is in the making. The European Union is a hybrid—neither a confederation, nor a federation, nor a suprastate. It is an organization with some characteristics of all of the above and some characteristics that are not included in any international organization Because of the sui generis nature of the EU, most categories used to define it tend to be problematic: we will try to take into consideration the context in which definitions and categories are used and the function that these definitions take in a particular representation. Because in the interviews I was also looking for explanations about the issues, the data permit a better understanding of people's perceptions about the EU than do the surveys—which would produce changes from one year to another of about 10 points difference one way or the other—for example, concerning support for further European integration. The interviews seem to me to present the advantage of uncovering the deepest roots of support or rejection for the EU. In addition to formal interviews, I was also acquainted with people's views on European Union through informal discussions.

The main documentary sources for this project were the documentation centers of the European Commission in Brussels, London, Paris, Madrid, Luxembourg, The European Parliament in Strasbourg, the web sites of the political parties and the national assemblies and senates (of France, Spain, and the United Kingdom), the library of Duke University (North Carolina), the libraries of Notre Dame and the Helen Kellogg Institute for International Studies (Indiana), and the library of Indiana University.

The specific purpose of the content analysis was to examine differences in newspaper coverage of issues dealing with the European Union in France, Spain, and the United Kingdom. Content analysis was conducted on the newspapers that were viewed as the most influential in each country, that is to say, *Le Monde* in France, *El País* in Spain, and *The Times* in the United Kingdom. In deciding which newspaper to analyze, I considered a combination of perceived influence of the publication on the differing readership of the country and the circulation (number of issues published per day). In the case of the United Kingdom it was difficult to say which newspaper, *The Times* or *The Guardian*, had more influence on the population and the elites. I choose *The Times* because it published a slightly larger number of issues than *The Guardian*. A sample of eighty-eight issues of each newspaper from May 2001 to September 2002 was subject to the analysis. To select the specific issues to be analyzed a combination of two sample techniques were used: composite and purposive. Seven issues per month with the same date of publication were chosen for each newspaper. The month of August was not included in the study. I constructed a composite week for each month.[20] However, when there were special events (such as meetings of the European Council, or some particular incidents that directly involved the EU institutions, etc.) in the EU then the sample of issues to analyze was chosen according to the dates of these events. The content analysis included the number of articles dealing with European Union issues and the type of coverage in terms of negative, neutral, or positive content. Negative content was defined as any coverage that presented the country members confronting each other, concentration on the negative impact of a particular EU policy or action, or a negative portrayal of EU officials. Obviously, the positive coverage included the opposite, that is, emphasis on the positive impact of EU policies or actions and the positive portrayal of EU officials. Neutral content refers to the coverage that I could not interpret as having a direct positive or negative content.

In addition, I made special efforts to watch television news in all three countries during my visits every year during the last six years, and particularly during the 15 months I spent doing research in Europe, from May 2001 to August 2002. I recorded only the basic topics being addressed in the news concerning the EU, but this observation was not systematic.

The unit of analysis was any article mentioning the European Union. The statistics used were simple percentages. The first step consisted of counting how many articles, if any, were written on the subject and how extensive was the coverage of European Union issues, and the second step in the analysis was to see what type of coverage was given to these issues.[21] The contents of the articles examined were placed in positive, neutral, or negative categories regarding coverage of European Union policies and/or declarations of EU officials. The most important dimensions studied were: major EU initiatives (such as monetary union), European Army, role of the EU in international affairs, incidents between member countries, equity/inequity in cost-benefit terms, identities, actions of the EU institutions (Commission, Court of Justice, Council, etc.), and EU officials. The collected data has been quantified (when possible) and summarized, in addition to being interpreted and structured in the text according to the established objectives and categories mentioned above. Of course, concentrating on these newspapers does not give a complete picture of how the EU is represented by the media. This analysis allows seeing only how these newspapers, which have a large proportion of highly educated readership, represent the EU. It serves as an important complement in the attempt to explain people's views on the EU in the three countries analyzed here, but the limitations of time and resources did not allow for a more extensive systematic research of other outlets, such as TV or newspapers with more popular readership.

The in-depth interviews enhanced the documentary research and allowed a better understanding of the interactions between individual experiences and their symbolic realm, in connection with the nation-state and the process of European integration. First-hand qualitative knowledge obtained through interviews is very valuable for understanding the multilevel and dynamic balance that characterizes the relations between individuals, groups, nations, and the EU. This technique of research allowed gathering data on people's perceptions beyond the official declarations of leaders, as reported in newspapers, and more in-depth information on perceptions than the surveys generally offer. It allowed me "to unlock the workings of social understanding and definitions and to make these a part of the explanation of historical processes and outcomes"(Ragin 2000: 2). Indeed, "qualitative research can account for the historical complexity that lies behind the interpretation/construction of a group or one's own identity," thus contributing to a better understanding of the narratives that inspire their discourses (Delgado-Moreira 1997: 15). The qualitative study also facilitates an understanding of the different and often contradictory cognitive and emotional values of diverse cultural identities for each individual. As Delgado-Moreira writes, "We can learn which identities are being mobilized on what grounds and to what ends" (1997: 16).

The challenge of this research was to deal with the complexity and diversity of interpretations regarding the institutions of the European union and its policies. Although some generalizations are unavoidable, I made a special effort not to mistake individuals for their discourse and tried to avoid identifying them with homogenous positions.

I also tried as much as possible to avoid preestablished categories during my conversations with the interviewees. As is well known, one of the problems with survey research and many methods of interviewing is that the categories given in questionnaires often force interviewees to respond within those established categories, which most likely are not their own. As it happens, with nationalism, the social representation of the EU is a question of invention, of continuous development of consciousness within a particular context that itself varies constantly. The EU, in other words, is continually invented and reinvented by all the actors. In this process the media and the political leaders play a major role in the debate, and more specifically, in agenda setting regarding the EU in each country.

That is to say, I am analyzing the EU in the making by looking at the different interpretations of events, policies, consequences of policies, EU summits, and so on, and how the citizens at large believe themselves to have been affected by the EU. This includes exploring the social practices and discourse through which the European consciousness is constituted and reproduced.

I am aware that in the process of explaining tendencies and grouping answers according to certain categories, percentages, and so forth, I am most likely simplifying a rather more complex reality. Unfortunately no researcher can escape this straightjacket if one attempts to make sense of what one is observing and studying.

The interviews were conducted in France and Spain in spring 1996–97 and 1999, and in spring and fall 2001. Anonymity of the interviewees was guaranteed. In the United Kingdom the interviews were conducted in fall 2001 and spring 2002. In-depth interviews followed the procedure developed by Sullivan (1992) and Seidman (1991), a procedure that is open but focused. To select interviewees, I used a combination of key informants and stratified quota sampling (cf. Neuman 2000; Wimmer and Dominick 2000). The concept of political leaders includes the top leaders of a party in the region, most of whom are also important national figures; these include general secretaries, congressman, senators, mayors, and high-ranking officials. In order to have a representation of different opinions and relays of the population at national and regional levels (political and labor union leaders), people from the following categories were interviewed: mayors, municipalities' upper-level staff, leading figures of political parties (including general secretaries, members of the parliament, and senators), members of the European Parliament, labor unions, and professional and business associations. A total of 181 leaders was interviewed (70 in France, 67 in Spain, and 44 in the United Kingdom). A total of 208 lay citizens (84 in France, 78 in Spain, and 46 in the United Kingdom) was interviewed, including individuals from the three main sectors of the economy (agriculture, industry, and service), equal numbers of women and men, and three age groups (18–30, 31–50, and 51 and older). The terms *lay citizens* or *lay people* refer to those respondents from the general public who do not occupy socially recognized positions of leadership. For lack of resources I could not continue interviewing more people in the United Kingdom. However, I believe that the variety of opinions on the EU in this country was still well represented in the limited number of interviews that I was able to conduct.

In France, I interviewed leaders from six national parties: the center-left Parti Socialiste-PS (Socialist Party), the conservative center-right and Gaullist UMP, the center-right Union Démocratique Française-UDF (French Democratic Union), the Parti Communiste-PC (Communist

Party), the right wing Front National-FN (National Front), and Les Verts (The Green party).

The UMP party was constituted in April 2002, just before the presidential and legislative elections. It was formed by the alliance of the Gaullist Rassemblement Pour la Republique-RPR (Alliance for the Republic), and a large part of the members of center-right Union Démocratique Française-UDF. The totality of the RPR is now members of the UMP (the RPR has disappeared). Before the elections a group of political officials of the UDF decide to integrate the recently formed UMP. After the elections to the presidency and the relatively low percentage of votes received by their candidate (6.84 percent), half of the elected members of the parliament of the UDF also joined the UMP. I started the empirical research for this book in 1996 when the UMP did not exist, but for the sake of clarity I will use the new name when referring to members of the then RPR. The union leaders belong to the three major unions: Confédération Générale des Travailleurs-CGT (Workers' General Confederation), Confédération Française Démocratique du Travail-CFDT (French Democratic Work Confederation), and Force Ouvrière-FO (Worker's Power). The business leaders were members of the main French Business and Industrialist association the Confédération Nationale du Patronat Français-CNPF (National Confederation of French Employers). The leaders interviewed, through their functions within their party, union, or business association, were also linked to the establishment of policies regarding the European Union.

I conducted the interviews in Ile de France (Paris and its suburbs), in the Haute Garonne (the majority of interviews were conducted in Toulouse and its suburbs), in Alsace (Strasbourg and its suburbs), in Lorraine (Mulhouse and its suburbs), in Lyon, and in Provence-Alpes-Côte d'Azur (Arles, Avignon). Leaders from other regions, such as Bretagne and Aquitaine, were interviewed in Paris.

In Spain, I interviewed leaders from the three main national parties and the main regional parties: the center-left Partido Socialista Obrero Español-PSOE (Workers' Spanish Socialist Party) and the Partido Socialista de Cataluña-PSC (Catalan Socialist Party); and the conservative center-right Partido Popular-PP (Popular Party) and the Catalanist Convergencia y Unión (Union and Convergence); and the leftist Izquierda Unida-IU (United Left), Iniciativa por Cataluña (Initiative for Catalonia), Izquierda Republicana de Cataluña (Republican Left of Catalonia), and Bloque Nacionalista Gallego-BNG (Galician Nationalist Block). The union and business leaders also include the top leaders of the union or association in each region. The union leaders belong to the two major unions: Comisiones Obreras-CCOO (Workers Commissions) and Union General de Trabajadores-UGT (General Union of Workers). I made an effort to interview those people who, through their functions within their party, union, or business association, were also linked to the establishment of policies regarding the European Union.

The regions of Spain in which I conducted the interviews are Andalusia (Sevilla, Granada, Cordoba, and Cadiz), Asturias (Oviedo, Gijon, Llanes, and Langreo), Catalonia (Barcelona), Galicia (Santiago de Compostela, La Coruña, Lugo, and Vigo), and the Community of Madrid, which includes the city of Madrid and its suburbs. Because of their economic, cultural, and political characteristics these regions represent different perspectives on the process of European integration. People from other regions, such as the Basque country, were interviewed in Madrid. Members of the European Parliament were also interviewed in Strasbourg.

In the United Kingdom, I interviewed political leaders from the three main parties: the Labor Party, the Conservative Party, and the Liberal Democrats. I attempted on several occasions through e-mail and telephone calls to arrange some interviews with the Green Party, but I was not successful. As stated earlier, due to limited resources I could not travel as much in the United Kingdom as I did in France and Spain, and therefore I arranged to interview people when they were in London for different activities. Representatives from all the regions of the country were interviewed in London and its suburbs, and Members of the European Parliament, in Strasbourg. At the level of the lay people the sample was rather biased towards those people residing in London and its suburbs. I did manage however to interview 14 persons from Wales, Scotland, and other parts of the country who were in London for business, for study, or for vacation. I interviewed also representatives of the larger confederations of business and industry.[22]

In the three countries, when quoting people who were interviewed in a region that was not their own, I mention both their constituency of origin and the place they were interviewed. I will specify the region and not the city. In the case of Spain when I refer to Madrid, it means Community of Madrid, which is an administrative region in itself that includes Madrid and its suburbs. The same is true for London, England: when specifying London I am referring to London and its suburbs; and for Paris and suburbs in France, this includes also the departments surrounding Paris (departments 78, 91, 92, 93, and 94).

The interviews were directed to assess people's perceptions regarding European integration (that is social-psychological and cultural questions) and the importance the mentioned segments of the population attached to this integration process. The interviews included some general questions on structural aspects of the EU, but more specifically, interviews were oriented to gather information on cultural identification, cultural pluralism, the meaning of European integration, how they saw their country's role within the European Union and its relationships with the European institutions, perception of cost benefits derived from EU membership, perception of equity/inequality derived from belonging to the EU for oneself and for the country, perception of the position the country occupies in the structure of the EU decision-making process, perception of the influence of the European Union on national political and economic arrangements, and the significance of Europe. Each respondent was interviewed for about one hour, with mostly open-ended questions. This research draws also on data from previous studies by the author (1993, 1996, 1998). To ensure the respondents' anonymity, the generic term *political leader, union leader,* or *business leader* is used instead of the position these people occupy in the party, labor union, or business association.

This work does not claim to extend the findings to other member states of the Union. Therefore, when using the term "member countries" in the conclusion, we are referring to the countries studied here: France, Spain, and the United Kingdom. All translations from French and Spanish are mine unless otherwise noted. The data presented regarding the interviews have been compiled from spring 1996 to spring 2002. When significant changes in the data occur there will be explanations in the text.

A BRIEF EXPLANATION OF THE EUROPEAN UNION INSTITUTIONS

There are three main political decision-making bodies that constitute the European Union. The Council of the European Union (also called the Council of Ministers) is the main policy-making body that most closely reflects the 15 member-states and their individual interests. According to the topic being debated the Council assembles together the ministers of finance, agriculture, foreign affairs, education, and so forth. Although it is the main legislative body, in a range of issues it shares the legislative power of co-decision with the Parliament, for instance in budgetary matters. The Council also coordinates the activities of member states in implementing common economic, foreign, and security policies (police and judicial cooperation, immigration, etc.). A directly connected institution is the European Council, made up of the heads of state, which meets twice a year usually. The European Council generally establishes the broad guidelines that the Council of Ministers and the other institutions will then follow.

The European Parliament enjoys far less power in the decision-making process than the Council, although its approval is necessary in the adoption of many European laws and the budget. It also approves the nomination of the members of the Commission and exercises political supervision over all the EU institutions. The Parliament is the only EU institution whose members are selected by voters of each member country in direct elections.

The European Commission is a quasi-executive body representing the European Union as a supranational organization. Its members are nominated by the nation-states after they have been accepted by the Parliament. The commission initiates most of the legislative proposals that it presents to the Council and to the Parliament for approval. It also insures that the treaties and laws of the EU are followed and accurately applied and represents the EU in the international arena, negotiating international agreements in trade and cooperation. The Commission implements the policies, programs, and budget approved by the Council and the Parliament. In addition to these main political institutions the EU also has a number of more technical institutions such as the Court of Justice, the Court of Auditors, the European Central Bank, and several major committees and agencies.[23]

ORGANIZATION OF THE BOOK

The book includes six chapters, written along chronological and thematic lines. Chapters 2, 3, and 4 describe and explain French, Spanish, and British perceptions and social representations of the EU. Chapter 5 analyses the enlargement process. Chapter 6 compares these countries in terms of perceptions, attachment to the EU, and concrete experiences with the EU, and concludes with a theoretical understanding of the main findings and suggests possible developments in the process of European integration. Part of the book draws on previous publications by the author, especially chapters 2 and 3. The excerpts that have already been published are reprinted here with permission.

NOTES

1. Aristide Briand was the first head of government to defend the idea of a united Europe, but in the first half of the twentieth century many voices demanded a united Europe. For instance, the philosopher José Ortega y Gasset asserted in the 1950s that the political configuration of Europe of national independent states did not respond to the reality of Europe: "Europe is not and will not be the internation because that means in the view of the historical record a hollow, a vacuum and no more. Europe will be the supranation." (Ortega y Gasset 1989: 236). Ideas promoting European integration on the basis of free common decision can be traced back to the beginning of the eighteenth century with the publication in 1713 of the *Projet de traité pour rendre la paix perpetuelle en Europe* (Project of a Treaty to Bring Permanent Peace to Europe) by the abbey Saint-Pierre (1761). Inspired by Saint Pierre, Jean Jacques Rousseau published in 1782 *Jugément sur la paix perpetuelle* (Judgement on the Eternal Peace) suggesting a confederation of princes. In the nineteenth century one could mention as well the proposition of Victor Hugo, which suggests in 1849 a "great sovereign Senate that would be to Europe what the parliament is to England" and a mention of the United States of Europe

(Cassen 2003: 8). Also in the nineteenth century Blöntschli proposed (1871) a European commonwealth, and the French lawyer Gaston Isambert a project of European confederation.

2. For a detailed story of the European Union since 1946 see http://www.europa.eu.int/abc/history/index_en.htm.

3. The sponsors of the European Economic Community, Jean Monnet and Robert Schuman, proposed as its basic criteria the integration of the states and the establishment of peaceful methods for resolving conflicts among them: "Out of all this will come forth Europe, a solid and united Europe. A Europe in which the standards of living will rise thanks to the grouping of production and the expansion of markets, which will bring down prices" (Robert Schuman Declaration 1950, cited in Fontaine 2000).

4. The Treaty on European Union (Maastricht Treaty) which took effect in 1993, had as its core the phased introduction of economic and monetary union. It also increased the powers of the European Parliament, enlarged the scope of vote by qualifying majority in the Council, and added two new pillars of intergovernmental cooperation to the one supporting the European Economic Community: Common Foreign and Security Policy and Internal Security.

5. The Treaty of Amsterdam allowed for the possibility of closer cooperation within the single institutional framework, to enable certain member states to work together, in the interests of the union, when not all of the member states wanted to, or could, do so at that point, on the understanding that they would be free to join the group at a later date. The mechanism for closer cooperation, however, was hedged with strict conditions that limited the practical scope for its application. In order to make the mechanism more workable, the Treaty of Nice removes the right of each member state to veto the launch of enhanced cooperation, currently provided for in the treaty. It requires a minimum of eight member states for establishing enhanced cooperation and provides for the possibility of enhanced cooperation in the field of Common Foreign and Security Policy (CFSP), except as regards defense. It ensures that enhanced cooperation occurs within the framework of the European Union, respects the role of the institutions, and allows the member states that do not participate immediately to join in whenever they wish. http://www.europa.eu.int/comm/igc2000/dialogue/info/offdoc/guidecitoyen_en.pdf.

6. The most salient aspects of the Treaty of Nice are: giving the parliament a more active role as co-legislator, modifying the decision-making process in the council, allowing qualified majority vote in areas previously decided by unanimity, a change in the weighting of votes (reinforcing the mechanism of enhanced cooperation already established in the previous Treaty of Amsterdam), and limiting the number of commissioners to one per member state (once the enlargement is completed, this will modify the workings of the Court of Justice in order to share tasks between the Court of Justice and the Court of First Instance).

7. The euro was already introduced in the commercial exchange between countries, banks, and so on in 1999 but was not used by the citizens in their daily transactions until January 1, 2002.

8. *Nationalism* is defined here as a consciousness of belonging to the nation-state, together with sentiments and aspirations for its security and prosperity. This definition is based on Anthony Smith's definition (1991: 72–73), although I added

the notion of attachment to the state as being important to the nation, in the context of the European Union. The tendency to equate the attachment to the nation (nationalism) with loyalty to the state (patriotism)—a conflation suggested by Connor (1994b)—is so dominant among both lay people and political and economic leaders that it would be futile to try to distinguish between them. Indeed, the interviewees perceive the state as either the political extension of the nation or its synonym, and the sentiment of national identity includes being part of the state. Furthermore, in the popular imagination this duality constitutes their collective consciousness. In any case, this distinction is not fundamental for the purpose of this research. Perhaps this distinction would have been relevant if I were studying the relations between the nationalist groups in the Basque country or in Catalonia as compared with the mindset of the rest of Spain or Europe. See the work of Keating (2000) for an extended analysis of this relation. Whether in Spain or the United Kingdom, the question that I was dealing with was the social representation of European Union, and whether the interviewees had a positive or negative image of Europe independent of whether their attachment was more to the state or to their nation within the state. Of course in a few cases the respondents expressed a strong attachment to what they called their nation (Catalonia, Basque country, Scotland, etc.). Another observation, not directly related to my main objectives but that deserves to be mentioned, was that contrary to what I hypothesized, there was not a significant difference among the people interviewed in terms of their attachment to Europe and attachment to the subnational arrangement (Catalonia, Scotland, etc.). Indeed, I thought that because of the desire for further independence from the larger nation-state, some of the nationalist interviewees would be more inclined to support further European integration. But in fact, the few people I interviewed who most identified with the subnational arrangement viewed Europe as a part of the complex of nation-states that are dominating them. This of course needs further research and further analysis that I will not do in this book.

9. Paragraph 4 of article 151 requires the community to take cultural aspects into account in its action under other provisions of the treaty and to promote cultural diversity. "Culture must therefore also be taken into consideration when developing Community action in its various forms, and especially when defining activities and policies. More specifically, and by way of example, culture must contribute to European citizenship, to personal and human development (through education), to economic and social cohesion among Member States, to job creation in Europe, to eliminating exclusion, and generally to enriching the quality of life in Europe." The specific aims and fields of intervention listed in article 151 of the treaty cover all aspects of culture and open up a broad range of activities to community action. Its aims are: "to contribute to the flowering of the cultures of the Member States, while respecting their national and regional diversity; at the same time to bring the common cultural heritage to the fore" (Treaty on European Union, 1992, Title XII, art. 151).

10. The various areas of intervention at the European Union level that are included in the first framework program in support of culture (Program *Culture 2000*) are defined as follows: "to improve the knowledge and dissemination of the culture and history of the European peoples; to conserve and safeguard cultural heritage of European significance; to support non-commercial cultural exchanges;

to encourage artistic and literary creation, including in the audiovisual sector (the latter area is covered by the *Media II* program, *audiovisual policy*, audiovisual broadcasting, and the guarantee fund for film and television); to highlight cultural cooperation with third countries and the competent international organizations, especially the Council of Europe" (European Commission 2000).

11. Accordingly, although I will certainly mention the concrete economic reasons and factors that might contribute to perceptions of the EU, including support or rejection of European integration, I will not discuss those factors in detail. This has been addressed in many other publications. See for example, Bosch and Newton (1995); Anderson and Kaltenthaler (1996).

12. When asking questions about the type of organization to lay people, when necessary (which it was in most cases) I explained at length what form of organization a federation would take compared to a confederation of nation-states, giving concrete examples, before been able to obtain some meaningful answer. I did this in the three countries studied.

13. The concept of national identity is related to the concept of social identity, which refers to the link between individuals and the social groups to which they belong. As Tajfel (1981: 255) defines it, "social identity is that part of the individual's self-concept which derives from his knowledge of his membership of a social group (or groups) together with the value and emotional significance attached to that membership." National identity is the same attachment, but to the nation-state.

14. These surveys basically measure people's satisfaction with the EU and whether they support further European integration in the abstract.

15. Indeed, as Díez Medrano and Gutierrez (2001: 6) write: "one may strongly support European political integration without strongly identifying with Europe." The converse of this is also true.

16. For further discussion of theories on European integration see Anderson (1995); Milner (1992); Rosamond (2000); and Steinmo, Thelen, and Longstreth (1992).

17. Culture is defined in sociology as the patterned ways in which human beings live together. This includes the ideas, symbols, beliefs, knowledge, and ways of doing things in a particular society (Hall and Neitz 1993).

18. Based on a quantitative analysis, Inglehart (1977) found a positive correlation between high levels of cognitive mobilization, education, and attachment to postmaterialist values and identification with Europe. During the 1990s Janssen (1991) and Duchesne and Frognier (1995) replicated in part Inglehart's propositions. Both studies largely confirmed Inglehart's hypotheses. (Janssen's work was not as conclusive regarding postmaterialist values.)

19. In trying to measure identification with Europe, the Eurobarometers ask how often people see themselves as Europeans. The answer to this question indicates to a certain degree that people see themselves as European, but I have my doubts about whether this really measures identification with Europe; furthermore, Europe does not necessarily mean for the interviewees the European Union. The other question that tries to measure national identity asks about how proud people feel of being of a country's nationality. I do not think this is really adequate since feeling proud of a country does not necessarily translate into attachment to national identity. For instance, a Spaniard could feel proud of France because of

particular foreign policies of France without feeling French. Also, one might not be proud of Spain (as often happens among Spaniards regarding certain Spanish government policies) and still feel Spanish.

20. Of the possible Mondays in a month I chose at random one Monday, of the possible Tuesdays I chose one Tuesday, and so on. Riffe, Aust, and Lacy (1993) have made a very convincing argument that a composite-week sample technique is the most appropriate, when dealing with newspaper content.

21. I started the research with the idea of measuring the exact column-inches of stories on the EU. However, I soon realized that such a detail was unnecessary for this particular research. Basically I made the distinction between just a small excerpt or a longer story on the topic.

22. In proportion to the other parties the Greens were the less represented in my sample. Although I made multiple attempts to interview leaders from the Green parties in France and the United Kingdom, I was able to secure only five interviews with political leaders affiliated with these parties: two interviews in the United Kingdom and three interviews in France.

23. The Economic and Social Committee, the Committees of Regions, the European Investment Bank, and the European Ombudsman are examples of important organizaitons that contribute to the functioning of the EU. A more detailed description of the EU arrangement can be found in the web site of the European Union: http://europa.eu.int.

CHAPTER 2

France: Between Universalism and Exceptionalism

In France, the idea of a united Europe is an old one. Indeed, already in the eighteenth century French social thinkers were suggesting the possibility of an arrangement that would provide for a united Europe. I have already mentioned some of these thinkers in the introduction.[1] The ideological founders of the European Union in the twentieth century were also French. After the establishment of the European Community in 1950, the position regarding this organization in France, among the main political forces, has been oscillating between a strong nationalistic stance (for example, during the De Gaulle presidency) with a market preference for an intergovernmental Europe (l'Europe des nations) and a certain degree of support for a supranational Europe (for example, during Mitterrand's presidency in the 1980s). Until the 1990s, the population was not consulted on questions of European integration, as it had not been consulted historically in any aspects that were considered by the political leaders *high politics*. The population, in general, has been willing to defer these activities to their elected officials, and surveys (Eurobarometers 1976–1991) reveal that in the 1970s and 1980s there was a large majority (above 55 percent) who supported the European Union (European Community at that time) and only a very small majority who were opposed (less than 15 percent). But the Maastricht Treaty, with its aim of political and monetary union, created a major public debate in French society, which made the population more aware of the implications of the European integration process for their lives. François Mitterrand, then president of France, decided to call for a referendum to ratify the treaty. This was the first time that any agreement or treaty regarding the EU was submitted to a referendum in France. As it happens, the referendum contributed to opening up the debate on the European Union to the population at large. Since then, the French public support for the European Union has oscillated between 44 percent and 54 percent, but the opposition has changed far more from one year to another (Eurobarometers 1992–2002).[2]

DIFFERENCE AND CONVERGENCE AMONG THE MAIN POLITICAL PARTIES

By the turn of the millennium, perceptions on the EU varied considerably, as would be expected, among the political parties and unions, but there are also sensible divisions within the same organizations, most particularly in the two main parties, the Gaullist UMP and the Socialist Party. There are also considerable variations between the leaders and the lay people. I will point out the specific differences as my analysis develops. First I address the representations of the EU among the leaders and the population at large.

The Socialist Party's (PS) leadership is divided between a majority who are pro-European integration—as it was intended in the treaty on European Union, and in the ensuing Amsterdam and Nice Treaties— and a minority who are anti-European integration. My interviews of the lay people and voting records during the 1990s show similar division regarding the integration process among PS sympathizers.[3] Members of the majority current that support further integration within the PS argue that the European Union has been instrumental in the economic expansion of France and has helped to maintain peace in Europe.[4] This dominant view on European integration within the Socialist Party was reflected in government policies when they were in power. As Schwork (1999) points out, the socialist government of Lionel Jospin adopted fiscal policies that closely followed the convergence criteria established by the EU. The following quote summarizes the position of the socialist leaders favoring European integration:

For the Jospin generation, the EU is considered a historical attainment. The EU can play a major role in the world's market. It can serve as a 3rd pole, with the Asian/Japanese pole and the U.S. However there are constraints resulting from this choice: loss of French sovereignty concerns us the most. Related to this issue, we are still dealing with the question of what decisions belong to the national level and which decisions should be taken at the European level. (Leader PS, Paris)

France giving up its sovereignty is precisely the main reason to oppose further European integration[5] for a minority current within this party, although this current has at the present a very limited influence. Indeed in the mid 1990s the most visible figure of this tendency was Jean Pierre

Chévénement, former minister in the Jospin administration, who left the Socialist Party with a group of followers, formed a new party, and ran for president in the 2002 elections. The arguments presented by those who are concerned about further European integration within the Socialist Party are several and include two major issues, one being the defense and protection of the workers, because they see Europe as too limited by economic agreements and liberalization of the economy and the loss of sovereignty and a certain idea of the nation. This position is exemplified in the following quote:

According to the republican concept of the nation, sovereignty implies the defense of democracy. And the process of European union as it is carried out presently is undermining democracy. Democracy is being flouted by both the independence of the European central bank and by the deregulation of the economy promoted by the EU, against which the French parliament can do nothing, just to mention two major examples. (Leader PS, Paris [Provence])[6]

Another issue that has instigated two major different interpretations within this party includes the question of cultural identity. Indeed this issue was a domain of concern mentioned by most PS leaders during the interviews, although there are different interpretations on whether the European Union plays a positive or negative role in reproducing French cultural identity. The minority current fears that in the process of European integration a globalized culture heavily influenced by the United States could end up obliterating national French culture:

I think that a certain form of organization at the European level is needed. As everyone knows the world is a single interrelated economy. Therefore, arrangements that integrate states in certain aspects are necessary, but we should not do this by giving up our national identity. Most people in the EU institutions, particularly in the Commission, have an open policy regarding cultural identity. In this context we could end up with a culture heavily influenced by the United States of America. (Leader PS, Paris)

The policies of free trade that the Commission favors are more and more close to the U.S. views on how capitalism should work. Look also at the strong presence in most countries of the EU of U.S. based information and entertainment programs on TV. So far, we the French are the only ones that do anything about it. The EU is not dealing with the issue at all, and this in the name of free trade. We cannot mix any merchandise with the cultural industry. (PS leader, Bordeaux/Paris)

Other leaders associated with the majority current believe that the European Union, on the contrary, may help to preserve national identities against the U.S. cultural invasion. This tendency sees a correspondence between French cultural independence and European cultural independence: "Acting at the European Union level is the key to counterbalance the U.S. cultural domination and to promote both French and European culture" (Leader PS, Toulouse).

In the same vein, the former prime minister, Lionel Jospin, suggested that there was no contradiction between the attachment to the French state and to the European Union. As he stated in the context of explaining the priorities of the French presidency of the European Union in 2000:

Far from denying the principle of nationhood, Europe is its extension. In embracing Europe, our country has acquired the strength needed to reach out to the world, to protect its interests and to bring the values underlying its identity to life. (cited in Schild 2001)

In fact, this has been the dominant argument of most of the French political leaders who support a more united Europe (not only within the Socialist Party). Europe is presented as part of French identity, not outside of it, or as a new identity that the French must acquire. Their argument is that France should be united to Europe because France is also Europe. European identity is presented as embedded in the French national identity. In other words, they see a direct connection between existing political culture in France, such as the ideas of republicanism, enlightenment, and the European Union, blending France and the other states of the Union in a community of progress and liberal democracy. In this view, the EU is to a large extent an extension of the French universal concepts of the republican state and democracy.

Related to the above different interpretations there is an ongoing debate also in terms of day-to-day policies. The most salient debate in the last six years has revolved around whether to accept the restrictions of the European integration process, in relation to the function of the economy (e.g. limited public deficits, and a much more market-oriented economy), and accordingly, applying policies of austerity that will affect the working class and the middle class, or whether to pursue a kind of national protectionism to shelter those groups from the economic hardship that might result from the free-market economic policies promoted by the EU institutions.

The conservative UMP is even more divided on the issue of European integration. This party was constituted before the elections of 2002. It is formed by a coalition of the Gaullist party Rassemblement pour la République (RPR) and a large group from the centrist and generally pro-European integration party, the Union Démocratique Française (UDF). In fact, the European Union has been the main cause of the RPR's dissension in the last two decades, and the debate still continues in the new party: the UMP. The official party line tends to support the European Union (in the sense that the EU is not viewed as undermining French sovereignty and specificity), especially since the early 1990s. In fact, Chirac's public declarations on Europe since then, although made with a reminiscent Gaullist touch, are similar to Jospin's, for instance the following statement in the context of the referendum to ratify the Maastricht Treaty:

The European Community is also a question of identity. If we want to preserve our values, our way of life, our standard of living, our capacity to count in the world, to defend our interests, to remain the carriers of a humanistic message, we are certainly bound to build a united and solid bloc . . . If France says Yes [to the Maastricht Treaty], she can better reaffirm what I believe in: French exceptionalism. (cited in Marcussen et al. 1999: 621)

However, my interviews show that many leaders of this party still perceive the European Union as a threat to French sovereignty and economic independence. During the 1990s there has been a relatively strong current around two leaders, Philippe Seguin and Charles Pasqua, who was sharply opposed to further European integration.[7] Today Charles Pasqua is not as prominent in the UMP, and Seguin, although still reluctant to accept the idea of a politically united Europe and European Union inspired policies, is less radical in his opposition. The interviews reflect, however, that there remains a considerable force within the UMP rather critical of what they call "the Brussels Technocracy." The views of this considerable number of leaders within the UMP, rejecting further integration, however, are not total rejection of a European organization. They even see a certain organization on the European scale "as necessary to ensure the nation-state immortality against the forces of globalization" (Leader UMP, Provence), but they strongly emphasize the primordial role that the nation-state must continue to play in the French destiny. In sum, most leaders of this party support the EU policies of free trade and other specific agreements on particular issues such as security and immigration, but there are sharp differences over questions of sovereignty—close to half of those interviewed were concerned about giving up political and military power to the EU. The following quotes typify these views, which express what Massard (1993) termed the difficulties of French people in accepting the supranational functions of the EU institutions:

As long as we are dealing with economic agreements and the single market, the European Union is a great idea. However, I am concerned about the project of political union. I do not see the need for a political union except perhaps to establish some specific agreements on immigration for example. (Leader UMP, Strasbourg)

The mechanisms of decision in Brussels affect France negatively more often than not. The too preponderant role of the Commission and the many and very technical regulations that are produced in Brussels are too overwhelming. In a nonintegrated Europe, France occupied a privileged position: agriculture, nuclear power, weapons industry. . . . In all these domains the European integration and the German or British pressures tend to undermine our country's particularity. In other words, the EU tends to strip French people from their national culture. (Leader UMP, Paris)

Although there are several different interpretations within the UMP regarding the meaning of the EU, one could view the major division as between a pragmatic group, which sees the European Union as the best alternative to insure French prosperity and international influence (whose visible figures are Chirac, Juppé, and Balladur), and a group (whose most well known leaders are Séguin and Pasqua) that is very concerned about French sovereignty and opposes integration beyond agreements on economic issues. However, even though these differences, in terms of degree of acceptance of how much Europe should influence France's internal affairs, hold contrary meanings when votes are cast concerning the European Union, these cleavages are not as fixed as they might appear.[8] Indeed, our interviews suggest that the differences within the UMP regarding the process of European integration are more along a continuum between two poles than a clear-cut, binary opposition.

The Union pour la Démocratie Française (UDF) is a confederation of center-right parties[9] that are largely supportive of the European Union, and in favor of further integration. Under the leadership of Giscard D'Estaing and François Léotard this party's elite has been historically largely committed to working within the frame of the European Union. The pro-European inclination of the UDF was also reflected in the 1992 National Assembly vote to approve the constitutional amendments required to ratify the Maastricht Treaty (77 out of 89 UDF deputies voted in favor of the changes), and to approve the Amsterdam Treaty in 1997, as well as in the interviews I conducted during the second half of the 1990s. This support for the EU is stronger than ever under the present leadership of François Bayrou. Only a minority group is opposed to the present process of European integration. The following is a typical concern of this minority group, expressed by one of its leaders:

The creation of a so called independent monetary power—that is to say separated from the political power—will prevent the states from establishing any corrective measures according to the economic and political circumstances and could bring about the end of the European democracies. (Leader UDF, Paris)

Although this group is relatively marginal within the UDF elite, it has a considerable influence in the UDF electorate. Indeed, the 1992 referendum and later surveys show that the support of UDF voters for the EU has been consistently around 60 percent, a proportion that is much less than one would believe by listening to most UDF leaders. Half of this party leadership has been integrated into the UMP. Some people joined the UMP before the presidential election (in the spring of 2002) and many more followed after their candidate received only 6.84 percent of the votes in the first round of the elections. Consequently, the force of this party in the French national assembly is now rather limited. It is still the third party in number of representatives elected, but far behind the UMP and the Socialist Party.

The Communist Party has been, since World War I, an important player in French politics, although its voting support has diminished sharply in recent years, and in the last election of 2002 the number of the party's representatives to the national assembly (French Parliament) has been reduced to about 5 percent. However, judging by the interviews of lay citizens and informal conversations, one cannot dismiss the weight of this party in French society. This party's influence among the working class is still considerable and broader than the actual support that they received in the last election (presidential and parliamentary elections). Although it is impossible to establish exact numbers, I can deduce from my interviews and informal conversations with workers that many of them, who are traditionally Communist Party supporters, often vote for Le Pen because they support his anti-immigrant stance,[10] but contrary to Le Pen's hatred for the communists, and as contradictory as this might appear, these people still see in the Communist Party a voice for their social concerns. The official stance of this party has traditionally been opposition to European integration. This is also the position expressed by the leaders I interviewed. Without exception, all of the leaders consider the economic measures recommended by the EU to have negatively affected the French workers. They point out the persistence of large pockets of poverty in France as in many other rich countries of the EU, and they also think that the economic choices of the EU have contributed to diluting values of solidarity. In addition, they are troubled by what they see as the deterioration of the welfare system and public services such as health, public transport, education, and so on, as the consequence of a "crazy and uncritical embrace of neo-liberalism" by the EU. The following quote is representative of the views expressed by the PC leaders I interviewed:

We always acted against the type of European construction currently happening, in particular against the economic criteria. The negative aspects of European integration definitely are more numerous than the positive ones, because there is an over-determination of the economic and financial criteria. (Leader PC, Paris)

In the same tone they blame the agricultural policies of the EU for weakening French agricultural tradition: "The destruction of our agriculture, based on family farming, is due to the capitalist ideology predominating within the EU" (Leader PC, Toulouse), suggesting that the Agricultural

Common Policy of the EU has not actually helped the small farmers but has been more useful for large farmers. From their point of view, the EU has only been positive, if at all, for multinational companies.

This party's view on sovereignty is very similar to the traditional Gaullist's ideas, which insisted on the independence of the French nation-state. Accordingly most interviewees did express concern over loss of sovereignty due to further European integration. However, in this aspect there was not absolute agreement; a small group of interviewees did not see the loss of sovereignty as a major concern and stated explicitly that if the policies were more socially oriented, they would certainly support more EU integration.

Furthermore, as with the majority of interviewees from the UMP and the Socialist Party, the leaders of the PCF also showed a strong concern over the United States of America's influence in the world and in Europe. Behind the free market trend of the EU they see the United States, as expressed in the following quote: "The finality of the European integration is not European but global, which implies submission to the U.S. conceptions of the free market economy and the commercialization of culture" (Leader PC, Toulouse).

In brief, the leaders of the Communist Party are all strongly opposed to the present process of EU integration, which they perceive as too market oriented. Although there were some differences regarding the concerns over sovereignty, all interviewees concur on the view that "the EU should direct its efforts to social policies," suggesting that the best social measures in force in certain member countries should be included in all the social directives of the EU. Furthermore, leaders of this party consider that the French parliament should be protected from direct influence of the EU "to safeguard French democratic institutions." At the same time, they want more power vested in the European Parliament. This party will support only a European integration that includes clear commitment to a more social Europe.

The Front National is the most anti-European Union party of the French political spectrum. This right-wing party is the most vocal regarding a possible loss of sovereignty and French identity as a result of European integration, and it is opposed by principle to any form of European integration. The leaders from the FN do not agree with any form of confederation and prefer intergovernmental agreements on specific programs and issues. The opposition to the European Union in the FN revolves around the rejection of what they see as a "European superstate that will destroy the French state," and French culture, as the following quotes exemplify:

To weaken the state is to weaken France. It means to deny thousands of years of history. By weakening the state we also affect the ways of life of citizens, because the state is the organizer of the society and insures a mission regardless of the laws of the market, such as justice, social protection, and public service. (Leader FN, Toulouse)

The process of European union, as it is conceived, is eroding French culture. There is a strong wave of Anglo-Saxon influence on the population. To lose cultural references is to lose cohesion and a means towards progress as well as individual power. Within the EU there is a dangerous drive towards deculturation, unique thought, and the politically correct unique lifestyle. (Leader FN, Paris)

Furthermore the leaders of the FN reject the opening of Europe to "Third-World immigrants," and the opening of European borders to foreign goods from the United States, Japan, and other Asian countries. In brief, they oppose most aspects that a form of European-level organization implies as well as what they label "the consequences of globalization." They will go as far as suggesting renegotiating the Treaty of Rome, and repealing the Maastricht Treaty and all the ensuing treaties. In 1999, this party split in two. One group called Front National-Identité Française (National Front-French Identity) was formed around the traditional leader Jean Marie Le Pen, and a second group called Front National-Mouvement National (National Front-National Movement) was formed around Bruno Megret. The choice of the names clearly expresses the connection between the survival of French identity and Nationalism. The Movement National is a very small faction and, given the low proportion of votes that they received in the 2002 French national elections, it is expected that this group will reunite again with the majority group of Le Pen. In any case, their discourse in the European Elections of June 1999 and in the National French elections of 2002 reflected that both groups continued to share the same strong anti-European stance as when they were united. The Front National ideas about immigration and Europe have a considerable resonance among French voters, as proved by its relative success in the presidential elections of 2002. It was able to get 18 percent of the votes in the first round and eliminating from participation in the second round the candidate of the Socialist Party, Lionel Jospin, who received 17 percent.[11]

Of the three main French labor unions, two of them, CFDT and FO, are ideologically in favor of further European integration, including political and economic integration. This positive view towards Europe in these two labor unions is perhaps due to the fact that they have a long tradition of engagement in cross-border cooperation. Indeed, even before the European construction began, a united front of French and German workers was constituted in the 1940s to oppose the Nazis. The French workers were affiliated with the union, which was later re-formed and gave birth to the CFDT. FO, in particular, originated as Résistance Ouvrière (Workers Resistance) during the German occupation of France. Consequently, when the European Coal and Steel Community was born in 1951, these unions were already used to cooperation across borders. CFDT and FO have now relatively well-established organizations at the European level. However, the support of these unions' leadership for more European integration today is not unconditional. All of those I interviewed are concerned about too much focus on free market economy in the recent treaties, as the following quote attests:

Due to the French policy adjustment to the requirements of the EU, the public sector, which used to guarantee job security, is being reduced. Also, public health, a traditional pillar in post-war French institutions, is being little by little dismantled. (Leader CFDT, Paris)

The other big labor union, the CGT, in large part because of its direct link with the Communist Party—and the ideological involvement of this party during the cold war on the side of the Soviet Union—was never structured at the European level. This union's leaders are more blatant than the other unions in their criticism of the EU. The leaders of the CGT are very concerned about the EU's emphasis on what they see as monetary policies and the overall free market orientation. The CGT opposed the ratification of the Maastricht Treaty in 1992 and today opposes further European integration that does not explicitly consider substantial social and economic policies in favor of the working class. This group thinks that the criteria for monetary union were anti-worker because they forced the French government to reduce public services and its public budget, and it does not see any compensatory measures sponsored by the EU. The quote below typifies the CGT views on the process of European union:

France has a unique system in Europe: a public service that plays an important role in economic and social redistribution. When the state cannot play that role anymore, it stops serving the society. There is an expectation from the state for public services that is less and less fulfilled and this is due to the influence of European Union policies. (Leader CGT, Paris)

All the leaders of the three main unions express a concern over the neglected social policies of the EU. However, the differences lie in the strategic approaches. The majority of leaders from the CFDT and FO push for modifications of the existing treaties but consider it important to work at the European level as well as at the national level. While the CGT and a minority of leaders from the CFDT are more radical in their criticism of the EU and the of fact that the latest intergovernmental meetings and treaties (Treaty of Amsterdam 1997, Treaty of Nice 2001) did not produce substantial changes in EU social policies, this intransigence constitutes, for them, more evidence of the EU's insensitivity to workers' demands.

The leaders of the most powerful French employers' organization, the

Mouvement des Entreprises de France-Medef (France's business movement)[12] are largely supportive of the EU, particularly regarding most of its economic policies, as prescribed in the Maastricht Treaty and the ensuing treaties. However, the business owners have a self-centered perception of this process. They tend to be divided, mostly in accordance with their business experience with the EU. If the regulations issued by the EU have affected them negatively, they tend to see the EU as an obstacle to their economic success. Especially medium and small company owners are concerned about the lifting of regulations that protected them from what they label as "foreign multinational companies' competition."

LAY CITIZENS: PERCEPTIONS AND EXPERIENCES

In terms of general support for European union, polls show that French citizens have evolved to be more positive by the end of the 1990s than they were at the beginning of the decade.[13] However, when discussing the EU policies in more depth and looking at the different socioeconomic groups' perceptions, one finds very diverse and complex interpretations of the relationship between French lay citizens and the EU. The opposition to the present process of European integration was strongest among the working class and those people whose livelihood is directly or indirectly related to agriculture. Antagonism toward the institutions of the EU was common among the farmers interviewed. As the owner of a medium-sized farm said: "The bureaucrats of Brussels not only are affecting the French economy with the international agreements, they are also trying to destroy our way of living. They are even attempting to regulate what we eat and how we eat it." This widespread negative view of the European Union among French farmers has been rather consistent particularly in the last 10 years, even though, through the Common Agricultural Policy, around 45 percent of EU budget is destined for farmers' subsidies. In fact, this policy is perceived among political leaders from other member countries such as the United Kingdom and Germany as benefiting France more than any other country in the union.

However, despite the Common Agricultural Policy, the European Union's agricultural regulations have forced France (as they have other countries of the Union) to reduce its agricultural production in many areas. As a result of these policies some small farmers had to abandon their traditional activity. Farmers interviewed believe they have been sacrificed to bring benefits to other sectors of the economy:

For us the European Union has been negative in every aspect. No matter what politicians say, I can see how most of the people I know in our region have been negatively affected. Because of the European Union the French government had to open borders to other countries, and had to reduce the production of many of our traditional crops to accommodate other interests. In fact, neither the French government nor the French people have any control over economic policies. (Farmer, Toulouse, Haute Garonne)

Another interviewee presented agriculture as the center of Frenchness (an idea shared by many people in France), and therefore, the argument goes, by establishing policies that question the traditional organization of the agriculture in this country, the EU is actually undermining French culture: "You see France has been agricultural for a long time. If you destroy the agriculture, you destroy France. The European Community is the end of French culture and of France as an independent country" (Farmer, Provence).

For most politicians interviewed from the PS, the UMP, and the UDF, these adaptations would have been necessary even if the EU did not exist. The EU, and particularly the Commission, constitute a scapegoat that allows the government to make the changes they perceive necessary even if they are unpopular. Politicians in power probably feel blessed to have the EU to blame, and particularly the Commission, which is perceived by the lay people as the main decision maker of the EU. All people interviewed knew something about the Commission and the European Parliament, but very few knew about the Council and its major role in the decision-making process.[14]

Among industrial workers there is also a prevailing negative perception of the EU, although it is not as widespread as it is among farmers. Given that French national laws have been since the 1960s rather favorable regarding social issues—such as the access of young people to the job market, length of work, protection of pregnant female employees, and anything that concerns health and security at work—most of the French workers do not see that Europe has anything to offer them. On the contrary, they see the EU as undermining the social fabric and the French welfare system, as exemplified by this quote:

The Europe that we are building in Brussels is not for the working class. The social charter is reduced to the minimum and barely applied, and most countries, including Germany, are opposed to the idea of a government or European agency capable of deciding policies independently from the financial powers. There is nothing in Europe for us. (Metal worker, Toulouse)

In general, French lay people (as well as many political and labor union leaders) are very attached to their constitutional system, public service (which they consider excellent), and social welfare system. The interviewees, although they are not as well informed about other countries' welfare systems, consider their social services, such as retirement conditions, protection of workers, education, and health care system as very good and are very concerned that these services might be undermined as a result of further integration.[15] French citizens have a deep sense of political, cultural, and economic boundaries, and they expect the French state to play a major role in resource redistribution and social organization. This is clearly reflected in my interviews and also in most surveys. For example, a recent Sofres (2001b) poll shows that French people think that the French national state should be responsible for: improving the economic standing of the citizens (52 percent), taxes (50 percent), employment and reducing unemployment (54 percent), education and professional training (57 percent), protection of wage workers (60 percent), and social protection (63 percent), at the same time they accept that macroeconomic policies should be decided at the European Union level (57 percent), as well as immigration (62 percent), foreign policy (67 percent), environment (57 percent), and consumer protection (54 percent).

The national state is viewed as a protector and arbiter. In fact, this conception of the republican state is rather widespread in France and transcends rifts among the different political components. Even neoliberal proponents such as Jacques Chirac (the current president of France) stated his support for this conception of the state in a speech shortly after he was first elected in 1995: "We have a social model that we want to keep," and he restated similar views during the 2002 campaign before being reelected. However, the difference in points of view among lay people concerned the extent to which the EU is affecting this widespread conception of the state. Thirty-four percent of respondents do not see that the EU will actually undermine French sovereignty. The recurrence of this view is exemplified in the following quote: "Well, we have been members of the European Union since the 1950s and I have not seen the French state losing its sovereignty, even after Maastricht. Nor have we lost national identity" (Mechanic, Arles, Provence). Sixteen percent of individuals did not express a clear opinion on this issue. Those opposing further integration over the concern of French sovereignty are a majority (42 percent). They fear that the European Union might end up obliterating their national and local traditions and cultural expressions. They reemphasize the "fundamental virtue of French national sovereignty" and the "obligation to keep alive and reproduce practices and landmarks of French history" (insurance company employee, Valence, Rhone-Alpes). A waiter in a Paris café stated: "We have to live in peace, and I think we must have agreements with the Germans and others, but I want to live in an independent country." The fear of weakening French national sovereignty is by far more widespread among the French lay people than among the leaders. Lay citizens' interpretation of French sovereignty is related to a large extent with what was examined above, that is, the autonomy of the French state in deciding welfare and social policies:

France is a republic, there was the French Revolution, the Popular Front, the Liberation, and all of this gave rise to an important public sector and social benefits resulting from the redistribution of wealth. The requirements of the European Union are undermining most of these traditions. (Bank employee, Paris)

There is also a concern among a minority of interviewees over the role of France in the European Union: "I cannot accept that Brussels dictates regulations to our country." Also typical is the following comment by a lawyer from Strasbourg: "The problem I have with the European Union is that the French government does not seem to be in charge anymore. This is clear in monetary aspects, but also in other policies." This sentiment of powerlessness is often accompanied with a reference to other countries as having the real power in the EU: "In the European Union, France's role in international politics has been considerably weakened in favor of Germany" (Store owner, Toulouse). On the other hand a minority of interviewees think that the national interest will be enhanced by the EU: "Because of the globalization process, I think that our national interest will be better defended in a strong European Union" (High school teacher, Strasbourg).

Furthermore, the majority of interviewees (52 percent) believe that the EU spent too much time on unnecessary regulations, and they are concerned that the standardization of products, like food and other goods, as a result of the integration process, might affect their traditional culture.

The French state, which is viewed as a stable and fundamental social institution, is connected, in the interviewees' perceptions, to the myths and symbols that constitute their sense of French identity. The perceived threat to national sovereignty is therefore often coupled with a perceived threat to national identity. However, as it is the case regarding concerns over loss of sovereignty, leaders and lay people differ considerably on the issue of national identity: 56 percent of lay people interviewed believe that France is losing its cultural identity as a result of European integration; only 38 percent of those in leadership share those beliefs. But even many of those who viewed the European Union in a positive light mentioned the national culture as a concern: "I think that the European Union is important for peace and good for the economy, but I believe that we have to find the way to keep alive our own unique culture (Cook in a small restaurant, Paris). Related to this feeling is the importance that many French citizens interviewed attach to French exceptionalism. They believe that France has an exceptional humanitarian tradition that should be safeguarded. Indeed, a number of relatively educated respondents see French culture as universal and consider that this view of the world must be defended. For instance:

At least since the Enlightenment, we have always been ahead of many other countries in terms of openness to the world and we give a lot of importance to art and culture. Even the most conservative governments have promoted art and culture. I am a little concerned that in Europe this is not as important, they seem to concentrate more on money matters. (High school teacher)

Finally, the possible loss of language was often mentioned in the interviews. Language is viewed as a basic cultural marker. French language is venerated as fundamental to protecting their cultural identity and national unity. Indeed, most people interviewed think that the existence of the French nation-state relies on having their own language. The quote below reflects this widespread belief among French people:[16]

Language is not the only thing that makes us French but it is an important aspect of people, culture, and evolution. Even the way we argue is influenced by language, and I think that we should make every effort to keep it alive, even within a more politically and culturally united Europe. I am not especially against further integration but I want my culture to be present. (Supermarket administrator)

In fact, the similarities in life styles and political values, including respect for human rights and democracy in France and in the rest of the member countries of the European Union, has made it more difficult for French people to appeal to a specific identity beyond the language differences. For instance, when I asked "What characterizes French culture?" people had difficulties pinpointing clear boundaries. I asked the respondents to state the four most important characteristics in their view. The question was open-ended and did not provide categories that could have led to particular answers. The responses most often mentioned were as follows: to speak French (49 percent), to be attached to a common French tradition and history (47 percent), to defend the republic (44 percent), attachment to individual freedom (42 percent), to enjoy good food (35 percent).

The issue of language has also created many contradictions among intellectuals. Writings in *Le Monde* throughout the years show how French intellectuals are struggling with their desire to defend French language and their interest in being present in the international arena.

People exalt the national values that they perceive as endangered by a supranational organization such as the European Union and the perceived growing influence of the English language: "French language is less and less important in EU affairs, and now with the enlargement, how would they deal with all the other languages from Eastern Europe? Most likely they will end up using English as the main vehicle" (High school teacher, Lyon).

In addition, many interviewees expressed concern over a certain Anglo-Saxon and/or Americanized domination of Europe, pointing to the linguistic risk in the process of European integration due to what they perceive as the growing use of the English language in Europe: "The increasing influence of American culture will be facilitated by the widespread use of English. The main line of defense, as we stand, is our language. France has to resist the growing influence of Anglo-Saxon culture" (University student, Toulouse). Other aspects of concern mentioned in the interviews include the "spy satellite system Echelon," the "ever increasing U.S. media products in Europe" (TV serials, films, news, etc.), and the "inability of the EU to confront the United States when necessary." They see that the "unilateralism that characterizes the United States international policies is even affecting the workings of all the international institutions" (Unemployed, Strasbourg). Respondents also mentioned "the U.S. frontal attack on the United Nations since the 1990s, including the refusal to pay its dues," (Bank employee, Paris) and "the blatant disregard for the UN resolutions when they do not follow their interests, a disregard as well for the suggestions of the World Bank, and I have recently read that the United States is also questioning the International Monetary Fund" (Engineer, Lyon). A recent survey from September 2002 (Duhamel 2002) revealed that French citizens perceive the United States as one of the four states most threatening to world peace (behind Iraq, Israel, and Pakistan). These results have probably been influenced by a perceived aggressive military policy of the George W. Bush administration, after the widely publicized and debated statements of the U.S. president on the "axis of evil" and other strong warlike statements in the fall of 2001 and during 2002, disregarding the views of the international community. One should not interpret this French viewpoint as a fixed antiAmerican sentiment, as too often U.S. commentators and journalists tend to do. Indeed, most of the interviewees who did express the above ideas do not consider the United States and its people as their enemy or as "primitive and violent warriors."[17] They made a very clear separation between what they consider the people and their government, often expressing the opinion that America was a lot friendlier to Europe and the international community under Bill Clinton than under George W. Bush. Furthermore, a study done in 2000, concentrating on views of Americans and American popular culture (not on U.S. policies), showed that most French citizens are relatively indifferent (neither negative or positive feelings) to United States citizens and 41 percent tend to see the United States in a positive light, while only about 10 percent consider the United States more as an adversary (Méchet 2002). The main question for these respondents was how to continue to be French in a Europe that they perceive as too Americanized in the economy, as well as in the culture, how to keep alive the values that gave France "relatively good social protection, an excellent and free education, and a striving political pluralism with many political parties that express the variety of opinion that should exist in a true democracy" (Student, Strasbourg).

In sum, the large majority of French lay people interviewed (56 percent) perceive the nation-state as representing a form of popular sovereignty. In contrast, the EU is perceived by a little more than half of the interviewees (52 percent) as a government of technocrats, distant from the people, which imposes restrictive policies on France. This representation is not foreign to the influence exerted on the population by certain political leaders. For instance, the monetary union together with observable developments within the European Union—such as expansive environmental policies, similar welfare systems, expanded human rights, collaboration against crime and terrorism, and closer than ever structure of the economy[18]—has been presented by opponents of the European Union (i.e. Seguin 1998) as evidence that the EU "unilaterally and hierarchically" imposes policies on the member states, hence undermining national sovereignty. During the 1990s, Philippe Seguin and Charles Pasqua continually warned against the bureaucratization of Europe.

The differences between those who are pro-European Union and its opponents rest also on what constitutes state sovereignty. The following quote from Jean-Marie Le Pen illustrates the views on this subject from the opponents to further European integration: "Sovereignty is the right to choose our own laws, to make decisions about taxes, to have our own government, our army, our judges, our police, our currency, and, above all, our house" (from a speech on January 17, 1998 at a demonstration in Paris). This is basically what we can consider a nationalist idea.

The pro-European integration side is rather diverse in assessing the effects of European integration on French sovereignty, as we will see in more detail in the next section. However, a very general common view is that sovereignty does not necessarily imply that everything must be decided at the nation-state level. There is some acceptance of the principle of subsidiarity.[19] For others, such as the socialist former minister Lionel Jospin and many other socialists and UDF leaders I interviewed, the European Union restrictions on sovereignty are a necessary trade-off for furthering French interests and political independence.

Since the Treaty on the Union (also called the Maastricht Treaty) in the early 1990s, French citizens have been almost equally divided concerning the value of further European integration. The referendum of 1992 showed that a large part of the French population (49 percent) was opposed to further integration, and further surveys in the ensuing years (Eurobarometer 49 1998; Eurobarometer 50 1999; Eurobarometer 54 2000; Eurobarometer 55 2001; Eurobarometer 56 2002; Sofres 2001), and my own interviews have shown only slight changes regarding the support for further European integration. The population at large is divided along educational and class lines. My interviews and all surveys confirm these same tendencies. The majority of citizens supporting further European integration is highly educated and occupies a generally high socioeconomic position.[20] Intellectuals also tend to support further European integration. These categories of citizens tend to be internationally oriented and cosmopolitan as defined by Hannerz (1990) and thus are more aware of similarities among the population of the EU member countries.[21]

In this section we have seen the plurality of views expressed by French leaders and lay people on the relations between France and the EU. The process of European union is viewed by a slight majority of French leaders from a variety of political parties and unions, and by a minority of lay people interviewed, as a necessity for the French state to flourish, while another considerable proportion (a large minority of leaders and the majority of lay people) see the EU as constraining the French people economically, politically, and culturally. One-fourth of the Socialist Party, half of the Gaullist UMP, one-fifth of the centrist UDF, and all the respondents from the PCF and the right-wing FN are among the political leaders adhering to the latter interpretation of the EU. All the interviewees from the labor union CGT, one-fifth from the CFDT, and one-fifth from FO also advocate this view.

The negative perceptions of the EU among the French people can be briefly summarized as follows: France's economic situation has been affected by the measures decided by the EU. France is losing national autonomy, sovereignty, and national identity, and other countries such as Germany or England have more influence on EU policies. These interpretations corroborate the theoretical premise inspired by Smith (1991) that a negative representation of the European Union frame of opportunities, such as economic and political restrictions, result in a renewed affirmation of the importance of the national state. This point will be further developed later.

In the next sections I examine the different understandings among political leaders, union leaders, and lay people, as to what the organization of the European Union should be, and which aspects of the dynamics of European integration might contribute to a negative social representation of the European Union.

THE MEANING OF EUROPEAN UNION: PRODUCTION AND REPRODUCTION OF SOCIAL REPRESENTATIONS

When people are supporting or rejecting the EU, they are basically supporting or rejecting a given idea they have of the EU. There is no clearcut, homogeneous interpretation of what the European integration implies. Among lay people especially, the knowledge of the EU is fragmented, partial, and inconsistent. Here, I focus first on attempting to comprehend the respondents' positions regarding support for an intergovernmental, confederate organization or for a supranational, federal form of organization. Then, I present the factors and policies that contribute to shape the meaning of the European Union for French people.

Recent Eurobarometers (Eurobarometer 49 1998; Eurobarometer 50 1999; Eurobarometer 54 2000) contain two general questions on unification: whether Europeans are for or against the efforts being made to unify Western Europe and whether they are for or against a Federal European Union. In my research, I attempted to understand what the French people thought was meant by unification, and I found the following trends:[22] Among political and union leaders who support France continuing as apart of the European Union (a total of 84 percent of the leaders interviewed), 72 percent thought that some form of confederation was the best alternative for the European Union, while 26 percent supported a federation (2 percent did not express an opinion). The interviewees who were more inclined to support a federation belonged to the Socialist Party and the union FO. The idea of a federation has considerable support among business leaders: one third of those interviewed supported a federation. Lay people were largely in favor of keeping a strong national government (72 percent).[23]

Furthermore, the concept of a confederation, as the respondents understood it, has many degrees of integration. A major tendency within the UMP favored intergovernmental agreements linked to the economy and certain specific policies, while the confederation tendency within the PS and the UDF supports a closer association, including foreign policies, cultural policies, defense policies, and economic policies. The union leaders from FO and the CFDT share this view. The leaders of the PC and CGT have similar views on the most appropriate form of organization for the EU. They will support a rather loose confederation with agreements that include economic and social policies, and autonomy for the French government in foreign and cultural policies.

The plurality of interpretations on what form the European Union's organization should take shows the difficulties of creating a political union. However, what seems to be rather clear is that most of the people interviewed in all categories tend to view the EU more as some kind of confederation of nation-states rather than as a federation. Most interviewees were very skeptical about a federation of the European Union. As one lay person said: "Due to the socioeconomic and cultural differences among the nation-members of the European Union, it is not possible in the near future to think about a federal form of organization"(Engineer, Toulouse). This shows that support for Europe in the abstract (as reflected in the Eurobarometers, 1996–2000) does not mean support for a federal Europe, or a politically united Europe. It means support for an organization that goes from a loose intergovernmental organization to a more closely united confederation with a common foreign, immigration, and economic policy, for a majority of those interviewed, and for a small minority of those interviewed, a federation with most major powers of decision making transferred to the EU institutions.

The fact is that the nation-state still constitutes the main referent for most French leaders and the population at large. This dominant interpretation is not alien to the specific characteristics of the French state or to the habits and perceptions of people acting within it, including the type of socialization. Indeed, the importance of a centralizing nation-state, a common political culture, ideals strongly characterized by *laicité* (separation of church and state and civic rights and responsibilities), and the values laid down during the revolution "*liberté, égalité, fraternité*" (liberty, equality, fraternity) are inculcated in the French population from their earliest education onward. There is a continuous reference to the French thinkers of the Enlightenment, Voltaire, Rousseau, Diderot, Descartes, and to the heroes from the past, such as Clovis or Jeanne d'Arc, together with the idea of France being the first country to produce a declaration of human rights that was then disseminated around the world, giving to the French a sense of universality. These ideas are included in textbooks, are disseminated by teachers, and are a part of everyday life. For instance, during the 1960s students often started the day in elementary school singing "La Marseillaise."[24]

Furthermore, historically the centralizing role of the state in this country has contributed to a sense of national cohesion and has played a decisive role in defining the civil society. The state has also played a major role in the economic transformation during the second half of the twentieth century. This is such that social demands have been traditionally directed towards it (Romano 1990). In brief, the state in France is not only viewed as a political structure, but it is also part of people's idea of what France is.

Consequently, even when addressing specifically European Union issues common to most members of the European Union, these issues find concrete expression only within the context of the national state. Issues such as human rights, protection of civil liberties, and social rights and benefits, are framed by the French citizens interviewed mostly in their relation to the French state.[25] Also, the political campaign and the results of European elections in the media or otherwise are mostly portrayed in terms of national issues. Therefore, in elections for the EU Parliament, national concerns clearly determine opposition to, or support for, a given candidate or party. The referendum on the Maastricht Treaty in 1992, and the debates in the Parliament concerning ratification of the Treaty of Amsterdam in 1997–98 and ratification of the Treaty of Nice in 2001 were marked by national issues and internal national political power struggles that were not always directly related to the content of the treaties.

Social representations of the EU are based on both concrete and symbolic experiences that the institutions of the EU themselves have not dispelled and have contributed to reproducing. The debates within the EU are conducted mostly in terms of national interests and are presented as such by the media (television, radio, and written media). Indeed, the main policies of the EU are decided by the leaders of the member countries, through the council, acknowledging and reaffirming the sovereign statehood as a crucial element in the EU policies. The Commission, which is often attacked by opponents of the EU, produces texts and recommendations but does not have the power to impose any measure without the Council's agreement. Furthermore, when implementing unpopular policies, the political leaders of the national governments often point to the European Union as the instigator of such policies, contributing thereby to negative sentiments about the European Union among the French population.

People resent the regulations coming from the EU and other constraints and do not see the benefits they receive from it. When the European Union is involved in actions to address concrete social problems in France, this is not known or recognized by the population. Indeed, because the structural funds and other aid coming from the EU are administered by the national state, they are not perceived as coming from the EU. The programs of rural development and the conversion programs for former industrial zones constitute concrete examples of the EU's direct involvement but are not acknowledged by the population at large. For example, the European Union funded almost entirely the restructuring of the mining and iron industry in France. This program offered the workers, in the words of a labor union leader, "major protection and compensation" and financed their efforts to acquire new qualifications. Yet, most workers did not know about which institution was financing these programs and assumed that it was the French government. They only knew what some politicians and some commentators on TV and in the popular press were publicizing. That is, that the European Union was behind what they perceived as "the annihilation of an industry."

The Common Agricultural Policy is a constant issue of conflict in France. This policy of agricultural subsidies initiated five decades ago to stimulate agricultural production is periodically revised under the pressure of other member countries such as the United Kingdom, Germany, and others to attempt to reduce the amount of the EU budget allotted for this item. However, every time that there is a suggestion that the Agricultural Common Policy has to be reformed, French farmer's associations organize strong anti-European Union campaigns, which have a great resonance within French society. This reaction has been observable during the decade of the 1990s, whether in the frame of the European Union intergovernmental conferences, or negotiations within the World Trade Organization.[26]

In addition, the European Union's lack of leadership role in international affairs, even on the European continent, also hinders allegiance to the EU among the population of France. The Balkan crises and Ireland are the most well-known examples during the 1990s. Because of the cacophony that characterizes the EU in foreign affairs, the EU could not play a decisive role in preventing the war in the former Yugoslavia, or later, in the establishment of a peace accord in Bosnia. For instance, the following criticism reflects the views of many who expected a lot more from the EU and from France:

What is the point of erecting heavy and complex structures like the Treaty of Maastricht, when Europeans are not even capable of acting with enough vigor to impose—if all else fails, by arms—respect for the simple principle of non-aggression and of non-expansion by force? (cited in Kramer 1994: 54)

The EU played a more active role in the Kosovo crisis but was still perceived as working under the leadership of the United States of America. The EU was also marginally present in Northern Ireland's peace process.

Beyond Europe, the EU has played a limited role in the Middle East, and it is not acting as a united voice in Africa. In fact, during the 1990s the EU seem to have stepped aside almost everywhere in the world, leaving the leadership to the United States. This might have been planned strategy (although I did not find any evidence that will confirm this hypothesis), but the way the public can represent and create an idea of the EU is based on what they see and read.

This lack of strong leadership in world affairs is not due to a lack of interest among European leaders, but to the particular organizational structure of the EU. As long as the European Union is only a club of governments negotiating issues as they come along, it will not be able to face the problems that lie ahead and to produce a sense of leadership that will portray it as a viable and important organization in the member countries' population. The European leaders are conscious of this, as reflected in the creation of the Common Foreign and Security Policy (CFSP) in 2000, and the appointment of Rafael Solana (the former NATO chief) as the EU Foreign Minister, but this is still at an embryonic stage. Governments continue to act very much on their own in most international affairs. Since this agency is a very recent creation, a few years will be needed before the public starts to be acquainted with its existence and researchers determine whether it is contributing to a positive representation of the EU among the population.

The economic restructuring due to the monetary union and other economic policies has also contributed to instigating negative feelings regarding the EU among French people. As one union leader suggests: "In order to get the euro, Europeans had to accept to be governed by an all-powerful central bank that is imposing free market policies. The monetary union will only continue to increase social inequalities and exclude many people from the mainstream" (Union Leader CGT, Toulouse). Indeed, the criteria considered to establish the monetary union (inflation, equilibrium of the budget, interest rates, and respect of change parities) were solely monetarists. Neither the situation of the job market, nor the economic activities (including industrial policies) were even mentioned. And since the euro is controlled by an independent entity, the European Central Bank, the so-called democratic deficit has increased while the technocratic conception has been enhanced. Those in power at the Central Bank, whose technocratic interpretation of the world is heavily influenced by a capitalist ideology, seem to have adjusted their policies according to the free market dynamics and tend to direct the European economy according to monetarist interpretations.[27] Furthermore, no social policies are being applied to minimize or counterbalance the effects of the neoliberal policies.

It equally has instigated concerns for national sovereignty, especially in that a large proportion of French people, including half of the leaders interviewed, believed that the euro was mostly a German project. The interpretation reflected in the following quote is rather widespread among political leaders from both the right and the left of the political spectrum:[28]

Look at the model of the European Central Bank: Germany. Germany, because of its economic weight, is already dominating Europe, and in a more integrated Europe it will be worse because we will not have anymore a powerful state to protect us from the laws of the market, or from the commercialization of culture, or from any other arrangements that will affect our existence as French people with a particular history. (Leader UMP, Toulouse)

Among the several possible combinations of the diverse conceptions of the EU, two major strategies stand out: a minimalist strategy (more or less neoliberal) which is above all interested in creating a free market zone, and another, more inclusive strategy, which in addition to economic integration, pursues social and political unity. For now the minimalist neoliberal tendency, which has created a common denominator, is clearly dominating the process.[29] It is this free market and technocratic Europe that has created feelings against integration among a large proportion of French lay people and a considerable and influential proportion of leaders. Obviously, although European Union officials often refer to solidarity among the citizens of the EU, in practice the struggle against inequalities and for social justice has not been the object of much dedication in recent years. Indeed, at the Dublin summit, held in December 1996, participants did not even discuss reforms aimed at obtaining complete freedom of movement of people within the union, or other social issues, such as changes in the domain of social benefits, that originally were included in the draft (El País 1996). The intergovernmental meeting at Amsterdam in June 1997 was not successful in agreeing on concrete social policies either. Only a commitment to work on reducing unemployment was decided, and the Nice Treaty in 2001 concentrated basically on enlargement issues. This is particularly relevant for France. Indeed, an attachment to some form of interventionist and protectionist European Union was consensual among French political and labor union leaders interviewed.

In brief, these difficulties in producing social policies to palliate the hardship created by the economic adjustments, together with the organizational practices and everyday experiences mentioned in the previous pages (including misunderstandings of the EU actions and policies) has not helped in creating a positive social representation of the EU. Therefore, allegiance for the EU among French people is still uncertain. Indeed, we have seen that large sectors of the population, political leaders, and labor union leaders see the European Union policies with marked skepticism. The majority of the French people are ideologically center-left and they are very wary of capitalism, although they do not believe in an extreme state-oriented economy of the type that existed in the Soviet Union. The French, however, support some moderate intervention of the state in social and economic policies. In fact, they are accepting of the traditional role that the French state has played for most of the twentieth century.

Finally, but not least, the media seem to play a major role in projecting a certain image of the EU and EU policies. An unstructured observation of TV news content in which I recorded only the themes addressed shows that news items were more often related to problems and difficulties that the EU encountered than successes. Also a more structured analysis of the newspaper *Le Monde*, whose editorial line tends to be supportive of the European Union, demonstrated that even in this newspaper a considerable proportion of news on the EU emphasized more the difficulties and tensions. In *Le Monde* the articles on the EU are published in the section on Europe. Of the three papers analyzed this is the only newspaper that has a special section on Europe. *Le Monde* published more articles on the EU than the other newspapers analyzed. Out of the 88 days considered in my sample, *Le Monde* had an article at least on 73 of the days. Given that there were up to four articles on the topic on certain days, there were a total of 94 articles published in *Le Monde*. Thirty-eight percent of the articles published in this newspaper had a negative representation of the EU. Although not all the negative content was always faithfully represented in the headlines, some examples of headlines illustrate the type of coverage very well. For instance, these are some of the recent headlines: "Six Months before Enlargement the Fifteen Still Disagree" (June 24, 2002), "Berlin Criticism Creates Doubts about Its Attitude on Europe" (March 13, 2002). However, most of the articles published in this newspaper, in the issues analyzed, were neutral (41 percent) or represented the EU in a positive light (21 percent).

On the basis of this analysis and on the informal unstructured observation of TV content and other media outlets, one can reasonably deduce that there is probably a tendency in the coverage of the EU by French media to expose more often than not the problems produced by the process of European integration. In certain cases the coverage is purposively oriented towards the negative aspects of this process, but in most cases it is due to the nature of the industry; that is, what determines worthy news seems to be the problems and difficulties and not things that are going well. But as a consequence the French are better informed of the difficulties, the tensions, and the insufficiencies that the EU encounters than they are of its accomplishments.

CONCLUSION

This chapter analyzed the social representation of the EU in France by looking at the context and the framework resulting from the dynamics of European integration, and attempted to understand the significance and meaning that leaders and lay people attached to this process. It also explored the social practices through which national identities are reconstituted in connection with the EU. We have revealed the range of social representations of the EU and recognized the key arguments of each group studied. Then we have discussed the actions and policies of the EU, which contributed to create these social representations.

The renewed activity of the EU during the nineties in establishing new treaties, the stated aim of which is to further political union and to include new members, has produced a debate with mixed and diverse reactions in French society. Whether based on rational ideas or irrational sentiments, a plurality of perceptions and interpretation have generated opposing discourse regarding the meaning and relevance of the European Union. Contrary to many issues, which have historically divided French society along party lines, the debate on the European Union divides the main political parties and, to a lesser degree, the labor unions despite these organizations' official stance.

Furthermore, identification with the nation-state still offers an appealing *grand narrative* to the French population. The idea of sovereignty revealed in the interviews indicates that nationalist principles are still engraved deeply in the French social consciousness, particularly evident in the us/them view of the world, and feelings of deprivation in regard to social policies, which permeates particularly French lay people's criticism of the EU. Economic difficulties and concerns regarding sovereignty and loss of national identity are explained by most of the respondents as the result of domination by other countries in the EU's programs and arrangements (Germany is often mentioned).

The notion of national identity does not have a precise and consensually accepted content and it is more often invoked than described. However imprecise, it still has a powerful meaning. Woven into the fabric of everyday life, this concept informs attitudes about territoriality and social representations, ranging from language to memories of recent and past history, and to concrete experiences with social welfare programs and other policies. Indeed, the constraints resulting from the European integration processes are perceived by half of the respondents as invading French cultural identity and undermining French sovereignty, confirming Smith's theory (1991) on the role of the structure of opportunities and the sense of deprivation in the heightening of nationalism. The growing power of the transnational corporations, the increasing political and economic influence of the decisions made at the European level, and the perceived grievances as a result of those factors—EU policies favoring a free market of goods and capital, the displacement of traditional industries, and the revision of social policies—are helping to foster a negative representation of the EU in France and reinforcing an attachment to the nation-state among large sectors of the society. In other words, to a certain extent, EU policies may end up reinforcing the nationalism they are supposed to supersede.

Furthermore, we have seen that there is a strong connection among the population between perceived national interests, notions of sovereignty, and the sense of national identity (Smith 1991). The type of EU organization that people favor reflects this view. Although there is not a single specific articulation, the bulk of the French elite as well as the lay people are strongly inclined towards an intergovernmental organization of the EU. At the most, some type of loose confederation seems to be the preferred form of organization for now. Very few of the political leaders, either from the left or the right, seem to be ready to accept real transfer of sovereignty to the European Commission or the European Parliament. The old Gaullist slogan, "a Europe of nations,"[30] is often repeated by Gaullists, but also by many socialists I interviewed, as well as the former Prime Minister Lionel Jospin (*Le Monde* 1998). Most French political leaders are associated with a strong centralized state[31] and fear that in a federal form of organization, the French state could lose its prerogatives.

All of the above does not imply that French people do not feel that they are Europeans. In the abstract everyone says that, of course, they feel European because France is in Europe but this does not mean identification with the European union. It seems that in the foreseeable future there will not be a European consciousness that will compete with French national identity. A possible development in the long term, as a result of continuous association, might be the redefinition of cultural boundaries, in which identities could be experienced as multiple layers (national and supranational), which in turn may help to increase support for a more united Europe, as the neofunctionalists (Haas 1968; Mutimer 1989) and other scholars (Tranholm-Mikkelsen 1991) anticipate.[32] However, for this process to happen, there must be experiences that link individuals to the larger community. The process of monetary union might be one such experience. The common currency might have a twofold effect in developing a European consciousness. In economic and political terms, it could result in reinforcing the position of the European Union in the world, as Keohane and Hoffman (1991) suggest, and as is the French leaders' ambition. Indeed, with only a few exceptions, French leaders that I interviewed want the European Union to become a coherent and strong leader in international affairs. At the same time, in cultural terms, the use of the euro in everyday dealings could contribute to the development of a supranational European symbolism. A survey of Sofres (2002) conducted in November 2001 indicates that the euro is perceived by the French as the most important symbol of the European Union.[33] They see the euro as the best symbol to represent Europe, far more even than the most common symbol for many years, the European Flag. Before January 1, 2002, the monetary union implied for almost half of the interviewees the abandonment of an important marker of French identity. But one year after the euro became part of the everyday life of the citizens—people carry this new currency in their wallets—the currency issue has ceased to be a reason for opposition to European integration. One important aspect here has maybe been the fact that after six months of circulation the euro gained in value against the dollar and was for the rest of 2002 more or less stable around U.S. $0.95. Furthermore, the fact that the national euros also carry on one side the various national symbols helped eliminate some of the original concerns regarding national symbolism.[34]

Identification with the European Union depends on its positive social representation. A more positive representation of the EU among the French population will depend to a large extent on whether the EU concentrates its energies on social policies as much as on economic policies.

Finally, it should be noted that France's role in the European Union depends on the political makeup of the government and the Parliament. Until now, the political divisions within France have not affected significantly the central role that the country has been playing in the EU. All the presidents of the last thirty years, D'Estaing (UDF), Mitterrand (PS), or Chirac (UMP), believed that France needed a more united Europe for France to play some meaningful role in the international arena; this was reflected in the actions of their governments, including when there was a coalition between the PS and the UMP.[35] However, the National Front's influence on the population and the convergence on European issues between the National Front and the forces opposing the EU within the Gaullist Party, the small movements on the right (such as De Villiers' *Mouvement pour la France*), on the one hand, and the Communist Party and the other parties of the left such as Lutte Ouvrière-LO (Workers Struggle) and the Ligue Communiste-LC (Communist League), on the other hand, could, at some point in the future, create sufficient opposition to the EU to prevent France from pressing for further integration.[36]

NOTES

An earlier version of this chapter appeared as "National Identity in France and the Process of European Integration." Reprinted from Dobratz, Waldner, and Buzzel, *The Politics of Social Inequality,* Copyright 2001, pages 307–333, with permission from Elsevier Science.

1. Other French intellectuals and prominent politicians worth mentioning who proposed a united Europe were Edouard Herriot and Paul Reynaud.

2. Public support for European Union is measured in the Barometers with mainly two questions: (1) is the country's membership in the EU a good thing? neither good nor bad? or a bad thing? and (2) does the country benefit from membership in the EU? In general, the positive answers tend to be very similar to both questions. That is, they have historically followed the same curve, although the percentage of people saying that belonging to the EU is a good thing is always higher than the percentage expressing that France has benefited from membership in the EU. For instance, between 1992 and 2001 the positive answers to both questions have only on two occasions differed by more than 8 percent (in the 1994 Barometer and in 1996 Barometer). However, the negative answers change considerably. The percentage expressing that the EU is a bad thing has oscillated from 1992 to 2001 between 12 and 19 percent, while the proportion of people who expressed that France had not benefited from belonging to the EU has oscillated between 27 and 45 percent. The percentage I presented in the text as being positive answers is an average of both answers combined.

3. In the 1992 referendum on the Treaty of the Union, according to a Sofres poll (*Le Monde* 25 September 1992), 74 percent of PS voters approved the ratification of the treaty, while 92 percent of the PC supporters voted against it. 58 percent of the UDF voters voted in favor of the treaty, and 67 percent of the RPR electorate voted against the treaty (the RPR is now integrated into the UMP). But this is not really a clear indication of support or rejection of the European Union. The debate was largely influenced by domestic issues and was heavily influenced by expressing support for or against defeating Mitterrand.

4. The use of majority/minority distinction that I am making refers specifically to the different views on European Union within the different parties, and only regarding the European Union, not other issues.

5. The concept of "further integration" means basically the idea of more political integration as it was laid down in the 1992 Treaty on the Union (also referred to as the Maastricht Treaty).

6. All translations are my own unless otherwise noted.

7. Charles Pasqua, although continuing to play a major role within the UMP, created a specific organization for the 1999 European elections called Demain la France.

8. Any decision made on the basis of a majority vote ends up presenting two sides: for or against. In other words, voters might agree with a particular aspect and reject another in a given issue, but when confronted with a choice between two alternatives they are forced to choose. Furthermore, the issues emphasized during a political campaign will force a particular choice. In reality, views and interpretations of the population and political leaders tend to be more complex, more vague, less defined, and less clear than a vote might lead us to think.

9. The two largest parties within the confederation are the Parti Republicain-PR (Republican Party) and the CDS (Christian Democratic Party).

10. After the arrival of the left (the Socialist Party with the firm support of the Communist Party) to power in 1981 a part of the right-wing voters—mostly small businesses owners—were radicalized and started voting for the FN and its leader, Jean-Marie LePen, in subsequent elections. The National Front Party (Front National-FN) was created in 1972, but it was only in 1983 that it came to count in the national political arena by winning a partial municipal election in Dreux, a medium-sized town in the region of Normandy, as a result of an alliance with the moderate right. Then in 1984 in the elections for the European Parliament the FN received around 11 percent of the vote. After those relative successes the Front National started to attract even more voters and became a considerable force by obtaining consistently around 15 percent of the popular vote in most elections. Only in the election for the European Parliament of 1999 did this party receive a low nine percent. In the presidential election of 2002, contrary to expectations and polls, LePen received close to 18 percent of the popular vote in the first round. He was second in the race with two percent less than the candidate of the UMP, Jacques Chirac, eliminating thereby the candidate of the Socialist Party, Lionel Jospin, from the second round. This strong show was possible not only because of the support of the small business owners but also because of the support of a part of the working-class voters who were unhappy with the policies of the Socialist Party, which has been in control of the government for most of the 1980s and 1990s. Indeed in the context of the economic crisis in the mid-1990s during the 1995 presidential election, his support grew considerably among the working class. According to a Sofres poll (2002), 30 percent of people who vote for the FN are working class. The economy is one important issue for the working class but also immigration. The workers have also punished the Communist Party because they see this party as too tolerant in immigration issues.

11. The elections in France require two rounds if a particular candidate does not get 50 percent plus one vote. This implies that in the second round, only the two candidates who received the most votes would be contending. For the presidential election it is obligatory that only the first two candidates should stay in competition. In parliamentary elections often those in third or fourth position tend to support one of the contenders who were first and second (although this is not automatically the case).

12. Until recently this organization was called Confédération Nationale du Patronat Français-CNPF (National Confederation of French Industrialists).

13. Surveys conducted from 1998 to 2002 show some notable variations in French views on the EU. However, the major tendencies remain the same. A slight majority support further European integration, and when it comes to questions of identity the French are divided in half. A Sofres (2001b) poll, conducted November 27–29, 2001, shows that a majority of French citizens (60 percent) think that France

has benefited from belonging to the EU. This is relatively high in relation to previous polls. However, a previous poll in February of 2001 (Sofres 2001a) also showed a positive outlook on the same question. Forty-eight percent thought that France had benefited from belonging to the EU against 37 percent who believed that France has not benefited from belonging. Regarding the image of Europe in France in the same poll (Sofres 2001a), the results show that 53 percent do not fear the consequences of further European integration, against 43 percent who do fear European integration. Furthermore, in a related question about attachment to further European integration there is a division in half; 49 percent do not want further integration and 50 percent agree with further integration. Furthermore, 42 percent are concerned about losing French national identity as a result of European integration and 52 percent do not think that there will be loss of French cultural identity.

14. Here my findings differ considerably from the Eurobarometers. Only 28 percent of French lay people I interviewed could explain the basic function of the Council of Ministers, while the Eurobarometers (Eurobarometer 50 1999; Eurobarometer 54 2000; Eurobarometer 56 2002) show that above 40 percent are aware of the Council and more than 60 percent consider it important. I found a similar proportion in the case of Spain (30 percent) and 18 percent in the case of the United Kingdom. Barometer findings are also higher in these two countries (72 percent of awareness in Spain and 22 percent in the United Kingdom). Again this difference is due to the type of question. The Eurobarometer questions ask if people are aware of the existence of the Council, and then of its importance, while in my research I actually ask people if they know what the Council is, and its role in the decision-making process of the EU. Of course my qualitative study cannot claim generalization in the same way that a quantitative survey based on a random sample of the population can.

15. This is also reflected in a recent survey (Sofres 2002). This study shows that French citizens believe that France has the best health-care system and the best retirement conditions, compared with the other countries of the EU.

16. As the work of Edwards (1985) shows, the tendency to value language as a fundamental marker of national identity is common in many societies.

17. A top manager of a large U.S.-based company was complaining to me recently: "Europeans perceive Americans as primitive people and violent warriors, or cowboys always ready to use force."

18. The agreement on the single European currency requires the member nations to comply with the following parameters: an inflation rate of no more than 1.5 percent higher than the three lowest national rates in the EU, long-term interest rates no more than 3 percent higher than the three lowest EU rates, and a budget deficit less than 3 percent of the GDP. Sweden has not yet met the criteria. Denmark and the United Kingdom exercised their right under the Treaty of the Union not to participate.

19. The principle of subsidiarity implies that the EU should act to extend its competency to those areas that are better done at the supranational level and leave the other actions and policies to be developed at the national level. The problem is that not everyone agrees on what actions, laws, and policies should be decided at the European level.

20. Since the Maastricht Treaty referendum in 1992, the cleavages have been

remarkably stable along socioeconomic and educational status: top-level and mid-level managers, as well as university and high school graduates tend to favor the process of European integration, while agriculturalists, blue-collar workers, low-level employees, and people with no degree or only a few years of high school tend to oppose European integration.

21. Upper-level employees in corporations, for example, often travel abroad for their jobs and have frequent contact with other Europeans. In fact, some businesses depend entirely on the international market that the European Union has created.

22. These numbers are presented as trends perceived in the groups interviewed. Their explanatory power relies on contrasting differences among the people interviewed only, and to the extent that they are representatives of the positions on the EU in the different parties and unions.

23. I found no significant differences between men and women regarding this issue. Among lay people, however, there was a slight difference according to age: Persons under age 30 tend to be more receptive to a federal Europe than persons age 31 and above.

24. I grew up in the South of France, where I experienced this practice firsthand.

25. This is not totally specific to French society: Habermas (1992) observes that in German society there is a general tendency as well to establish a connection between universal values and the nation-state.

26. The hostility of the French farmers to the word *Europe* or *European* is a tradition and is acknowledged by everyone. What is more revealing, however, is that, even though French farmers constitute only a small minority of the French work force and have a relatively limited weight in economic terms, they still maintain broad support in French society. A survey conducted in the early 1990s during a negotiation of the EU with the United States showed that 82 percent of the French supported the farmers in their rejection of the agreement with Washington, and 69 percent wanted the French government to veto the agreement even if that measure would have provoked a crisis within the EU (IP-SOS-Le Point 1992). This support seems to have diminished slightly by the end of the 1990s but is still relatively strong.

27. The central bank is the only European institution with the power to affect all countries of the Union and no institution counterbalances its power. It should be noted, however, that the Maastricht Treaty extended the powers to the Parliament by reinforcing its capacity to amend projects proposed by the European Council in several domains and by bestowing on the Parliament the right of veto on several themes (consumer protection, transports, telecommunications, energy, education, etc.). This is called the co-decision-making process.

28. In fact, although Germany has played a central role in influencing the model of monetary union, the decision to provide Europe with a single currency was first suggested by the French government in 1988. Then, in 1992, following German reunification, the president of France, François Mitterrand, strongly pushed Helmut Kohl and the other members of the EU to create the monetary union as soon as possible. Although the project of a monetary union had been in the making for years, mostly in terms of the economic advantages, the decision to establish it at that particular moment was evidently political. Indeed, the German reunification, which was not expected so soon, rushed and modified the process of European Union as it was conceived since the 1960s. The process of European integration

was initiated in the 1950s, when Germany was subjugated and divided. France and England were losing their empires, and no one in Western Europe could be hegemonic in an era rather frozen by the cold war. However, in 1992, the German reunification gave rise to fears that a too-strong Germany might want to lead Europe or even break apart from Western Europe and switch its allegiance to Eastern Europe. To ward off this danger Mitterrand asked Kohl, who accepted, to firmly tie Germany to the European Union by establishing a monetary union.

29. In fact, the Treaty of Maastricht, which laid down the basis for the present process of European integration, already had a more technocratic than democratic conception of Europe and expressed the primacy of economics over politics and social issues.

30. The term *nation*, as De Gaulle and the other politicians use it today in France, refers to what we define in the social sciences as the nation-state. I must specify that the use of *the Europe of nations* by Jospin and other French politicians doesn't have exactly the same meaning that it did in de Gaulle's time. Indeed, de Gaulle used the term in combination with a sense of French grandeur and uniqueness as well as referring the *mission civilisatrice de la France* (civilizing mission of France), in which destiny would spread the values of the French revolution: liberty, freedom, and democracy.

31. The administrative decentralization, which was made in progressive steps during the second half of this century, did not really change the centralized role of the French state.

32. Some core values of *Europeanness* often mentioned include: Roman law, Christianity, democracy, Renaissance humanism, individualism, rationalism, the free market, and private property (Smith 1991).

33. Cognitive psychological theories (Boski 1989; Egan 1997; Fiske and Taylor 1984) show that as individuals become involved in institutions, and make use of the corresponding myths and symbols, their self-identification changes accordingly.

34. The idea of using national symbols in the euro coins was in this aspect very definite in helping to subsume opposition on the basis of national identity: "You know to me it was like when we changed from old francs to new francs. I was not sure of the value for a while, but the euro is also French, I do not see it necessarily as a bad thing. In fact it is good that we do not have to change money when we go to most countries of Europe" (Retired postal worker, Provence).

35. In the French political system, the president is elected for five years (until the mid-1990s it was seven years) and the parliament (Assemblée Nationale) for four years. This means that it is possible that a president from a given party would govern with the ministers from the opposition party. The president has to form a government with members of the political party who win most seats in the parliament. The president nominates the prime minister (who is the leader of the majority party in the parliament), who then chooses the different ministers that form the executive branch of the government. When a president is from one party and his government from the opposition party there is *cohabitation*.

36. These parties, the LO and the LC, reached 10 percent of the votes in the 2002 presidential election. If this influence continues they would be a force of importance not only because of their electoral weight, but also because they represent mostly students and the younger population, which tend to be rather combative.

CHAPTER 3

Spain: Enchantment and Disenchantment

The chapter examines how Spanish people (general public and leaders) view the European Union and themselves within this organization, in the intertwined areas of economics, politics, and culture, and attempts to explain how these social representations of the EU are produced and reproduced.

A brief overview of newspapers, political speeches, and scholarly works reveals that very few Spaniards rejected the idea of belonging to the European Union (at that time the European Community) in 1985, when the treaty of membership was signed. Spaniards from all political allegiances and socioeconomic backgrounds were largely content to become part of a select club of developed and democratic nations, after being isolated from Europe for a half century during the Francoist dictatorship (only some small far left groups showing some reservations).[1] Membership in the European Union was presented by the political and economic elites as a unique opportunity for economic development and the consolidation of democracy.[2] Besides, for the two years following the treaty (which was effective in January, 1986), Spain became the top recipient of foreign investment worldwide, resulting in the highest rate of economic growth in the community (above 5 percent from 1986 to 1989). In fact, according to data provided by the Instituto Nacional de Estadística (1996), between 1985 and 1995 the Spanish economy grew 3 percent a year on average, and per capita income increased by 41 percent (the greatest growth occurring from 1985 to 1991). Average per capita income rose from 66 percent of the European Union average in 1986 to 72 percent in 1991. From 1992 on, the average income continued to grow, but at a slighter slower pace and with ups and downs. In 2001 it was at 82 percent of the EU average. The structural funds and the cohesion funds provided by the EU[3] contributed decisively to the improvement of infrastructure, such as roads, bridges, and agricultural works. In sum, the first years of Spain's membership in the European Union brought a qualitative transformation of the economic structure and the creation of significant wealth. Further- more, a few years after becoming member of the EU, the country was no longer portrayed in the foreign media and by other European citizens as a backward, rural, conservative society. It was more often than not de- picted as a modern, secularized, liberal democracy. All these circum- stances reinforced Spaniards' satisfaction with membership in the EU, as reflected in various surveys conducted in the late 1980s and early 1990s (i.e., Eurobarometer 30 1988; Eurobarometer 32 1989; Eurobarometer 34 1990; Eurobarometer 36 1991; Eurobarometer 38 1992).[4]

From 1992 to 1996, however, this support had considerably eroded among the population. While at the end of the 1980s well above 60 percent of Spaniards felt positive about belonging to the EU, with a peak approval in 1990 of 78 percent (Eurobarometer 36 1991), by 1996 this proportion had declined to 51 percent (Eurobarometer 46 1996). From 1998 to 2001 the support for the EU started to increase again but did not return to the high level of support of the earlier years; in the fall of 2001, only 57 percent of Spaniards expressed support for European Union membership (Euro- barometer 56 2002). Thus, if we accept the validity of these studies, one could categorize Spanish people's relations with the EU in three major periods: the first, just after membership, of great enthusiasm (1986–1991), then a period of disenchantment (1992–1996), and then a third period that we can call conditional support for the EU (1997–2003). The field research that produced most of the material that I am using in this book was done between the spring of 1996 and the spring of 2002. It corresponds roughly to the latest period. Next, I examine the interpretation and understanding of the European Union according to political parties, labor unions, busi- ness leaders, and lay people. First, I briefly summarize the major tenden- cies in each of the above groups regarding the EU, and then I address their positions concerning the organization of the EU, followed by an attempt to explain these social representations, with emphasis on those that are triggering negative reactions to the EU.

THE VIEWS OF THE LEADERS

In general, my interviews confirm what many surveys have reflected in the 1990s: the Spanish political and business elites tend to largely sup- port the European Union. This quote from the 1992 Christmas speech by the King Juan Carlos (a very influential institution himself), summarizes very well many of the responses I received from political and business leaders regarding their views on Europe:

We are in Europe and in Europe we shall remain because we are Europe, because Europe needs us. We will thus become more and more integrated in it, without obsession or haste but conscious about the fact that we must proceed along this path with confident and prudent steps. We must persist in this effort because the modern world needs Europe and, also, because Europe's process towards unity will not be halted, regardless of obstacles that seem at first, like on other historical occasions, insurmountable. These are to be expected in such an ambitious and multifaceted enterprise. The fact of belonging to Europe enriches our national identity. (Discursos 1996, cited in Díez Medrano and Gutiérrez 2001: 765–66)

However, as we will see, this support has many different meanings. The in-depth interviews reveal the complexities, diffuseness, and variety of representations of Europe among the leaders. In analyzing the details we found that there is no consensus on the positive and negative aspects of EU membership even among the leaders of the same political party. Yet, certain tendencies predominate, and I will try to review these in the following paragraphs.

The Spanish Socialist Party (PSOE) has been historically very pro-European Union. The totality of leaders I interviewed from this party regard Spanish membership in the EU as utterly crucial. Former Premier Felipe González even wrote "that the European vocation is a sign of identity for our country" (1998). According to these leaders, the European Union has decisively supported and facilitated Spain's economic expansion and political modernization, and as one PSOE leader from the Basque country explains, "The European framework has given Spain the stability and the tools to develop and consolidate as a more articulated country, without a serious crisis." With very few exceptions, socialists were also proud that after years of isolation "for the first time in this century, Spain is participating directly in the development of Europe." These leaders value what they see as the opportunity afforded to Spain of "participating in the historical project of building the European Union" (Gonzàlez 1996: 8). Although some deplore that they would have to give up part of Spanish sovereignty, they see it as a necessary trade-off in order to face the challenges posed by the intensification of the globalization process in recent years. With only one exception, the interviewees from the socialist party stated that the EU is the best alternative to confront the negative aspects of globalization: "The European Union, and the monetary union in particular, is absolutely necessary for Spain, even if this entails giving up a little bit of sovereignty." The argument here is that: "in order to maintain equal rank with the United States, Japan, and with China, as well as to be able to face the power of large corporations [the union is a key necessity]" (PSOE-PSC leader, Catalonia). This has been the central argument in the PSOE for the past six years. Even those who were critical of the EU and had some reservations about many of its policies argued that Spain could not compete in the world economy alone: "No western European country has the economic weight and power to defend its interests properly in the world market" (PSOE leader, Madrid). The suggestion was also made that the EU could contribute to regulating society in order "to maintain in Spain and in Europe social justice, and a good welfare system" (PSOE leader, Madrid).

Regarding the monetary union, a large majority do conceive Spanish participation in a unique currency as very positive and see it as a very important step in the process of European integration, as the following interviewee asserts: "A unique currency benefits each country economically and reinforces the EU's economic weight in the world" (PSOE leader, Andalusia). However, on this issue there has been a certain discontent among a significant number of leaders who believed that the price to pay in terms of limiting social benefits was too high for Spain, and particularly for the working class. Some even suggested that the PSOE lost the elections in 1996 because they started applying the restrictive policies that made possible for Spain the integration into the common currency.

Judging by the interviews, the Spanish socialist party has in fact very few *euroskeptics*, at least during the period analyzed here (1996–2002) and it is less divided on this aspect than the French Socialist Party. Therefore, the debate within this party regarding the European Union has not been particularly intense in the last six years. Nevertheless, a sizeable number of leaders interviewed (36 percent) do question the role that Europe has played in defining social policies and consider that there should be a stronger stance of the socialists on this issue. The following quote summarizes and reflects several comments made by interviewees from this party:

I think we lack clear and programmatic ideas with a defined social-democratic content and a commitment to use the European Union to accomplish those objectives. I mean, to really work with the institutions of the European Union in addressing problems of poverty and social injustice that are produced by the capitalist system. The social democratic parties of Europe have dominated European politics for most of the 1980s and 1990s and we have in fact been good managers of the capitalist system, not doing enough to combat its excesses. (PSOE leader, Andalusia)

This small minority does not see that the European Union has been, on the whole, positive for Spain. They point to the dismantling of the social welfare system, which was still underdeveloped in comparison with most of the other countries north of the Pyrenees. They argue that the pressures coming from the EU demanding the liberalization of the economy ended up reverting to the tendency of expanding the welfare system initiated in the mid-1980s by the Socialist Party, then in power. To be sure, all interviewees from the Socialist Party agreed that the social pillar of the European Union has to be developed, but the divergences exist on whom and what to blame for not developing the social integration in parallel with economic integration.

Indeed, the economic paradigm that has predominated in Europe for the last 12 years has been strongly influenced by neoliberal ideology. The basic argument has been that the logic of the global market made it necessary for the EU member countries to reduce the labor costs, including the cost of welfare policies, in order to enhance their global competitiveness. This view has certainly stirred concrete policies that have started to undermine the welfare system. The leaders of the PSOE consider that it is time to review these policies and see the EU as the necessary instrument and political space for these revisions to be effective.[5]

The widespread majority belief in this party is that it is at the European level that a social contract must be established. Nevertheless, there is a minority of leaders who thinks that the Spanish state cannot wait for a European Union, whose policies have in fact contributed to undermining a process still in progress: "I doubt that the European Union would be able to significantly influence social policies in the near future. The recent history shows rather the opposite" (PSOE leader, Asturias). The members of the Socialist Party who hold this minority view, although only a few, (22 percent of those interviewed from this party) are scattered in all the regions of Spain and seem to have a considerable resonance among the socialist sympathizers. In the same tone, a leader of the PSOE in Andalusia questions the efficiency or the desire of the EU to stimulate social programs in Europe: " . . . the EU has been rather good at establishing economic agreements which have integrated considerably our economies but the standards of living are still far apart between the south and the north, and in the case of Spain it is due to a rather primitive welfare system if we compare it with the rest of Europe."

The conservative Partido Popular is relatively divided on the question of the European union. Although the official party line obviously has tended to support the European Union since this party came to power in 1996, my interviews show that many leaders still perceive the European Union as a possible threat to Spanish sovereignty and independence. In fact, 52 percent of the members of this party that I interviewed expressed concerns about going too far in the integration process, as expressed in the following quote:

I support the idea of the European Union in terms of agreements among states, particularly on economic matters, defense matters, peace agreements, and the fight against crime, but I think we should try hard to keep our own state and keep Spain as an independent country with its own army and particular culture. (PP leader, Asturias)

As one might expect, the interviews reflect some divisions within the same political parties regarding the European Union, but they are not as clear-cut as in the case of France. In the party in power, the Partido Popular-PP (Popular Party), there is a conditional majority support for European Union. In this party I found more euroskeptics than in the Socialist Party. These individuals expressed concerns over sovereignty: "More often than not, Spain has to accept the propositions of its more powerful partners. In that context, there is a clear loss of national sovereignty" (PP leader, Madrid), and over the Spanish economy, as exemplified in the following quote:

Because of the requirements of the European Union, I see Spain's productive capacity being dismantled little by little and [Spain] becoming basically a big supermarket for products that come from all over Europe and the world. We will be left with only the tourist industry, like any third world country. The European Union does not fulfill Spain's needs, as it does for France and Germany. (PP leader, Galicia)

These negative evaluations of Spain's membership in the European Union were expressed by 56 percent of the people from the Popular Party that I interviewed. When asked whether being part of the EU was a good thing, more than 80 percent responded positively in the abstract, but then many expressed their specific concerns, which are reflected in the above quotes. Others made references to the difficulties that Spain encountered in continuing to develop its agriculture, and reducing unemployment, often implying that the EU policies were to a certain extent responsible.

Forty-two percent of the Popular Party seems to embrace Europe in a very positive light and consider that overall Spain has benefited considerably from being a member of the EU. The following quote from a leader of the PP in Catalonia is a good example of this approach: "I know that not everyone in my party shares my view, but I think that with some problems here and there, being part of the EU has been great for Spain and we should continue working closely with the institutions of the EU and the other member countries." This minority group of the PP is not concerned over a possible loss of sovereignty. The following argument, which evokes views similar to the Socialist Party, is an example of this approach:

Even though we cannot say with certainty that the EU has been efficient in preventing the negative aspects of the free global market, I think it has the potential to compensate for the loss of national sovereignty. In any case, we have to recognize that Spain, and probably no country in Europe, can confront by themselves the power of the larger countries, such as the United States or China. (PP leader, Madrid)

The leftist parties included in my sample: Izquierda Unida-IU (United Left), Iniciativa por Cataluña (Initiative for Catalonia), Esquerra Republicana de Cataluña-ERC (Republican Left of Catalonia), and Bloque Nacionalista Gallego-BNG (Galician Nationalist Block), and the labor unions, tend to perceive the European Union as an organization that gives primacy to economic agreements among corporations and is detrimental to the people, particularly the working class: "The European Union is basically the union of capitalists and the power of decision is too much based on the nation-state" (Leader ERC). The leaders of the most important party on the left (Izquierda Unida-IU) and of the two main unions (UGT and CCOO) oppose the European union because of the market policies applied since the Maastricht Treaty. They categorize the EU as a bureaucracy at the service of the capitalist corporations and the most economically powerful member countries. In other words, the social concomitants of neoliberalism that dominate in the EU gave people on the left an inducement to assert their national identity on the basis of economic well-being for the working class. Those leaders feel that the globalizing forces of the EU are not pro-working class; therefore, they see dealing with the national government as the best alternative for this social class. Izquierda Unida leaders express that Spain is not playing an important role in the Union: "The problem with Europe is that it is really run by France and Germany. Spain is a secondary actor" (Leader IU, Andalusia), and that the country is losing national sovereignty, and national identity: "I think that we cannot deny that the European Union is changing some of our national characteristics" (Leader IU, Madrid). From the economic and social point of view most of the left (except for the Socialist Party) are rather critical, but not to the point of demanding withdrawal of Spain from the EU. They judge the EU in terms of their perceptions of policies and how they perceive that these policies have affected the working class. In other words, the arguments of the left also vary considerably. For instance, for those people I interviewed from IC, the working class and the labor unions should pressure for change at the EU level, as well as at the national level. Three interviewees from IU share this opinion, while the rest of the left are more oriented towards keeping a certain power of decision on social issues at the national level. They believe it would be "easier and more beneficial for the working class" to work with the Spanish government than with the EU. In any case there is some agreement among these parties in considering that "the EU has depended almost exclusively on economic agreements," of which the most visible and recent example is the monetary union, whereas "political agreements and social matters have been neglected." They present the persistent high unemployment rate in Spain as an example of the lack of interest by the EU in addressing social problems: "Unemployment is one of the most urgent problems in Spain, we read in the newspapers where they talk about it but nothing is done" (Leader IU, Madrid).

Furthermore, even though the structural and cohesion funds of the European Union are being invested in those regions of Spain that have been traditionally backwards or have suffered as consequence of the structural changes in the economy promoted by the EU and the central government, some regional political leaders believe that not enough has been done, particularly in Asturias, Galicia, and Andalusia. The following quote express these frustrations:

If we look at the consequences of European integration for the whole country, maybe there are some sectors and some regions that have benefited by being part of the European Union, but for Galicia it has been a loss. For instance, agriculture, cattle production, fishing, and the shipbuilding industry, basic and historical sectors of the economy in our region, have been either totally neglected or forced to reduce production. (Political leader, Bloque Nacionalista Gallego-BNG [Galician Nationalist Block], Galicia)

Moreover, representatives of the regionalist and the nationalist groups (such as members of the Basque Nationalist Party, the Republican Left of Catalonia, and the Galician Nationalist Block) expressed that the European Union was not dealing appropriately with the regions and the autonomies. They complained that all negotiations were made through the central government in Madrid.

The labor union leaders, although in large majority not opposed in principle to the European union, have many reservations about what has been accomplished socially speaking as a result of European integration. Contrary to the situation of the labor unions in France, in Spain there was not a major difference between leaders from the major different unions regarding the European union. All the interviewees expressed criticism of the EU policies. However, when discussing benefits and disadvantages of the European Union, the union leaders considered the Spanish government as being as responsible as the EU for policies that negatively affected the working class, and these cleavages were similar in both labor unions: Confederación General de Trabajadores-CGT (Worker's General Confederation) and Unión General de Trabajadores-UGT (General Worker's Union).[6] A recurring concern of the labor union leaders was unemployment. This was equally voiced in 1996, when I started my field research, as in 2001, even though according to EU publications, Spain's unemployment rates went from 20 percent in 1996 to 12.9 percent in 2001: "Unemployment is the major problem that Spain has to confront, and the present government is not confronting it because the main priority is to keep pace with the application of neoliberal policies promoted by the EU"(Union leader CCOO, Madrid). Half of the labor union leaders interviewed were also concerned over the Spanish government losing the ability to determine social policies because of the EU: "The policies that our government is adopting are clearly influenced by the decisions taken by the bureaucracy of the EU, under the leadership of Germany" (Labor union leader, UGT, Andalusia).

However, only a minority of the political and labor union elites interviewed (26 percent) see the EU as threatening Spanish cultural identity. This concern is reflected in the following statement: "There is no doubt in my mind that being part of the European Union has come at a great cost to our culture" (Leader CCOO, Madrid). The large majority of political, labor union, and economic leaders, although also concerned about the importance of defending cultural identity, do not think the European Union is a threat to Spanish national identity: "Spain has a strong cultural tradition. Although the English language, for example, is very influential, Spanish will not disappear. I think that European nations can strive for unity while maintaining their national identities" (Union leader, UGT, Andalusia).

Business leaders are mostly divided according to the size of the business they represent. The representatives of large companies tend to be largely in favor of European integration: "The European Union has opened up markets for our products. This has been great for us and especially for the Spanish economy"(Industrialist, Madrid). There is also a perception that the opening of borders has allowed them to gain markets: "Before, because of the tax on imports, our production was limited largely to the Spanish market. Now we have more access to the other countries of the Union, and as a result our business has increased enormously" (Business representative, Madrid). While four of the five representatives from small companies interviewed saw the EU in a negative light and believed that their survival would depend on some type of support by the national state against competition from foreign companies, "We entered the European market with primitive structures. Therefore we cannot compete on equal footing with big European corporations. Neither the Spanish government nor the European institutions are doing much for us" (Representative of a small businesses organization, Asturias). Small business representatives expected that the government would assume the role of adjusting national and local economies to the demands of a more integrated market at the European level and suggested some form of protectionism in certain areas.

This overview of some of the main points made by all the leaders will be completed with the examination of lay people's views (those who do not occupy any recognizable position of leadership in Spanish society).

LAY CITIZENS: UTILITARIANISM AND SYMBOLISM

When lay people were asked about their views on the European Union the answers were very diverse and conditional, with a majority suggesting that being part of the EU was necessary even if it was not perfect. Contrary to what I expected, a small minority of those I interviewed (9 percent) were rather hostile to the EU and tended to be strongly anti-European. The majority of the people interviewed were in-between; they opposed Europe in certain things and agreed with other things. As stated in the introduction to the book, I will examine here most particularly the social representations of the EU that are producing negative reactions in the population. Among lay people, the opposition to the present process of European integration is strongest among those whose livelihood is directly or indirectly related to agriculture, the fishing industry, and the coal and steel industries. In Galicia and Asturias, for example, regions that have endured the restructuring of their industries (coal and steel, shipbuilding) and other important activities such as fishing and agriculture in the past decade, people tend to see the European Union as a disadvantage, more than in other regions such as Andalusia, Catalonia, or the community of Madrid.

Lay citizens expressed an array of grievances, mostly economic, including perceptions that Spain's economic situation is not really better as a result of membership in the EU: "I see that being part of the European Union has not produced more jobs, and the cost of living is going up." As in the case of France, the agricultural issue produces skepticism regarding the EU. Lay citizens interviewed tend to believe that membership in the EU has been negative for Spanish agriculture and has contributed to increasing the price of consumer goods. A 2000 survey (CIS 2000) confirms this tendency. Thirty-five and a half percent of respondents believed that membership in the EU had little benefited Spanish agriculture, and 25.7 percent believe that agriculture had not benefited at all, while only 22.3 percent thought that membership in the EU had benefited Spanish agriculture. Similar results were expressed regarding the fishing industry (34.1 percent said it had benefited little and 27.3 percent saw no benefit, while only 14.6 percent believed it had benefited), and cattle production (33.9 percent said it benefited little, 23.8 percent saw no benefit at all, and 18.7 percent saw a benefit). The perceptions were more positive regarding tourism, business, and manufacturing.

These perceptions are based to a certain extent on concrete experiences and or direct observation in many regions of Spain. The European Union's agricultural regulations have forced Spain to reduce its agricultural production in many areas. For instance, Spanish wine producers were required to uproot many vines. Similarly, milk producers had to drastically reduce their production; many medium-sized and small farmers were forced to abandon their farming. It is no coincidence that the people in Spain most strongly opposed to the EU are the farmers. They believe that they have been sacrificed—used as a means of exchange—to bring benefits to other sectors of the economy. They think that agriculture has had to pay a high price for the construction of highways and other infrastructure. The available data on commercial exchange between Spain and the other countries in the Union seem to support those claims. The balance has been negative in most areas of the economy and particularly in agriculture.[7] In 1986, the year Spain became a member of the European Community, it sold $2.2 billion more than it bought from the other 11 members (El País 1996). Gradually imports grew larger than exports in most sectors of the economy (the inclusion of new members in 1995 did not significantly modify this tendency). Since 1990 the trade balance with the EU has always been negative, and it has increased considerably in the late 1990s. In 2000, Spain had a deficit of 19.165 billion euros with the EU and a 17.985 billion deficit in 2001 (Instituto Nacional de Estadística-INE 2002).[8]

However, in macroeconomic terms, membership in the EU contributed to economic growth in general. If we include in the analysis both the commercial exchange and resources received by Spain from the structural and cohesion funds, there is a net positive balance for 1986–2000 (Instituto Nacional de Estadisticas 2002). For the managers of the state apparatus this data is eventually what counts the most, but most people, as we have seen, do not necessarily make that distinction (most people logically tend to see the economy in micro terms). Furthermore, as already stated elsewhere in this book, the funds coming from the EU are administered by the state, and with the exception of some signs at construction sites, stating that the financial support of the EU funded that particular work, not much publicity is done by the state apparatus specifying the origin of these funds. Lay citizens hear from politicians that a given restructuring of an industry, which forced a certain number of workers to retire, and because of which some lost their jobs, was due to requirements of the EU, or that such and such a policy is in response to EU regulations, and so on. They do not see the overall picture or they even feel angry that other sectors of the society have benefited while they had to endure the cost of policies supposedly initiated by the EU.

Another grievance often mentioned by the interviewees is the high unemployment rate. As we have seen, this issue was also of foremost concern to both political and union leaders. In fact, most political leaders and the population in general consider this the major problem that Spain has to confront. A survey from April 2002 (CIS) reaffirms decisively this tendency: 70.5 percent of respondents considered unemployment the main problem of Spanish society,[9] well above any other issue (for instance the second most important problem mentioned was ETA terrorism (58.2 percent). However, in terms of whom or what to blame as the cause of unemployment there has been a considerable change of perceptions. A study done in 1995 by the CIS found that 40 percent of Spaniards interviewed in 1995 believed that membership in the EU had contributed to unemployment, while only 27 percent thought that Europe had helped to create employment in Spain (CIS 1995). However, a more recent survey, conducted in May 2000 (CIS 2000) indicated inverse results; only 18.1 percent thought that it had contributed to increased unemployment, while 41 percent of the population believed that the EU has contributed to reduce unemployment in Spain. However, on the other hand, most respondents have little trust (39.8 percent) or none at all (16.3 percent) that the EU could solve the problem of unemployment, while 34.7 percent think that the EU will contribute to solving this problem (CIS 2000). This idea that the EU is not really contributing to solve the problem of unemployment was also evident in my individual interviews and has been rather consistent throughout the last six years.

Contrary to the Spanish government expectations in the late 1980s, membership in the European Union did not reduce unemployment in Spain. In fact, for 12 years after membership, the unemployment rate rose, even during the years of high economic growth in the late 1980s. In 1998, 18.4 percent of the working population was unemployed according to Eurocom (1999). The reforms put into effect to keep the country in conformity with the monetary union requirements[10] and with the policies promoted in Brussels had not helped to reduce unemployment substantially. Only in 2000 did the unemployment rate start to go down. However, by the end of 2001, although better than it had been for years, it was still the highest in the EU, at 12.9 percent.[11]

Although the various political parties, unions, and business organizations hardly agreed on the pace and extent of the policies that should be applied in Spain, the two predominant political parties (PSOE and PP) that have most strongly influenced state policies during the last ten years have applied similar policies, largely inspired by EU recommendations. These policies have been oriented toward reducing deficits, which have resulted in limiting the costs of human resources—wages, social security, retirement, and other related social benefits (such as unemployment compensation). The implementation of these policies has produced strong reactions from the labor unions and their allies on the left.[12] There have been many confrontations between labor unions and the government, including general strikes. First, there were protests against the PSOE in 1994–95 and then, since 1997, against the Popular Party. In short, the policies that were carried out to fulfill the monetary union requirements and to continue to keep the country's economy in accordance with the parameters established by the EU have lessened support for the EU among the working class, and this support is not likely to strengthen in the near future.

On the contrary, one might expect more conflict and a growing opposition to the European Union among the working class and their political allies, especially after enlargement, which will bring into the EU countries that can offer even lower labor costs and a relatively low-cost welfare system (if any).

While economic problems do play an exacerbating role, they are not the only factors eroding support for further European integration, and reinforcing the attachment to the nation-state.[13] As noted earlier, in addition to perceived economic grievances, other aspects in the symbolic realm have created negative feelings toward the European Union. Representations of sovereignty and national identity constitute the most salient aspects.

Sixty-four percent of the Spanish lay people interviewed believe that the European Union strongly influences Spanish policies while Spain has little say in the European Union. For instance: "I do not think we count much in the EU. Just look at which country controls the most important offices in the European organization. We are hardly getting secondary offices" (Miner, Asturias).

Most Spaniards interviewed expect that their government will provide a structure to ease the insecurities of their existence and will represent them honorably. When these expectations are not met they criticize the government, but they also take refuge in the traditional ethno-political divisions, blaming the other countries of the union for what they perceive as conditions unfavorable to Spain: "I think that Spain cannot really influence the other countries. We just follow policies established by others, especially Germany, France, and what is even worse, by the U.K." (Restaurant owner, Catalonia, Barcelona).

Furthermore, respondents perceive the European Union not only as a foreign power but as an organization beyond their control: "If we are unhappy with our government we can always vote for a different party, but with the European Union we do not have any mechanism to let our voices be heard." Even though the European Parliament has seen its power increase significantly in recent years since the Treaty on European Union, most Spaniards still perceive the European Parliament as a useless entity: "The European Parliament is more a decorative institution than anything else" (Bank employee, Andalusia).

The EU is seen as a distant and vertical power. It is not perceived as providing a meaningful context for social action and participation. This is clearly demonstrated in my interviews, but also in surveys.[14] By contrast, Spaniards see the local and national context as offering more institutional mechanisms to defend themselves from the uncertainties of the globalization process. Forty-seven percent of people interviewed mention the state and not the EU as providing for development and welfare programs. The fact is that although the vast majority of Spanish people are not opposed in the abstract to European integration, they still consider important the defense of national identity and the nation-state, while the EU is viewed in some respects as favoring the interests of other countries. Their reaction is a defense of what they consider their interests, which they see as better defended by the national state. In addition, many of my respondents, 44 percent, do not believe that there is a culture common to all Europeans, while only 28 percent think that there is a cultural commonality. The rest felt that they did not know enough about the other countries of the European Union to properly comment on that particular aspect. In the Eurobarometer 50 (1999) there was a question that attempted to measure whether people believed that there is a European cultural identity shared by all Europeans; the findings showed a similar tendency to my interviews: 50 percent of Spaniards did not think there was a cultural identity shared by all Europeans while 33 percent answered positively.[15]

In the minds of most lay people, the attachment to national sovereignty is often coupled with a perceived threat to national identity: 41 percent of those interviewed expressed concern about losing cultural identity as a result of European integration.[16] Their concerns are typified in the following quotations: "with the European Union we are changing; we are losing our national characteristics"(Government agency employee), and:

Spain is not the same now. People are more and more interested in things that come from the outside. You can see the cultural penetration in the way people dress, in what they watch on TV, in what they buy, in the music they listen to, and even in what they eat. Also, the English language is everywhere. A lot of people feel good about being part of Europe but they are also giving up their culture. In fact, through Europe what we really get is the culture of the United States of America. (Bank employee, Madrid)

The reference to U.S. culture was often mentioned when referring to Europe. It is indeed observable that through commercialism and mass media, the U.S. culture is more tangible, more present than any incipient European culture. The presence of U.S. culture has increased in recent years, as Spain has opened up to Europe.[17] In other words, a considerable proportion of people interviewed (34 percent) articulated a chain of influence equating the EU with globalization, which is in turn equated with the free market and with a U.S. view of the world. Individuals' sense of national identity appears as a mechanism of differentiation in order to oppose globalization and the domination of the free market, which is perceived as leading to deteriorating social relations by this group of interviewees. However, there are other interpretations of this process that do not consider the EU as the negative agent of cultural change. As this interviewee argues:

Indeed, the Spanish culture is not the same that it was forty or fifty years ago, but that is not due to the European Union only. The national culture is changing because of many external influences. We are in a globalized world and even the Franco dictatorship could not prevent cultural penetration. By opening to exchange with the world we are exposed to many influences that little by little make us different, for better or for worse, but I think that the EU is not to blame. (University Professor, Madrid)

The identification with Europe has different meanings depending on what is emphasized. When asked if they feel European, all interviewees will give an affirmative answer, but when given the choice of ranking their feelings of belonging they clearly express that above all, they feel Spanish, and a few would say that they feel as European as Spanish (only 4 percent of those I interviewed). Several surveys on Spanish population identification with Europe in the last five years have consistently showed that Spaniards feel first Spanish, and then European (Eurobarometer 1999; Centro de Investigaciones Sociológicas 1997–2000; Diéz Medrano and Gutierrez 2001). These surveys found that the ranking has been consistently the same: first Spanish identity, then regional identity, and finally European identity. More specifically, these studies reveal that in most regions of Spain, people feel that they are first Spanish, then Asturian, Galician, Castilian, or Andalusian, and then European. In certain regions, such as Catalonia and the Basque country, the attachment to the region is almost at the same level as the attachment to the Spanish nation. My results differ considerably from these surveys regarding whether people feel European and Spanish at the same time. In these surveys the proportion of people who feel this duality is far higher than in my own findings (generally, above 20 percent).[18] This is perhaps due to the fact that my analysis emphasized identification with the European Union, not with Europe in general, as these surveys presented the question. Although in the minds of many people it might be equated, some people do make a difference. It is logically possible that a person could feel European (in the geographical sense for example) and a European citizen in the administrative sense, but not necessarily identify with the European Union. For instance, according to Eurobarometer 56 (2002), Spaniards are proud of being European (72 percent expressed this opinion), but this does not necessarily translate into wanting further European integration, (even though one could reasonably expect at least some correlation). Likewise, evidence of a certain European consciousness, some elements that people share as Europeans and that they can feel in certain situations, does not necessarily mean support for further integration or identification with the EU, for example, when one travels to other areas of the world, as the following quote illustrates:

I feel closer to other Europeans when I am on another continent. For example when I traveled to the United States, to Africa, and to Asia. From there I can see all the things we have in common. For example, the organization of the urban and rural space; where the main buildings are in a city. I don't know, I never got lost in Germany or Sweden for example, even though I did not speak any of those languages. (Teacher, Cantabria)

To be sure, most of the people I interviewed (both leaders and lay people) emphasize the importance of their national identity, but they are not overly concerned about loss of national identity. Most people do not think that the EU will undermine Spanish identity. As in France, this issue is more important for lay people than for leaders. In fact, in Spain there is an even sharper contrast between leaders and lay people than in France in their concerns over questions of identity. Indeed, very few leaders have expressed apprehension over the possibility that the EU would end up undermining Spanish identity.

Whether or not they regard the EU as a threat to cultural identity, interviewees have proven to be particularly attached to the idea of Spanish sovereignty. Their *imagined community* (Anderson 1991)—the nation-state—is perceived as a stable institution and in some ways as a preexisting social reality. National identity and Spanish sovereignty are represented in their minds as the position and the status of Spanish people in the European Union. However, for 6 percent of interviewees these issues were less important. These people thought that the best way to build Europe was to create a state at the European level, and they felt that giving up sovereignty was not necessarily a bad thing.

In sum, for the large majority of Spaniards interviewed, the main concern is not as much national identity as sovereignty, in the sense of being influential in the European Union, a feeling that they are not a full-fledged and important force in Europe. Several experiences regarding Spain's relations with the European Union have caused these feelings during the 1990s. In 1993, for example, the Spanish government hoped to obtain the headquarters of a relevant EU office such as the Agency for the Environment. Instead, Spain was assigned the Office for Harmonization of the Internal Market, a much less prestigious organization. This was widely presented in the media as a failure for the Spanish government. Again, in the second half of 1993 and in early 1994, during the negotiations for admission of the Nordic countries, the EU accepted none of Spain's main propositions regarding institutional reforms. Then, in 1995, Spain was engaged in a confrontation with Canada over fishing rights; many respondents believe that Canada was able to impose most of its conditions because Spain could not obtain solid backing from the EU. Also in 1995, in a confrontation over fishing rights with Morocco, the European Commission was unable to modify Morocco's position in favor of Spain. Only in one recent case was Spain supported by the EU: on July 10, 2002, a small group of Moroccan soldiers occupied an uninhabited strategic tiny islet in the Mediterranean Sea, called Perejil (considered a Spanish territory but disputed by Morocco). During this crisis the Spanish government had the immediate support of the EU Commission, urging Morocco to end the military occupation of this islet and threatening Morocco with sanctions.[19] This support was relatively well publicized in the Spanish media, although perhaps one case is not enough to change people's minds, but at any rate I could not verify the possible effect of this recent case.

The interviews' results suggest that all these perceived setbacks affected Spanish thinking about the European Union as strongly as would economic adversity, if not more so. Seventy-five percent of the lay people interviewed believe that when problems arise, Spain does not obtain solid support from the European Union. Many political and union leaders also expressed this idea. For instance, 64 percent of the politicians from the United Left, 25 percent of the Socialist Party, and 34 percent from the Popular Party shared this sentiment. These incidents, coupled with the perceived economic grievances, have most likely helped to revitalize nationalist feelings among Spaniards.

In addition, coverage of issues by the newspapers plays an important role in defining social representations of the EU. As stated earlier, I analyzed the newspaper El País, a paper viewed generally as rather supportive of the EU. This newspaper, compared to Le Monde (the newspaper I analyzed in the previous chapter on France), had fewer articles on the European Union. The stories on the EU were generally included in the international section of the paper. Out of 88 days considered in my sample, El País had at least one article on the EU on 64 days. Given that there were up to four articles on the topic on certain days, the number of articles could be greater than the number of days studied. Thus, El País had a total of 73 stories on the EU. Forty-two percent of the articles published by El País had a negative representation of the EU, while 44 percent were neutral and 26 percent represented the EU in a positive light. Overall compared to Le Monde and to The Times (which is analyzed in Chapter 4), El País had a more balanced coverage of the EU, representing the EU in a less negative light than the other newspapers. The following headings illustrate El País's type of coverage: "The EU Limits Economic Liberalization because of the Social Demands of France." (March 17, 2002). This headline and the content of that article, although relatively neutral, can still bring people to think that the country members are still fighting among themselves over this particular topic, especially when in the same issue there is another article titled: "Aznar Affirms That the Reform of the European Economies Is Irreversible." The following headline exemplifies a more positive coverage showing unification and agreement: "The EU Agreed on a Unified Plan to Repatriate Immigrants" (June 23, 2002).

In short, even this paper, which is considered the most supportive of European integration among major Spanish newspapers, presents a relatively high percentage of information that relates to the problems that the EU confronts, such as lack of understanding among the different members, cacophony over economic and international issues, the fight over national interests, and so on. Therefore, one could deduce that in general people receive more negative than positive or even neutral information on the EU from the Spanish information outlets.

DEFINING THE EUROPEAN UNION

Whether critical or supportive of the EU, there are many different understandings about the meaning of European integration and the European Union. I tried to address those interpretations related to the organizational model of the EU. Specifically, what were the respondents' positions regarding support for an intergovernmental organization (confederation) or for a supranational, federal form of organization?

Most of the people interviewed in all categories tend to view the EU as an association of different nation-states, that is, some type of confederate organization. Only a minority among both the leaders and the lay people would favor a federal form of organization. Overall I found the following trends in my interviews among those who support some form of European integration: Sixty-six percent of political and union leaders preferred a form of confederation, while 30 percent were inclined to constitute a federal Europe (4 percent did not have a tangible preference).[20] The interviewees who were more prone to support a federation belonged to the Socialist Party. Among the business leaders, 36 percent tended to support a federation, while 63 percent favored a confederation.

A majority believed that a federal organization was not possible in the near future because of what they considered the "vast socioeconomic and cultural differences among the countries that make up the European Union." Others opposed the idea of Europe on ideological grounds: "The idea of a federal Europe is a dream of a minority. I do not believe that it would ever be possible, but in any case, the state has served us very well and the EU should continue to be a union of states, not a federation, and the state should continue to be at the center of the decision-making process" (Leader PP Madrid). There is a marked desire among most Spanish political leaders to influence and control the process of integration from the national perspective.

Lay people generally showed a resolute attachment to a national government. Seventy-one percent favored a loose form of confederation, while 21 percent were in favor of a federation (8 percent did not know). A federal Europe seems impossible to some respondents and undesirable to others: "The nations should not abandon their sovereignty, for it is their essential liberty " (teacher, Andalusia), and "I do not like very much the idea of a federal state because it will end up eliminating cultural differences" (Store manager, Andalusia).

Age does make a difference in this issue: of the 21 percent of lay people who supported a federation, 69 percent were less than 30 years old. The following quote illustrates ideas expressed mainly by students interviewed: "Yes, I would like the European Union to become a federal union because we (the populations of The EU) have the same interests and that will help to reinforce the role of Europe in the international scene" (Student, Galicia).

The perceived structure of opportunity offered by the EU, and the competing interests between the national representatives of the EU member states, widely publicized by the media, have reinforced an attachment to the nation-state and much support for an intergovernmental organization. In other words, the majority of Spaniards see the EU through the prism of national interests. If there is a perception that policies of the EU negatively affect Spain, then public opinion is negatively affected. The inverse process could theoretically happen if EU policies were represented as positively affecting Spain. In practice, however, this would be rather difficult, because policies are conducted through the national member states and are represented as such in the media and by politicians.

Although multiple identities are possible, national identities are still perceived (and socially represented) as offering more of a refuge to the population at large than a European identity. This happens because the national states through the Council still determine policies, and politicians in power take full credit for them. Rarely is the EU as an independent organization represented as doing positive things for the Spanish population. National politicians in power present the EU in terms of advantages for their own country, not in terms of advantages for the whole population of the EU. This is the logic of the system; politicians must rely on their national constituency to stay in power or to be elected.

In sum, increasing economic exchange and other activities at the European level has not produced a trend toward a postnational identity in the population at large or among the political and union leaders. National concerns determine their interpretations of the European Union. Interviews seem to indicate that only a tiny minority of the population is starting to experience a different feeling of belonging, something that we could categorize as more international and European, perhaps cosmopolitan. This has happened (and to a rather limited extent) particularly among the few people engaged in international research (one of the main areas of collaboration across states in the EU) and among executives in large companies. In their daily work, these people already experience some sense of belonging to a supranational organization.

As seen in the previous sections, the wide preference for an intergovernmental organization of the EU, the attachment to the national state, and the mistrust of the EU are based on some concrete experiences or observed situations in their cities or communities, on symbolic experiences, and more generally (and connected to the above), on the perceptions that the institutions of the EU themselves have helped to create. Indeed, the debates within the EU are conducted mostly in terms of national interests, and through the Council, the nation-states remain the major actors in EU agreements. The present organization of the EU is based on settling disputes among different countries to reach common agreements. In this process, citizens of the member countries often perceive that their national aspirations are not met, thereby renewing feelings of national identity.

Furthermore, the European Union has historically followed a conception more technocratic than democratic, and economic concerns have taken precedence over political and social matters. Additionally, the formation of a European citizenship, although formally specified in the Maastricht Treaty, has remained more a "legally sanctioned economic category" (Deflem and Pampel 1995: 137) and a free-movement "market citizenship" than a citizenship with the full rights of equal participation (De Longe 1995). In other words, political citizenship is not yet guaranteed beyond the nation-state. As this Spanish member of the European Parliament said:

We often hear our leaders talking about more Europe. But what does that mean? More often than not the foreign ministers and other ministers do not go beyond the words and general statements. Maastricht, Amsterdam, Nice, Laeken, Barcelona, are European cities where big summits took place but also where the distance between challenges and political responses were exposed (MEP PS).

In sum, Spanish membership in the EU has not contributed to a substantial reduction of nationalist reflexes among Spanish citizens. It might even have helped to reinforce these feelings. The national state is still perceived as the best institution to defend Spanish interests in the world.

The interviews reveal that social policies and rights of citizenship are important contributing factors to develop identification with the EU. Such was the case of the euro. Although Spaniards have been rather supportive of the euro in general it was noticeable that in the interviews conducted at the end of 2001 and particularly in the spring of 2002 the number of people who saw the euro as undermining national identity was far less than in previous years. As in France, people liked the idea that the euro coins use both national and European symbols.

CONCLUSION

Almost all the Spanish interviewees agree in the abstract about the relevance of the European Union for obtaining peace and developing solidarity among the countries of Europe. Furthermore, they tend to identify with the European Union slightly more than France and considerably more than the United Kingdom (as we will see in the next chapter). However, this view does not translate into a desire to create a federal Europe or to be unconditionally supportive of further integration. The large majority of those interviewed (leaders and lay people) are very much attached to an independent nation-state as the basic constituent of their identity. The Spanish nation-state is viewed as a political community that represents its citizens' collective identity and sense of sovereignty.

The nation-state still inspires a sense of unity and belonging for Spaniards and constitutes the "overarching normative ideal of collective identification" (Schlesinger 1994: 319) even beyond the boundaries of social classes. We saw that the working class representatives (labor unions and United Left Party) and most lay people interviewed tended to equate class solidarity with national solidarity.

However, that is the only point in common among all the interviewees. Indeed there are several cleavages in terms of how the EU is represented in the Spanish population. The representations of the EU in Spain result from a combination of psychological variables and social representations that change according to the sectors and other dimensions that cannot be completely explained by general surveys or analysis of political votes, or even by in-depth interviews. I will attempt to summarize here the major cleavages found and develop further in the conclusion of the book the main theoretical points. First there is a clear difference in these interpretations between the leaders and the lay people. Then among the leaders there are divisions that cannot be clearly defined along party lines. There is, however, a cleavage that differentiates the left (IU) and the extreme left from the moderate left (Socialist Party) and the conservative parties. All the interviewees from the left (IU and extreme left) consider that the EU is basically promoting policies that are contributing to the creation of inequalities. The leadership of the extreme left parties do not see any interest in Spanish membership in the EU, but the interviewees from IU are somehow divided: half of those I interviewed consider that membership in the union is still important. Then the larger parties, the PP and the PS, also have divisions within the party. In the PP, which is roughly divided in two regarding support for further political integration, these divisions are related to questions of sovereignty in terms of what should be decided at the national level and what should be left at the EU level (the issue of subsidiarity comes into play here). In the Socialist Party there are fewer divisions than in the PP, but there are a minority of people who are not enthusiastic about further integration. This group's major criticism and concern is that the EU is not doing enough in terms of social policies.

There are also divisions among lay people: about 46 percent of interviewees are relatively satisfied with membership in the EU, 42 percent are rather unhappy with the EU, and a small minority is unclear about what to think. The EU is blamed by 42 percent of lay people for many grievances. For instance, the EU is perceived as having influenced policies that have restricted job opportunities in the areas of agriculture and industry. These perceptions have led those engaged in these areas to feel alienated from the European integration process. Furthermore, a large proportion of Spaniards believe that they are not treated fairly by the European Union. They describe a perceived disadvantage of Spanish citizens as produced by the domination of the other member countries in the EU's decision-making process. In other words, perceived economic and political grievances are connected to feelings of national identity and sovereignty to shape social representations of the European Union. Lay people refer to everyday experiences and concepts of national sovereignty to continually reaffirm a Spanish national identity, however inarticulate this concept may be in their minds. However, it does appear to them more concrete and intense than a European identity.

This form of nationalism is inspired by the old, reflexive *us/them* view of the world. People look for past or present affronts and explain economic and other difficulties according to this binary view. Indeed, although contemporary Spaniards tend to admire other European countries, many feel at the same time a feeling of relative deprivation in relation to other members of the EU, especially in relation to those member countries that are economically and politically more powerful.

Furthermore, the invocations of national identity are a means through which the Spanish population tries to address the crisis of identity produced by the drastic changes occurring at present in that country, most of which are perceived as originating in the process of European integration. Likewise, the idea of cultural specificity emphasized by the interviewees is combined with an ideology of democracy: people feel closer to their representatives within the national state. The Spanish nation itself is conceived as "a horizontal comradeship" (Anderson 1995: 7) as opposed to the European Union, which is perceived as more vertical and foreign.

These results do not imply that a new layer of European identification could not be developed by Spaniards—identities are already experienced by most Spaniards as multiple layers, which include the local, the regional, and the national. These results indicate rather that in order to develop a stronger identification with the European Union there should be a more positive social representation of the EU. This would imply developing policies that provide a sense of dignity (Greenfeld 1992), meaningful ways of life across the full spectrum of human activity (Tamir 1993), and concrete experiences that link individuals to the larger community. Accordingly, the European Union must become part of the Spanish citizens' everyday lives; it should be perceived as capable of alleviating what people view as the major problems in their society.

NOTES

Reprinted by permission of Sage Publications Ltd. from A. M. Alarcon, "Spain in the European Union: A Qualitative Study of National Identity," in *International Journal of Cultural Studies*, Copyright Sage Publications 2000.

1. This chapter concentrates on developments during the 1990s. For details on Spain's relations with Europe during the transition to democracy in the 1970s and earlier, during the Francoist regime, see Alvarez-Miranda (1996), Maxwell (1995), Moreno Juste (1990), Hooper (1987), Vàzquez Barbero and Hebbert (1985), and Salmon (1991).

2. Becoming part of the European union was almost a consensus in Spain. One could see a continuous reference to the European Community during the first half of the 1980s by the leading politicians as well as in the media, particularly on TV and newspapers. The following excerpts from two leading newspapers at the time reflect the strong push and desire to be part of the European Community: "Spain is not waiting to become part of Europe, since it already is part of Europe. And a founding nation, indeed, of everything European" (ABC 1985) and "whatever people may say, Europe is incomplete without the Iberian Peninsula" (*El País* 1979).

3. According to data published in *El País* (1996) from the Instituto Nacional de Estadisticas, the total amount of structural and cohesion funds was $1.1 billion U.S. transferred to Spain between 1986 and 1995. Half of that amount was transferred in the first five years after membership.

4. To measure support for European Union membership in the Eurobarometers, it is asked whether membership in the EU is a good thing, a bad thing, or neither good nor bad. In 1987, 63 percent of Spaniards interviewed thought that membership in the European union was a good thing. This average increased to 74 percent by mid-1988, it went down again to 63 percent in 1989 and increased again to 78 percent in the fall of 1990 and stayed above 70 percent until 1992. The other measure of support for the EU includes the question of whether people thought they benefited from membership in the EU. The same tendency could be observed in the answers to this question. After two years of membership, Spaniards started to perceive some benefits from belonging to the EU and the percent that thought that Spain benefited from belonging to the EU went from about 28 percent in 1988 to 51 percent in 1990 and oscillated between 51 percent and 58 percent until 1992, when the percentage that thought that Spain benefited from belonging to the EU went under 40 percent. It was only in 1998 that more than 50 percent of the interviewees believed again that Spain had benefited from belonging to the EU.

5. The PSOE is also responsible to a certain extent for the application of these neoliberal policies in Spain at the beginning of the 1990s, when they were in control of the government.

6. Historically the CGT has been affiliated with the United Left and UGT with the Socialist Party, but by the mid-1990s this connection was not so clear-cut; the UGT especially has often confronted the PS leadership. Since 2001 there seems to have been a renewed reconciliation between UGT and the PS.

7. For example, according to data provided by the Instituto Nacional de Estadística (INE), the balance in agricultural products between France (the biggest producer of agricultural goods in the EU) and Spain used to be well in favor of

Spain, but since joining the EU, the Spanish market has been invaded by foods such as fish, meat, milk, cereals, and fruits imported from France. While the export of agricultural goods from Spain to France increased by 190 percent from 1985 to 1993, sales from France to Spain increased by 860 percent.

8. In November 2002, $1 U.S. equaled .975 euros.

9. In fact, by the end of the 1990s, fighting unemployment was considered the main problem to address by the populations of the EU member countries, considered together (Eurobarometer 50 1999).

10. To be included in the European Monetary Union, a member nation must have complied with the following requirements: (1) an inflation rate no more than 1.5 percent higher than the three lowest national rates in the EU, (2) long-term interest rates must not be above 2 percent of the average of the three lowest EU rates, (3) the state's budget deficit (including central, regional, and local governments) should not exceed 3 percent of the Gross Domestic Product (GDP), and (4) the public debt ratio of the member states should not exceed 60 percent of the GDP.

11. The average unemployment in the EU is 7.8 percent, in December 2001 (8.5 percent in the Euro zone), Netherlands 2.2 percent, Luxembourg 2.5 percent, Austria 4.2 percent, Ireland 4.2 percent, Portugal 4.3 percent, Germany 8 percent, Finland 9.1 percent, France 9.3 percent, and Spain 12.9 percent (Euro-Op News January 2002).

12. The implementation of policies with a neoliberal flavor has been far from smooth in Spain. This is especially striking when comparing this process with the relatively nonconfrontational adjustments in the Scandinavian countries and other northern European nations such as Germany and the Netherlands.

13. Spain is somewhere between a nation-state and a multinational state (as defined by Connor 1994b). A minority of people in the Basque country and in Catalonia claim to derive from a different ethnic background than the rest of Spain. However, most people, even in these regions, claim allegiance to both: their region or community and to the Spanish state. Therefore, I think that the most appropriate, if not perfect, term for the purpose of this research is the nation-state. I define the term *nationalism* as "a consciousness of belonging to the nation-state, together with sentiments and aspirations for its security and prosperity." This definition is based on Anthony Smith (1991: 72–73), although I added the attachment to the state as important to the nation in the context of the European Union. The state is perceived by all the interviewees as either the political extension of the nation or its synonym, and the sentiment of national identity includes being part of the Spanish state. Furthermore, in the popular imagination this duality constitutes the collective consciousness. The tendency to equate the attachment to the nation (nationalism) with loyalty to the state (patriotism)—a distinction suggested by Connor (1994b)—is so dominant among both lay people and political and economic leaders that it would be futile to try to distinguish between them. In any case, this distinction is not fundamental for the purpose of this research. Perhaps this distinction would have been relevant if I were studying the relations between the nationalist groups in the Basque Country and in Catalonia with the rest of Spain or with Europe. See the work of Keating (2000) for an extended analysis of this relation.

14. In Eurobarometer 50 (1999) a question was asked about how people would feel if the EU were to be scrapped. Forty-nine percent of Spaniards answered that they would feel indifferent, while 37 percent would feel very sorry. However, only 5 percent answered that they would be very relieved.

15. In the Eurobarometer, people are asked to say whether they agree completely, slightly agree, slightly disagree, or completely disagree with the statement "There is a European cultural identity shared by all Europeans." The percentages presented refer to the sum of slightly disagree plus completely disagree and completely plus slightly agree.

16. A survey done in 1999 by the ASEP differed considerably from my findings. They found that only 33 percent of Spaniards thought that European integration would have a negative impact on their identity (national and regional), although the survey produced similar results regarding those who believed that it would be unlikely that the EU would have a negative impact on national identity (my data found 52 percent, ASEP found 56 percent). The differences should be expected given that my research was qualitative and used open-ended questions as opposed to a structured questionnaire with already printed possible answers.

17. Spanish people with a leftist sensibility, even moderately leftist (approximately half of the population), have traditionally regarded the United States with concern, and readily considered the United States imperialistic, but this view was not overtly antagonistic. However, recently even those who are not on the left seem to have espoused a negative view of the United States. For instance a CIS survey in April of 2002 reveals that only 5.2 percent of the Spanish population consider that the United States is acting to create peace in the Middle East, while 21 percent considered that the EU was contributing to peace, 12.8 percent said that the United Nations was contributing to peace, and 28.1 percent of those surveyed responded to the statement: no one is doing anything for peace.

18. The most recent survey that included this issue (CIS 2000) shows that 62.2 percent of respondents felt they were, above all, Spanish citizens, 23.1 percent both citizens of Europe and Spanish citizens at the same time, and 6 percent, above all European citizens. The recent Eurobarometers (2000–2002) show significantly different proportions, both from my findings and the CIS findings. This is due to the way the questionnaire was conceived, which does not really allow for meaningful, exact comparisons of specific data. But what is predominant in all these surveys and my qualitative study is the attachment of Spanish people first to Spain. The findings from the Eurobarometers mentioned show systematically that people feel first Spanish and then European (52 percent in 2001, 53 percent in 1998), then Spanish only (38 percent in 2001, 34 percent in 1998), then European first and Spanish second (4 percent in 2001 and 6 percent in 1998), and finally European only (3 percent in 2001 and 4 percent in 1998).

19. The European Union issued a statement backing Spain's position and urging Morocco "to immediately withdraw its forces" from the island and "warning that continuing the crisis could seriously damage Morocco's relations with its northern neighbors" (Daly 2002). There were several newspaper reports and intense TV coverage for several days. In the news, reporters cited officials that threatened economic sanctions in concert with the European Union and tighter restrictions

on Moroccan immigrants. The news also reported that Romano Prodi, president of the European Commission, telephoned the Moroccan prime minister, Abder-raman Yusufi, to demand the withdrawal of Moroccan soldiers from the island.

20. These numbers are presented as tendencies perceived in the groups. The sample is used for comparative and descriptive purposes; it is not intended for statistical analysis.

CHAPTER 4

The United Kingdom: To Be or Not to Be . . . in Europe

It is quite true that the so-called races of Britain feel themselves to be very different from one another. A Scotsman, for instance, does not thank you if you call him an Englishman. But somehow these differences fade away the moment that any two Britons are confronted by a European.

George Orwell (1953, p.47–48)

Becoming a member of the European Economic Community-EEC (as the European Union was called at the time) and increasing cooperation with other Europeans has been a long, difficult process for the United Kingdom. Indeed, ongoing tensions and intense debate have accompanied the issue of European integration since the United Kingdom first applied for membership in the 1960s. De Gaulle, then president of France, opposed U.K. membership because he believed the British were more committed to the United States and the Commonwealth than to Europe.[1] In 1973, the United Kingdom finally became a member, but the debate within the country continued, and it intensifies every time that there is a new proposal or treaty at the European Union level.

Those who favored British membership in the European Economic Community in the 1970s argued that membership was a means to reverse decline and revive lost influence. For instance, Edward Heath, British prime minister at the beginning of the 1970s, argued in 1971: "Why should we go in?. . . . We must go in, if we want to remain Great Britain, and have the chance of becoming a greater Britain. . . . Today we don't occupy the place in the world we once did. . . . For 25 years we've been looking for something to get us going again. Now here it is" (*The Times* 1971, July

9: 5). An editorial published in *The Times,* referring to the government document that argued in favor of U.K. membership in the European Community, echoed this view: "[The White Paper] . . . marks the start of a new and much more promising phase in British History, a phase in which the British revive their own strength and prosperity in contributing to the collective strength and prosperity of Europe" (*The Times* 1971, July 8). The title of *The Times* editorial, "Towards a European Britain," is also a revealing sign of British views on Europe. Indeed, for the pro-EEC politicians, membership was economically necessary, because they believed that the United Kingdom and the Commonwealth could not rival the power of the European Economic Community, the United States, the Soviet Union, or Japan. However, membership, in their minds, did not imply any surrendering of sovereignty or loss of national identity. Again, quoting Edward Heath: "The French are not less French; the Dutch are not less Dutch for being members of the community for 20 years. . . . Nor shall we be any less British. The other countries have their own royal families. So shall we" (*The Times* 1971, July 9: 5).

Those against U.K. membership in the EEC claimed that British sovereignty would be lost and argued against the power of the European Union institutions. "Farmers worried about fewer defenses against European agricultural imports" (Amey 1973); workers feared a "wholesale invasion of Britain by workers from across the channel" (Murray 1973); even some university presidents feared that the EU bureaucracy would "wreck the English education system by assuming administrative control" (Jessel 1973).

Disputes over Britain's relationship with Europe have persisted right up to the present day. In the following pages I will examine the social representation of the European Union among leaders and lay citizens. I will follow a format similar to the two previous chapters on France and Spain.

LEADERS' REPRESENTATIONS OF THE EU

As in France and Spain, the debate over European integration does not break down along party lines in the United Kingdom. There are divisions within all the parties as well.

Prominent members of the Labor Party (LP), which has been in power for the last eight years, hold divergent views on the issue of European integration. Those in favor of participating further in the European institutions, such as the prime minister, Tony Blair, and a slight majority of the Labor Party, argue that being in Europe is a way for Britain to be more influential, not only in Europe but in world affairs as well. As Tony Blair said during a speech defending the need for the United Kingdom to participate in the common currency: "The United Kingdom must be in the center of influence of Europe in order to have influence and power in the world"(cited in Garton Ash 2002: 13). This was the same argument used at the beginning of the 1970s by Heath, then British prime minister. In fact, the similarities of the arguments in the United Kingdom debate on European union throughout the years are remarkable. Judging by the frequency that the political leaders interviewed during my own research mentioned the need for the United Kingdom to influence world affairs, and to play a civilizing role in the world, this argument has wide resonance in British society. Speeches by the prime ministers in the last 20 years, from Thatcher to Major to Blair, reflect a desire for a United Kingdom with global reach.[2] This widespread desire influences the Labor Party leaders' view of EU's role in foreign policy. Most of the interviewees from this party are still very much attached to U.K. independence and exceptionalism. Only four of the interviewees said that they would not mind having a unified foreign policy to be able "to counterbalance the power of the United States and China." As a Labor Leader from Scotland put it: "There should be a collective voice in the EU. We should be able to tell the international community that they should follow the law and the agreements they have signed. The only way to do this in a consistent manner is through a united foreign policy." Furthermore, this minority group pointed to the relatively sharp discrepancies that often emerge between the Europeans and the United States in dealing with international issues to justify the need for a European Union common foreign policy.

In terms of general support for membership in the European Union, a slight majority of Labor Party leaders interviewed were in favor of strengthening the European Union, most especially the adoption of the euro by the United Kingdom, and further economic integration. This next statement by a Labor Party MP exemplifies this view: "The European Union is good for the U.K.—no doubt about that. Our main support lies behind a single market, and our priorities at a European level revolve around a single market that ensures a level playing field and which allows us to be competitive in the world." Regarding the relations with other countries outside of the EU in trade issues, the majority of the interviewees from the Labor Party considered that the EU should somehow speak with a single voice. In particular, regarding the relations with the United States, several interviewees expressed concerns that are echoed in the following quote: "Americans are on some of the trade issues quite frankly outrageous, they are very protectionist even if at the WTO and in other international forums they have a different discourse. They are pressuring us on the CAP policy for example, and they are subsidizing their agriculture far more than we do." (Labor Party leader, West Midlands). The political leaders interviewed in the United Kingdom mentioned the United States more often than their counterparts in France and Spain, even when my questions did not mention U.K. relations with the United States. This probably reflects the duality in which Foreign U.K. policy is enmeshed. Political leaders see themselves between two blocks. "Because of our special relation with the United States, some conservatives say that we should move away from Europe and concentrate on the United States. In fact, we need to face both worlds, but our future lies within Europe. It's as simple as that" (Labor Party leader, London). Indeed, labor leaders see themselves as connected to the Commonwealth and consider important their special relationship with the United States, but at the same time, six out of ten interviewees want to continue an association with Europe and believe that U.K. exceptionalism would be empty without the European Union.

Those who desire to work within Europe in this party argue that it is in the United Kingdom's best interest. For these interviewees, supporting Europe means being part of a large organization that would advance U.K. interests:

I think we should improve coordination, and understanding of what each nation state is going to contribute to the EU and what we are going to do collectively. This is the key you know. The U.K., much that we like to think we're successful on our own, we're only going to be successful in part for being in Europe. (Labor Party leader, Wales)

I support membership in the EU because the national interests of the U.K. are better defended inside than outside of the EU. And despite what many euro-skeptics Tories say, so far we have been very good at getting what we wanted from the EU. (Labor Party leader, London)

There is also a relatively strong anti-European movement within this party, whose members suspect that every new agreement endangers British sovereignty and autonomy. For instance, Denzil Davis, Labor Party Member of the Parliament, referring to the Nice Treaty, signed and ratified by the government of the United Kingdom, warned that "British democracy has been transferred to a centralized Europe" and that the Nice Treaty "would continue and accelerate the transfer of power from this house [U.K. Parliament] to the central institutions of the European Union" (Kallenbach 2001). Even more than in France and Spain, the recurring themes of the debate on Europe in the United Kingdom have been the question of sovereignty and national identity. Several interviewees expressed the opinion that the international institutions of the EU, particularly the Commission and the Parliament, were having too much influence in the decision-making process. They considered that the Commission, for example, initiated too many regulations and that in a real democracy the norms and legislation should come from below, that is, in this case, from the people and their representatives in Parliament. Several mentioned the need for clarification of the concept of subsidiarity: "We are far from understanding what really should be decided by the country and what should be decided at the European level. We really need to clarify that"

(Labor Party leader, London). The question of national identity was also addressed by some interviewees, who considered that the euro could undermine an important marker of U.K. identity and history—an idea that, as we will see in the following pages, was shared by many people from all parties analyzed here. A common argument on the issue of national identity was that little by little the European Union was creating mechanisms that will end up obliterating U.K. traditions and culture: "Many regulations established by the EU do affect our ways of doing things. We want to keep our measurement system, our ways of driving, our farming organizations . . . " (Labor leader, suburbs of London). The social charter was also an issue of debate and a reason for opposing the EU among a minority group in the Labor Party. All interviewees from this party did agree on having general directives for health and safety in the workplace emanating from the EU, but a considerable minority considered that social policy (welfare, unemployment, workers rights, etc.) should be a matter for national governments. "I think that in the area of social policy the principle of subsidiarity should be applied. The EU should act only on those issues that have transnational implications" (Labor Party leader, London).

More Conservatives oppose more aspects of European integration than members of the Labor Party. The leading group (not necessarily in numbers) within this party, represented by the supporters of the present leader, Ian Duncan Smith, has adopted a position of strong opposition to further integration with Europe. Although most of them do not necessarily advocate a complete withdrawal, they want to limit the level of involvement with Europe to some agreements. For instance, Duncan Smith and his followers oppose U.K. membership in the common currency. Echoing some of Thatcher's ideas, one interviewee stated that the euro was "a step in the process of creating a European superstate." The general argument of those opposed to further integration within the Conservative Party is well defined by the following declaration of Michael Ancran, the foreign affairs spokesman for this party: "We have long made clear our view that further political integration would create a 'one size fits all' Europe, which would seriously undermine the basis for a sustainable, prosperous and harmonious Europe in all its diversity, which is our aim" (Kallenbach 2001). Most of the interviewees from this party also expressed concerns about the Common Agricultural Policy and were partisans of a reduction in the financial resources allocated to this domain of EU action. As a leader who considered himself among the moderates on questions of European integration put it: "I am convinced that we should limit the amount of money we put into the Common Agricultural Policy but I am aware that it is not a simple matter. This has to be negotiated also with the United States at the level of the WTO; because the United States is subsidizing heavily its agriculture and if we do not do it in agreement, the EU farmers would be at a disadvantage." According to several interviewees, this moderate tendency within the Conservative Party represents close to half of the party. A pro-EU group of Conservative Members of Parliament has even been created around the figure of Ken Clarke, former conservative chancellor. This group considers further integration in certain areas, such as monetary and economic union in general, as a necessity, and a few also supported some type of unified foreign policy. This tendency is reflected in the following quote: "I know that there are people within my party that are even asking to withdraw from most of the EU engagements and establish some type of association on a case by case basis. That alternative would be the same as total withdraw. It would be a suicide for the United Kingdom, a stupid turning away from reality." Another interviewee suggested the need for the EU to concentrate on environmental issues: "The EU should focus on the major environmental problems on the continent and try to work on solving those problems. In this aspect the EU is better equipped than any government independently, to be successful. I think they could easily take governments and people with them on this issue."

On the issue of losing national identity, which is a major concern for most Conservatives, there is no consensus. In fact, two interviewees, although acknowledging being in the minority within their party, do not regard Europe as a bad influence: "It might be possible that in our association with Europe with time, for example by adopting the single currency, we might end up being influenced a little by Europe, but so be it, I do not have a problem with that, because I also feel European myself" (Conservative Party leader, London).

Other Conservative leaders expressed rather drastic views on the United Kingdom's association with the EU, proposing a partial disengagement or even withdrawal from the common agricultural and common defense and security policies. Two of the interviewees showed an inclination to withdraw completely from the EU. The following statement is representative of the ideas expressed on this issue: "I am not against some type of association with the European Union but I would be happy if we withdrew from the present organization, then we could establish some agreements as we have with other countries around the world" (Conservative Party leader, London). One leader even compared the EU bureaucracy to the repressive bureaucracy of the former Soviet Union and said that the only alternative for England was to withdraw from the EU, thus repeating and even going beyond Thatcher's latest idea (2002).[3] There is a considerable variety of thinking within the Conservative Party, but this small group of radical euroskeptics (who often express xenophobia against other Europeans) is perhaps louder than the moderate voices.[4] They often attract media attention, and other politicians interviewed consider them relatively influential in British society. Commenting on whether the EU should join the common currency, one interviewee connected the question of sovereignty and national identity to a loss of economic independence: "Participating in the common currency would clearly be a loss of sovereignty for our country. And not only that, but our life is already changing, we are already losing some of our culture now, if we become more involved with the EU by participating in the common currency, it would be the end not only of English sovereignty by putting our financial future in foreign hands, but also [the end of] our cultural identity. The pound is a symbol of Britain's greatness" (Conservative Party leader, Wales). In sum, three major tendencies seem to predominate within the Conservative Party. The dominant group supports the status quo in terms of level of integration. They reject monetary union and further political union and would agree on some modifications of the mechanisms and policies that govern the single market in order to fine-tune its functioning. A second group does not oppose the monetary union and would like to see further integration in certain areas such as foreign policy and environmental policy, while a third group would like to withdraw from most arrangements within the EU framework. The major difference between those supporting the present continuing membership in the EU and the euroskeptics who would like to withdraw from some of the present arrangement lies in the question of what is better for a United Kingdom with global reach: inside or outside of the EU? For the euroskeptics it is better for the United Kingdom to be independent from Europe to have more power in the global scene.

The other party with strong presence in the U.K. Parliament, the Liberal Democrats, also shows evidence of some divisions on the issue of European Union, although less sharp than in the other parties. Menzies Campbell, Liberal Democrat foreign affairs spokesman, supports further integration and said: "I have no doubt that we have benefited very considerably from our EU membership. Our future best lies in a close relationship with the EU" (Kallenbach 2001). This upbeat view of the U.K. relation with the EU is also reflected in the following quotes from two of my interviewees, who defended the idea of a cultural identification with Europe as a positive process: "I do not see myself as different from other Europeans, and life in England is not so different from the rest of Europe. We must emphasize all the aspects that we have in common, which, in my opinion, are more than what differentiates us" (Liberal Democrat leader, Wales), and "I feel as much European as I am English. When I think of allies, I think France, Germany, etc." (Liberal Democrat leader, London). Interviewees from this party believed that the U.K. exceptionalism could be meaninglessness without the European Union but still refer to their special partnership with the countries of the Commonwealth and with the United States as an important element of British particularity and identity. The following quote expresses an opinion shared by all interviewees from this party: "I think our special relationship with the United

States enables us to be a bridge between the EU and the United States. Also, it enables us to influence in some ways the United States government."

In economic terms the support for Europe varies considerably in this party, although there was a prevalent concern about too much EU influence on the choice of economic policies:

I am pro-European, but it is clear that the U.K. economy is closer to the U.S. We have less social costs, which have allowed us to have lower rates of unemployment than in most European countries. And I would be concerned if further integration means significant change in that approach because I think it would hit our ability to create jobs quite heavily. (Liberal Democrat leader, London)

At the same time, interviewees from this party echoed the idea that from the economic point of view the United Kingdom does not have the ability to be really independent: "What happens in the EU would have a very direct and significant impact on the U.K. economy" (in London). Therefore, they allege that the U.K. choice is not between complete independence or membership in the EU. Membership in the EU is deemed necessary, but the United Kingdom should attempt to negotiate the appropriate terms of EU economic policy and push for a policy that will not be too restrictive.

In the same irresolute tone, interviewees addressed the issue of U.K. membership in the single currency. They tended to be more in favor of the United Kingdom joining the single currency: "We would gain more economically and possibly politically than we will lose by giving up the control over our interest rates," but they were also concerned about the risks in terms of economic independence: "By joining we lose our ability to manage the interest rates and with it a certain control of our economy." However, they also stressed the benefits and the economic value of the common currency, such as reduced costs in terms of transactions and the benefits that have historically characterized the euro zone, of low interest rates and low inflation rates.

At the same time, three out of five interviewees from this party thought that the EU should play a major role in foreign policy and defense: "I would be very happy with greater involvement of the EU in areas like foreign affairs and defense because small nations cannot greatly influence international affairs and cannot have enough resources to maintain a strong army." Interviewees also mentioned the environment as a predominant area of action for the EU: "If we really signed up to a very progressive environmental policy, people will see the benefit of Europe and actually may be encouraged to think more European."

As in the other parties, the question of sovereignty is also a question of debate with the Liberal Democrats. However, the difference between the interviewees from this party and most of the Conservative Party and a sector of the Labor Party is that the Liberals consider that the United Kingdom could resist whatever would be considered any excessive infringement of the EU on national sovereignty. Although they concur with the perceptions that if the EU adopted a more federal type of approach then there might be a possible threat to national independence, the interviewees from this party do not believe that for the foreseeable future the survival of the British nation-state is at stake, even if the United Kingdom adopted the euro:

In practical terms you can say that if the U.K. is no longer controlling and defining the direction of our economy and other areas there should be some erosion of sovereignty, or perhaps of national identity, but that has been happening not only as a result of European integration, and in any case I do not see that the EU would affect the U.K. core identity significantly; that is more a myth than a reality. I think that the idea that we can relate our national identity with the pound is a myth that the Conservative Party uses. (Liberal Democrat leader, London)

On questions of social policy, interviewees from this party would like to see as little intrusion as possible coming from the EU. The argument is articulated around the idea of subsidiarity. Interviewees believe that the EU should leave the question of social policies to the nation-state. They consider that in this area the EU has gone as far as it can go with the social charter included in the Treaty of the Union in 1992, which the United Kingdom finally signed in 1999. One interviewee recognizes that even if there is a concern over social dumping in other EU member countries, national independence on social issues is dear to the Liberal Democrats:

It might be true that the U.K. has perhaps more inequality, and certainly less social costs than in other European countries, such as Germany or France, but I think that this should be a choice that the U.K. should be able to make. Even though social dumping could be a concern in other EU countries, I still believe that each nation should be free to establish how many hours people work, how much time off people can have, and so on.

In summary, only a minority of British political leaders is opposed to some type of association with Europe, but this minority is more significant than in the other countries analyzed in this book. The main debate during the past two years revolved around the issue of the United Kingdom joining the euro zone. Out of 44 politicians interviewed (including MPs, MEPs and local leaders), 18 were opposed to the euro. Nine were from the Conservative Party, 6 were from the Labor Party, and 3 were from the Liberal Democrats. Opposition to the euro is based on a mix of rational reasons and nationalist feelings. The major argument expressed by all those opposed to the euro was the loss of the U.K. control over its economy; half of those even suggested that the euro would be the beginning of a federal state and the end of the United Kingdom as a national state. Losing control over its economy and fiscal policies is the beginning of the end for the British state, they believe. Another reason expressed was that it would not work. Also mentioned was a lack of convergence between the economies of the different countries and the risk of centralization. And finally there was also a question of national pride. Having its own currency is a means of cultural integration and an important symbol of belonging.

In terms of foreign affairs there is much support among U.K. political leaders for the European Union to take on certain international roles, such as keeping peace, but when I specifically addressed the question of a more united foreign policy, the U.K. political leaders and the population at large showed more resistance than in France and Spain. Seventy-two percent of the leaders interviewed (there were not sizable differences according to the parties here) thought that every country should establish its own foreign policy and use the European Union organization in certain cases to pull together resources, but only considering the EU role on foreign policy on a case by case basis, rather than an overall umbrella above the national state.

The labor unions in England are less concerned about European integration affecting workers' interests than the labor unions in France and Spain. The leadership of the British Trades Union Congress (TUC), the most important labor union in the United Kingdom,[5] tends to be in favor of closer association with Europe, which represents a radical change of position since 1990. Until then it was rather opposed to most European policies. Now, the union leaders see the European Union as promoting the interests of the British working class. Indeed, as the United Kingdom delayed adoption of the European Union Social Charter for many years, the welfare system declined and wages stagnated. The social charter was finally adopted in 1999, two years after the return to power of the Labor Party. In fact, the labor unions have lost considerable ground during the 18 years of Tory rule (1979–1997), and they did not regain much under the five-year rule of Tony Blair's modernized Labor Party. They are also actively supporting the adoption of the single currency by the United Kingdom; TUC secretary John Monks commented on the Blair government's backing of the single currency: "I very much welcome the Prime Minister's positive message on the euro today . . . the time is surely right to step up the campaign for hearts and minds" (TUC 2002: 1). The TUC leaders believe that workers have much to gain and little to lose from a closer union with Europe: "We should be able to have in the U.K. the European standards on social issues, for example: health and safety at work."

However, the leaders from this large labor union have a view that goes beyond the defense of workers' rights. On the question of Europe they express even broad objectives on what Europe should be. For instance: "We are interested in a social and citizens' Europe. We believe that we can better influence Europe by being more integrated. Besides if we want to face the negative aspects of globalization it is at the European level that this should be done." They argue that the success of their fight for social justice and fair treatment of workers in the United Kingdom cannot be separated from a successful European Union, and from the struggle to answer the aspirations of workers throughout the European Union. The TUC therefore participates actively in the European Trade Union Confederation. Their push for more integration of the United Kingdom with Europe is also responding to real, immediate issues.

The business and industrialist representatives in the United Kingdom do not differ much from the other countries. They have a pragmatist and utilitarian view of the EU. The representatives of the most important U.K. business and industrialists' association, the Confederation of British Industry (CBI), were rather enthusiastic in support of the single currency and in the pursuit of further economic integration. They consider that by adopting the euro the United Kingdom will eliminate the continuous problems that most of the industry confronts due to the uncertainties created by the fluctuations of the pound versus the euro. Even people from sectors that do not traditionally support the EU, such as farmers' associations, are recognizing the problems created by the differential pound/euro. Indeed, the hard facts of the economy seem to be affecting how people in this sector perceive the common currency. McCoy (2002) writes in *The Financial Times* that "British farming has been devastated by the impact of the strong pound against the euro, which has cut prices, damaged exports and hit support payments." In the same article, the Milk's Committee Chairman, Robin Christie, cites "the exchange rate differential as one of the major factors for leaving grassroots dairy farmers with a 10-year low milk price of 16 pence per liter before seasonality deductions, which was totally unacceptable and unviable." Ben Gill, president of the National Farmers' Union of England and Wales, is also cited as saying that "the nightmare of foot-and-mouth came on top of incomes already driven to rock bottom by, among other things, the ongoing high sterling/euro rate" (McCoy 2002). However, farmers as well as small business owners are still unsure about the benefits of the European integration for them. As in the other countries examined here, they perceive "the many regulations of the EU" and especially the competition from the outside as a threat to their survival. Particularly the U.K. farming industry is receiving considerable advantage as a result of the Agricultural Common Policy, but most farmers are still reluctant to see the European Union in a positive light.[6] These sectors tend to focus on certain policies, directives, and regulations produced by the EU that they perceive as too restrictive.

Furthermore, the main support of the United Kingdom's larger businesses, and in particular the representatives of the CBI (which includes also among its affiliates small and medium firms) are behind the completion of the single market. They are, however, less inclined to accept other European Union policies, especially those that give more rights and better conditions to the workers:

We accept that there is a role for a social charter, and that there should be some European standards on social issues because that would be unfair competition; however there are aspects that should be left to the national governments. I think that social policies encroach in areas that should be the responsibility of the national governments. Here I am referring to the concept of subsidiarity. There should only be European level action in cross border issues.

This is a common theme among business representatives. The problem with this concept is: what constitutes cross border issues? According to the labor unions and particularly the U.K. unions, as represented by the TUC, social issues are cross-border issues, and according to business representatives in other countries of the EU, social issues are also cross-border issues. These argue that given the lower expenses on social welfare in the United Kingdom, this country is in fact lowering the cost of labor, creating thereby social dumping, which in turn results in unfair competition for the other members of the EU. The representatives of the CBI consider that the argument of social dumping is flawed:

One can see that some companies relocate even to countries of the EU that have rather high social standards. Furthermore, if it were true that countries couldn't compete because of such high social standards, they would be faced with a deteriorating export economy for example. In fact, France, Germany, and all the countries with high social standards also have an amazingly competitive national market. This indicates to me that there is absolutely no evidence that high social standards can't withstand competitiveness.

An additional argument presented by another business representative on this issue seems to contradict the one above, but both reveal the strong opposition of the U.K. business community to EU regulations beyond some general mechanisms to allow the free market to work: "This idea of social dumping is largely French and Belgian protectionism. They want to export social standards to prevent what we think is perfectly legitimate operation in a free market situation where certain countries can have advantages in certain areas and can make different trade-off in certain social policies." Business representatives interviewed insisted that the EU should play a major role in economic integration, understanding by *economic* basically facilitating the rule of the market. Also they insisted on *flexibility*, suggesting that Europe should allow more decision making by the business community in every country. They also rejected the idea of the European Union influencing social policies and were strongly against the social charter decided at the EU level: "It is undemocratic to try to impose a social charter from above rather than creating a community from below especially in areas of national competence." They criticized as well what they called "the continental social model that kept higher unemployment in most European countries than in the U.K." The CBI is very active at the European Union level, as are most industrialist and business associations from the members of the EU.[7]

LAY CITIZENS: BRITISH EXCEPTIONALISM

In the public at large we have observed that in France and Spain there are a considerable proportion that have a tendency to exclude themselves from the rest of Europe, and to see the other countries in terms of *us* and *them*. This is even more so in the United Kingdom. Among lay citizens interviewed, 52 percent stated that they do not feel very close to other Europeans: "You see, we might be geographically close to Europe but I think we British are different and, although we should live in peace with Europe, I do not want Europeans to dictate what we British should do" (Small store owner, suburbs of London). A few spontaneously said that they felt closer to Canadians, and even to U.S. citizens: "Well I do not see that we have much in common with most Europeans such as the French or Italians for example, except that we are more or less in the same continent and, especially with the French, that we were enemies. We British are Anglo-Saxons, that's why we are probably closer to the United States and more especially to the other countries of the Commonwealth such as Canada" (Employee, insurance company, London).

The concept of national identity among the population of the United Kingdom is as vague as in the other countries, but it has an anchor image of racial distinction, such as Anglo-Saxonism, that makes this view, although abstract, relatively palpable in the minds of those expressing it.[8] In other words, it is a useful image that people refer to in order to explain the distinction between us and them, between the United Kingdom and the continent. A large fraction of those interviewed reflected in their statements very little empathy for the other members of the European Union. This attitude is also reflected in the Eurobarometers; for instance in the Eurobarometer 56 (2002), people were asked whether they felt European only, European and British, British only, or British and European; 71 percent responded that they felt British only and 22 percent British and European, by far the least European feeling of all the EU members. The same tendency was observed when asked whether they agreed or disagreed that there is a European cultural identity shared by all Europeans. Fifty-eight percent slightly or completely disagreed with that statement and only 28 percent completely or slightly agreed. These views were accompanied by similar proportions (43 percent) with distrust of the European Union and a marked drive to limit the scope of action of the EU institutions. In fact, as all surveys done in the last 20 years demonstrate (i.e. Eurobarometers 1982–2002), the United Kingdom has traditionally been the most against European integration of all the member countries. When measuring support for U.K. membership in the European Union, U.K. citizens were consistently well under the EU average during the last 20 years. Particularly in the last 6 years the percentage of U.K. citizens that thought that membership in the EU was a good thing oscillated from 36 percent in 1996 to a low 25 percent in 1999, and to 33 percent in 2001 (the EU average in the same period oscillated between a low 48 percent in 1996 and 54 percent in 2001), while those who thought that membership was neither bad nor good varied from 27 percent in 1996 to 31 percent in 2001. The proportion of those believing that membership in the EU is a bad thing is, however, still a minority, declining from a peak of 29 percent in 1996, to 20 percent in 1997 and 22 percent in 2001. The same tendency can be observed in the other question measuring support for the EU. In the last six years the percentage of the general public that considers that the United Kingdom has benefited from membership has oscillated between 40 percent in 1996 to 25 percent in 1999, and to 36 percent in 2001.

These negative views of Europe are derived from many apparent flaws in the EU. For instance, many Britons worry about the negative economic consequences of further integration. As in the other countries, there is a perception of economic deprivation. Farmers complain about EU regulations and policies, small business owners fear the competition from other countries of the EU, and workers feel that they might lose their jobs as consequence of unfair competition from Europe. One must notice, however, that the industrial workers interviewed were not as opposed to Europe as people from other sectors of the economy. Perhaps this is due to the influence of the larger labor union confederation of the United Kingdom, the TUC, which supports the European Union, including the adoption of the euro and European social policies.

The majority of U.K. citizens also showed discomfort with what it perceived as the imposition by the European Union of the continent's norms and values, mentioning, for example, the push for decimalization and for the establishment of the metric system. Seven out of ten lay citizens interviewed expressed opposition to the monetary union. Some tried to explain it in economic terms, but it was clear that the opposition to the euro among the population at large was based more on questions of sovereignty and identity. Common statements included references to the practical use of the euro and to questions of national identity, "The pound is a basic sign of our identity as British" (Housekeeper, suburbs of London), and "I think the pound has served us very well, why should we change to a money with no country" (Government employee, London), as well as allusions to U.K. history: "You see, to me the pound is a representation of our history, it is part of our memory as country" (Bus driver, London). Opposition to the euro among my interviewees was more widespread than opposition to the EU in general, perhaps because the euro is palpable and the consequence of monetary union is more directly and immediately observable than the diverse policies of the EU or the perspective of further integration. Also, the topic of the euro was in the news very often during the previous three years (from 1999 to 2002). At the same time, some British citizens said that they knew that even though they did not like the idea, the political elites would probably end up adopting the euro. "Most likely in a few years we will end up with the euro, politicians will do whatever they like. In fact, many businesses already accept the euro"[9] (Taxi driver, London).

In addition to a relatively strong opposition to the euro, there is opposition among the U.K. population to what they consider the interventionist tendency of the Commission. For instance: "I am very concerned about the bureaucrats of the EU to impose on me their values, for example they want to impose on England the metric system. That is not acceptable" (Bank employee, London). The interviews confirm that lay people in the U.K. have widespread caricatured images of the EU. Many mentioned the freedom-infringing measures of the EU such as wanting to impose "the shape of a cucumber" or "the banning of tobacco chewing," and many others. Newspapers and popular television shows reinforce these caricatures. Half of the interviewees referred to the inefficiency and bureaucratic heaviness of the EU. The main criticisms are that the EU is a "rambling, inefficient bureaucracy" or that it is an "unnecessary expensive bureaucracy." A few also mentioned that there "was probably corruption in the commission," explaining that "officials must be receiving kickbacks from big companies," and a sizeable number of interviewees showed some suspicion that the EU officials were involved in some type of illegal activity.[10]

This should not be interpreted, however, as a total rejection of Europe in general by Britons. Although interviews demonstrate a concern for maintaining British identity and a strong desire to decide at the national level most policies, citizens also express some recognition that there are values such as democracy, respect for human rights, and concerns for the environment that they share with other Europeans, and to a certain extent they feel proud of what Europe represents. For instance Eurobarometer 56 indicates that 47 percent of British citizens feel "very proud" or "fairly proud" of being European (although this should not be interpreted necessarily as equating Europe with the European Union). Furthermore, although a negative view of the EU by U.K. citizens is clearly predominant and tends to be more often diffused in the media, there is also a considerable proportion of U.K. citizens that sees themselves as Europeans and supports the European Union. One third of the lay people interviewed expressed some type of connection with Europe and believed that they shared some cultural traits: "I could say that I am European, even though we have some specific culture as British people, but so have the French, the Germans, and so on" (Unemployed, London). Also "Yes, I see myself as European. I like many things in the continent, the food, the sun on the Spanish beaches . . . Let's say that when I cross the channel I do not feel anymore so much in foreign lands" (Mechanic, Scotland). Several of the most educated people interviewed pointed out that the United Kingdom could help to connect United States-Canada and Europe, an idea that was also often expressed by politicians: "I believe that the U.K. could position itself as a bridge between the two continents [Europe and North America], but I think that the U.K. is a very European country and I find myself very European" (High school teacher, Wales). A minority sees the idea expressed by the euroskeptics of leaving the EU as a "crazy idea": "Turning our backs to Europe would be a suicide." "We cannot deny that there are major cultural differences between the United Kingdom and most of Europe, for instance, in political traditions. We do not have a Christian Democrat tradition and all the social elements that go with that influence. But the reality is that we are in Europe and we have to learn to live in this context of a more socially oriented society" (Economist, London). Another common idea among U.K. citizens is that the EU must be "transparent." This opinion was expressed in these terms by only two interviewees, but many complained that although they were not in principle opposed to the European Union, they would like to have a better idea of what the EU "was doing" and "how it was doing it."

One prevalent concept among the United Kingdom citizens' interviewees (even among those who do not oppose to the EU) is the tendency to see their own history and particularly their norms and values as special and different from the rest of Europe. People interviewed tied U.K. national identity to traditional religion more than in the other two countries and identify U.K. identity with the monarchy far more than in Spain, the other monarchy in my study. In fact, the king or the monarchy is rarely mentioned by Spanish politicians or by the lay people as part of their national identity. In the United Kingdom many people perceive the monarchy as warrant of stability and order. The works of Colley (1992) and Greenfeld (1992) give an excellent account of how this sentiment developed in England from the seventeenth to the nineteenth century.[11]

As in the other countries studied in previous chapters, there are considerable differences between leaders and lay people in their interpretation of the EU. Leaders tend to be more positive than the population at large when they evaluate the benefits of EU membership.[12] The next section examines more specifically the organizational preferences of the EU and the concerns over sovereignty and national identity.

SOVEREIGNTY AND POLITICAL ORGANIZATION
OF THE EU

In the United Kingdom the vast majority of both leaders and lay people support an intergovernmental structure for the EU. All the U.K. political leaders interviewed but two remain much attached to a continuation of a strong nation-state. Even the most enthusiastic pro-European Union of the U.K. political leaders interviewed was reluctant to create a federal Europe: "I'm a democratic socialist, and I want to work internationally, I am a pro-European in that sense. However, I don't really believe in a federated Europe, but I do believe that we can work together, and work as a great corporation on a whole range of issues" (Labor Party leader, Scotland). On this issue there is an agreement among all the major parties. The majority of pro-EU leaders interviewed expressed the desire to work within Europe, but clearly in the context of a Europe of nation-states: "I am very supportive of the EU but I would be very unhappy if the European Union would take the direction of a federation as a Swiss type of federation (Liberal Democrat leader, London). The interviews reveal much concern over losing national sovereignty among both leaders and the population at large. But arguments against federalism also include questions of economics:

I think that the economic benefits of federalism are greatly exaggerated. In fact it could lead to the very worst things that I fear. Federalism will require some type of centralization, which in turn will require large economic units. The central bank would inevitably take measures that would produce economic divergence rather than convergence and I think that the poorer regions will get poorer and the better off regions will inevitable suck in more of the resources. So, we need to be very careful about that. (Conservative Party leader, Northwest)

Rather than what tends to get the publicity, which is people saying it is the end of the nation state, federalism renders the nation-state control of the economy powerless, which is much more worrisome. (Labor Party leader, London)

However, there are differences among leaders regarding the much-publicized concern over a possible loss of national identity as a result of European integration. As we have seen, there is a group within the Conservative Party that often has expressed the fear of losing U.K. national identity. In the other two major parties this is not so important. In fact several interviewees from the Labor Party and the Liberal Democrats consider that this question is basically a "cheap demagogical tool of some conservatives to win votes" (Labor Party leader, London), or a question of age differences: "The loss of national identity is a myth, which works well with the Conservative Party supporters who tend to be much more elderly" (Liberal Democrat leader, Northwest).

Among the public at large, there is little debate about the type of association that should prevail between the United Kingdom and Europe. Very few support federalism, and there is widespread concern that the Commission has too much power to influence U.K. policies. A large majority is highly skeptical of what they perceive as the "expanding power of Brussels." Only two interviewees were inclined to create a unified federal Europe: "I think that we should be even more integrated in organizational terms. We should aspire to a federal Europe in a model similar to Switzerland" (Bank employee, London). In fact, the general attitude towards the European Union and to the possibility of a federal Europe does not seem to have changed that much since the European Community was created in the 1950s. The following quotation from Winston Churchill in 1950 echoes a view that has been rather consistent throughout the years among the U.K. Conservative political leaders (even though the United Kingdom has now lost its empire):

Where do we stand? We are not members of the European Defense Community, nor do we intend to be merged in a federal European system. We feel that we have a special relation to both. Thus can be expressed by prepositions, by the preposition 'with' but not 'of' —we are with them but not of them. We have our own Commonwealth and Empire. (cited in Marcussen et al. 1999: 625)

Europe is viewed as "the continent," as that "other race" in contrast to Anglo-Saxon exceptionalism. While in Spain and France politicians discuss openly giving up some sovereignty to create a more united Europe, the question is rarely considered in the United Kingdom, even though in practical terms they sometimes have to accept European Union directives. When the idea of federalism is brought up in the United Kingdom it is almost always considered in negative terms. "We do not want a super-state" is a common criticism of U.K. politicians, including Prime Minister Tony Blair, when responding to calls for further EU integration. In the United Kingdom, it would be political suicide for a candidate to suggest openly giving up some sovereignty to the EU. Even those who support U.K. membership in the EU, and an economic association with Europe, still want the major decisions to be in the hands of the U.K. government and Parliament and believe that each state must have the possibility to opt out of certain agreements or parts of the agreements. The United Kingdom has been able to exert this opt-out option regarding the social charter included in the Maastricht Treaty (they finally agreed on the social charter in 1999), the euro, and the Schengen Agreement, which abolished border controls between the current member states. In short, the terms "federalism" and "supra-state" are often mentioned by politicians and the public at large when discussing European Union issues, but these concepts are used primarily to mobilize public opinion against a particular EU agreement, such as in the debate on adopting the common currency. Even the idea of harmonizing certain laws has minimal support in the United Kingdom: "A united Europe should be about reducing the legislation rather than increasing legislation at the European level. I do not think that a European-wide judicial system would be possible, not even desirable" (Liberal Democrat leader, London). Leading figures of the Conservative Party are already rather concerned about what will come out of the Convention to create some type of EU constitution that started in the spring of 2002. They already predict a centralization of power by Brussels. For instance, William Cash, a Conservative Party member of Britain's House of Commons and the party's lead spokesman on legal affairs, declared: "There is a lack of connection between the people and the elites on a huge scale." He estimates that only five of the 105 delegates drafting the EU constitution share the demand for a "more democratic, transparent Europe" and that all the others are committed in advance to further EU integration: "I emphatically say we are heading for a European super-state" (Sands 2002: 1). It is noticeable that the idea of a more transparent, democratic Europe is opposed here to further integration. The same people who are opposed to giving more power to the European parliament defend a more democratic Europe. What Mr. Cash and many others in the United Kingdom imply by this concept is that only at the nation-state level could a democracy be possible. They want all the powers to remain at the national level.

Objections to transferring political sovereignty to the European Union are often justified on the grounds that the EU lacks parliamentary accountability, as this quote exemplifies: "In the U.K. we have a long tradition of liberal democracy and we are very attached to the values of a strong Parliament. The EU has not really a mechanism of checks and balances. The EU Parliament has a very limited power" (Labor Party leader, London). However, historically the government of the United Kingdom has not been supportive of giving more power to the EU Parliament. On the contrary the emphasis has been on keeping the Council in charge. This has not changed much throughout the years, whether the Conservative Party or the Labor Party was in power. These views are reflected in this quote from former prime minister John Major in 1993: "Britain has successfully used the Maastricht negotiations to reassert the authority of national governments. It is clear now that the Community will remain a union of sovereign national states. That is what its people want: to take decisions through their own Parliaments . . . It is for nations to build Europe. Not for Europe to attempt to supersede nations" (*The Economist* 1993).

The strong intergovernmental position of the U.K. government is even clearer in Prime Minister Tony Blair's 2002 proposal to "get the Council of the EU member states' government leaders to elect a kind of president of the union for a five-year mandate." Blair claims that his plan attempts to achieve continuity of political guidance and direction in the Council's action. Indeed with the addition of ten new members in 2004, the traditional system of rotating the presidency every six months could become problematic. However, the smaller states are opposed to Blair's proposal because they fear that representatives from the larger nations would dominate the Council. Those arguing against Blair's plan suggest that continuity in political action is ensured not only by the presence of a single person in office, but also by the concrete existence of a shared political and strategic line. The European Union's government leaders, who are by their very nature heterogeneous and changeable, do not have such a line. On the other hand, the European Commission and its president could create a shared political and strategic line, but this would imply giving more power to the Commission, which is considered by most U.K. politicians as the federal and centralizing power of the EU. If Blair's plan were approved, the intergovernmental approach to European integration would be enhanced while the federalist and supranational approach would be severely limited. Indeed, the Commission would be even more limited than it is today, confined to a basic technocratic role, as a kind of advisory board to the president of the Council. This plan could also undermine the role of the Parliament. Indeed, the power Parliament recently acquired (in 1997 under the Treaty of Amsterdam) of approving or disapproving the Commission's president would have no democratic value. Furthermore, the election of the president by a fluctuating Council of Ministers would not address the problem, so often denounced by many who support an intergovernmental European Union, of a democratic deficit. Citizens of the member countries will not yield any additional influence in the workings of the Union because of this change. The real objective of Blair's proposal is not to stimulate the European Union's political unification—far from it. Instead, he hopes to disrupt as much as possible any institutional reform that could reinforce the power of the supranational institutions: the Commission or the Parliament.

Business representatives, including those supporting membership in the European Union, consider that the national state should establish its own laws: "It is outrageous that the Commission can promote legislation that national parliaments do not want. The Council and the nation-state should continue to be the main players in the union."

Most U.K. leaders, in the interviews and in their declarations in the press, still talk of Europe as an external power that can make their country more powerful in the world. Europe is a means for the United Kingdom to promote its power, but without surrendering sovereignty to Europe. In other words, Blair, more blatantly perhaps than other European leaders, praises U.K. association with Europe in these terms: "The United Kingdom has lost an empire but has found a role in the contemporary external politics, a fundamental partner" (Garton Ash 2002: 13). He reproduces here the same idea expressed earlier by other U.K. leaders, such as Churchill (see the quote earlier in the chapter); the United Kingdom is in a partnership with the European Union but not part of the European Union, the United Kingdom is "with them but not of them."

THE ROLE OF THE MEDIA

In the United Kingdom there is a myriad of newspapers openly anti-European Union. The European Commission representation in the United Kingdom publishes a Press Watch section on their web site that analyzes articles published in different British newspapers, particularly *The Daily Express, The Independent, Daily Mail, The Times, Daily Express, The Sun, The Sunday Telegraph, The Daily Telegraph, The Mail on Sunday, Daily People, Sunday People, Western Daily Press, The Newcastle Journal,* and even the news aired by the *British Broadcasting Corporation.* They try to counter and explain all the inaccuracies that are published in these newspapers, showing how some of the British press publishes incorrect news about the EU, but they also note that "when stories aren't factually incorrect, they are so full of bias as to leave readers bewildered." (European Union Representation-Press Watch 2001). I examined the publications of the last two years (2000–2002). Most of these newspapers (with the exception of *The Times* and *Independent*) seem to have a clear agenda of undermining anything that has to do with the European Union and European integration. They have concentrated on criticizing the supposed regulations coming out of the European Union (as reported in the EU Representation-Press Watch 2002 titles, "Papers Still Blind to the EU's Bigger Picture"), often confusing institutions and systematically attributing to the EU regulations that have nothing to do with the EU. In fact, it is rather entertaining reading all the vicious but stupid reporting contained in these newspapers, for example: "Certain Breeds of the Queen's Favorite Dog Could Be Outlawed Under a Controversial EU Convention Being Considered by Ministers" (*Daily Mail* 2002: 5). This gives the impression of another example of intrusive Eurocrats getting involved with unimportant things and unsettling not only British citizens but also a major institution of the United Kingdom, Her Majesty, the Queen. Another typical article "Fire chiefs in the North-East are rejecting a European safety directive to stop staff sliding down stations poles . . . The new EU safety directives state that firemen should be ordered to walk down the stairs instead." (*The Newcastle Journal* 2002: 4). As the EU Representation-Press Watch (2002: 3) points out, "the most relevant pieces of European law are the council directives of 1989 and 1991, which encourage improvements in the health and safety of workers" in general, but there "is nothing in either directive, which specifically relates to fireman's poles." Furthermore, there is nothing new about those directives. Indeed, more than 11 years have passed since the last one was issued.

There are more than 60 similar stories reported in the Press Watch of the European Commission in the United Kingdom. over two years, but these examples will suffice to illustrate the type of coverage of the EU by the popular press. It is clear that in the United Kingdom there are more articles in the press against European Union than in favor. With the few exceptions already mentioned, it seems that from the U.K. media point of view the only good European story is a bad news story.

As stated earlier in the introduction, I also analyzed in more detail news reported in *The Times*, a relatively serious newspaper, which is not opposed in principle to the EU. Compared to *Le Monde* or *El País* (analyzed in the previous chapters on France and Spain), *The Times* had fewer articles on the European Union. Out of 88 days considered in my sample, *The Times* had at least one article on 59 days (while *Le Monde* had at least one article on 73 days and *El País* on 64 days). Given that there were up to four articles on the topic on certain days, the number of articles could be greater than the number of days studied. *Le Monde* had a total of 98 articles, *El País* 73, and *The Times* 68.

Fifty-two percent of the articles published by *The Times* had a negative representation of the EU, while 30 percent were neutral and 18 percent represented the EU in a positive light. The articles on the EU are published in the section "World News" of the paper. Following are some recent examples of headlines that reflect a content that could instigate in the readers negative feelings about the EU: "Blair Admits Frustration over Summit" on the Barcelona EU summit (March 17, 2002), "EU Force Undermined" (March 15, 2002), "Thatcher Insists Britain Must Never Join the 'Doomed' Euro" (March 19, 2002), "Blair Out of the Picture After Losing on EU Policy" (EU summit in Seville July 24, 2002). These titles reflect a predominant tendency in the press (even in relatively serious papers like *The Times*) to concentrate on conflict and drama and contribute considerably more to a negative idea of the EU than a positive one.

Finally, of the three papers analyzed, *Le Monde* is the only newspaper that has a special section on Europe. The other two, *El País* and *The Times*, include the topic of the EU on their international or world sections. This gives a sense of how each of the newspapers places Europe. In *Le Monde* the issues of European Union are not totally domestic but neither are they foreign. By placing news on the EU in the international section, *El País* and *The Times* induce their readers to see the European Union as distant and foreign. This might be unintentional (and could be just the result of historical habits that have never been questioned), but the context of news articles does influence the way they are interpreted by the public.

In the next section I summarize and examine briefly the most salient of the social representations of the EU in the United Kingdom, and their implications for this country's association with Europe. I will develop further the larger implications and consequences for the future of the EU in the final chapter.

CONCLUSION: BETWEEN TWO WORLDS

The specific arguments debated in England are whether the United Kingdom is strong enough to surrender some sovereignty (as little as possible) for the sake of a place in the largest free market in the world and to be able to influence the path of the European Union rather than to be changed by it. Blair's government seems to want more influence in European Union affairs, without giving up any type of sovereignty.

Most interviewees, including those opposed to the European Union, recognized that the European Union has some role to play in Europe. But there is much ambiguity among leaders regarding the level of engagement of the United Kingdom with the EU. This ambiguity is reflected in the interpretations of the widely mentioned concept of subsidiarity. Although this concept was interpreted differently in terms of more or less *Europe* in U.K. policies, there is a predominant view emphasizing that the U.K. government should continue to play a major role in most areas of the economy and politics. Many interviewees have a view of subsidiarity that relegates the EU institutions, such as the Commission and the Parliament, to the status of advisory boards, and concentrates all the power in the Council. The idea here is to eliminate from the picture the most federal institutions and give all the power to the nation-states. This explains also the opposition to the common currency among large sectors of the political elite. Indeed, the European Central Bank is probably the most federal institution of the EU.

The predominant image of the EU, shared by most U.K. political and business leaders, is of a vast, deregulated market for goods and capital, and with the nation-states as facilitators for the creation and functioning of this market. The problem with this vision is that in the same way that the national currencies needed some type of stability in order for the national economies to function properly, so does the euro. The common currency needs further political unity, including harmonization of the tax system, in order to remain competitive as a world currency in the long term.

In international affairs, there is acknowledgement among the majority of political leaders and many lay citizens that no European country could influence the world without the others, but only a small group of leaders and citizens interviewed believed that the EU should have a unified foreign policy. We have seen that U.K. leaders and citizens were very much attached to the exceptionalism of the United Kingdom. More than in the other countries, the debate on the EU in general and on the euro in particular is very much dominated by questions of national identity and sovereignty.[13] The euroskeptics from different political parties hinge on this feeling and on a widespread interpretation of the "U.K.'s glorious recent history" to resist European integration, and even British participation in the European Union.

Historically, worldwide crises or changes have forced nations to redefine themselves, and in the process, to confront questions of sovereignty and national identity. The most recent of these defining moments in Europe were during the twentieth century World War I and World War II, the independence of the colonies,[14] and the creation of the European Economic Community, for both the member countries more directly, and those who had trade relations with the EC. The United Kingdom has been forced to deal with the EC first as trade partner and later as member. The Treaty on the Union and the ensuing agreements during the 1990s have more than ever instigated an intense debate in the United Kingdom about the EU. As we have seen, the debate has been revolving around questions of sovereignty, national identity, and the appropriateness and conditions of U.K. participation in the EU. The ongoing debate on the adoption of the euro as the U.K. currency is the most tangible and recent example.

Furthermore, U.K. political leaders emphasize the importance of the country's independence in international affairs and world politics. However, in reality Blair's government's mirroring and almost blind following of U.S. policies during the last six years could make the United Kingdom irrelevant in world politics and even in European Union affairs. Many European leaders note with suspicion Blair's echoing of George W. Bush's views.[15] U.K. leaders interviewed argued that the special association with the United States was not "really threatening to its associates in Europe," and that the United Kingdom acted as a bridge between the United States and the EU. However, one might ask: Does the United States need a bridge in its relationships with the European Union?

In fact, there is a widely shared idea among EU politicians interviewed that the U.K. government disregards the European Union too often. For instance, the government of the United Kingdom is viewed as serving U.S. interests more than the interests of Europe. In fact, the fundamental partner of the United Kingdom in international affairs seems to be the United States rather than the EU. In the war in Afghanistan, and in the 1993 conflict between the United States and Iraq, Tony Blair played a rather active role on the side of the United States.[16] His declarations were more warrior-like than the other Europeans and often in open contradiction with the other European leaders, and even with many members of his own party. This quote express opinions articulated by half of the interviewees from the Labor Party: "I think the U.K. people have a vision that is closer to the other Europeans in general, than to the U.S. in international issues, on the middle East for example, but the government of the U.K. seems to be prisoner of the United States. I do not understand that myself" (Labor Party leader, Scotland).

Furthermore, the U.K. government often opposes European Union-wide initiatives. A recent example is the opposition to the European project of satellites, Galileo.[17] Empirical evidence suggests that the fundamental partner of the United Kingdom in international affairs is not the EU but the United States. Indeed, the U.K. government has often tied its national interest to the United States, which confirms Charles de Gaulle's concern when he opposed U.K. entrance in the European Economic Community in the 1960s. As one interviewee asserts: "the problem with the U.K. is that we look in two directions at the same time. We cannot have it both ways. Either we associate with Europe and we play a major role in the process of building a more united Europe or we just stay outside and try to associate with the United States or others" (High school teacher).

In fact, many politicians in France, Spain, and even in other countries of the EU consider that the U.K. government often acts against the interests of other Europeans. For example, in 2002 the parliament of Belgium complained that the British were using Echelon to spy on their European partners. They presented several examples, such as an intrusion in the computer system of a research center as well as the case of the Belgian "voice recognition" company, Lernout & Hauspie, which went into bankruptcy, after the *Wall Street Journal* published a negative article on the basis, according to the Belgium Parliament, of information provided by Echelon. The Belgian parliamentarians point out that spying on its partners in the EU is contrary to European laws.[18] In addition, there have been for several years complaints from French officials and politicians that the Government Communications Headquarters (GCHQ) of the United Kingdom are spying on the other Europeans (using the satellite network Echelon) for the benefit of the U.S. government, more specifically for the National Security Agency (NSA), which in turn uses the information to help the U.S. private companies to get international contracts to the detriment of the Europeans. In other words, complaints are that the U.K. government uses the satellite network Echelon to spy on Europeans to steal contracts that are under negotiations by European companies. Another widely publicized case, which drew protest from French officials, was the loss of a large contract by the European consortium Airbus to the profit of rival U.S. company Boeing in 1999 (this allegation was particularly bizarre given that U.K. companies have a big stake in Airbus). The accusation at that time was that a very large contract that was on the verge of being signed by the Saudis was derailed thanks to Echelon. Supposedly, Boeing, on the basis on the information collected by Echelon, was able to offer the Saudis a better deal. In sum, these incidents coupled with the foreign policy that the United Kingdom has followed in recent years (closely tied to U.S. foreign policy) have contributed to engendering distrust among other European leaders about where the United Kingdom stands in its commitment to the European Union. The impression that the United Kingdom gives to other European leaders is that it wants to get the best of all worlds. As one French interviewee said: "The U.K. government wants rights and advantages, but not responsibilities. Europe is made up of compromises; we all have to give up something in order to win more." Can the United Kingdom continue to look in two directions at the same time? The reality is that economically, even though the United Kingdom is an important partner with the United States, it might be forced to look more and more towards Europe. In fact, it seems that the government and the economic elites have decided to adopt the euro and are planning a referendum for 2004–2005. This would require being able to convince a rather large number of people who are opposed to the euro. In order to do so the U.K. government would have to adopt a more positive outlook on the EU and probably stop the negative rhetoric regarding the evil supra-state. They cannot expect to win the hearts of the British population on the euro and criticize the EU at the same time.

NOTES

1. De Gaulle stated: "Moi, je veux l' Europe pour qu'elle soit europénne, c'est à dire qu'elle ne soit pas américaine" (I want Europe to be European; that is to say that it would not be American) (Peyrefitte 1994: 61).

2. Margaret Thatcher often referred to past glory to reassert the international British civilizing mission: "It was the British people who took the lead in asserting liberty as a fundamental human right and who devised political institutions to protect and promote it. We have planted that doctrine and those institutions in every quarter of the globe"(The New Statement and Society 1989: 8–11).

3. In her recent publication *Statecraft*, Margaret Thatcher (2002) suggests the conditions and mechanisms under which the United Kingdom should withdraw from the EU.

4. Many of the views expressed by this minority of the Conservative Party would most likely be considered extremist views in France or Spain, while they seem to be considered almost mainstream in the United Kingdom. Indeed, some of these views do not differ significantly from the arguments on Europe put forward by the French extreme right party, the Front National. In fact, in may instances, this radical wing of the Tories might be even more radical than the FN. Thatcher even wrote in her latest book (2002), that Europe was the source of all the world's problems (not including, of course, the United Kingdom in her definition of Europe).

5. The Trade Union Congress (TUC) represents the vast majority of trade unionists in the United Kingdom. The unions that are not affiliated are small organizations representing specialist staff and in many cases employees of a partic-

ular organization. Substantial organizations that are outside the TUC include the Police Federation, which is barred by law from affiliating to the TUC (TUC 2002).

6. In fact, farmers do request funds from the EU. *The Financial Times* reports that Mr. Gill has written to Farming and Food Minister, Lord Whitty, to request funds from the EU. He is quoted as writing: "The parlous state of livestock and dairy incomes reinforces the urgent need for the Government to claim whatever compensation is available for the competitive disadvantage and exchange rate losses that have accrued to U.K. farmers." He is referring to compensation made available by the European Commission to make up for exchange rate fluctuations. "Only in this way can it be ensured that U.K. farmers are not further disadvantaged by the influence of the exchange rate policy" (McCoy: 2002: 1).

7. The European level equivalent of the CBI is the Union of Industrial and Employees Confederations of Europe-UNICE.

8. There is a recurring tendency in the United Kingdom to use the concept of race to define a country, and specifically the United Kingdom. Many U.K. politicians associated the concept of national identity with an outdated nineteenth-century concept of race. Declarations of two prominent politicians such as Blair and Thatcher illustrate this point: Blair characterizes the British "as an island race proud and independent, although with much European blood in our veins" (Garton Ash 2002: 13); and Thatcher in an explanation of why the Falkland Islands war was necessary, stated: "the people of the Falkland Islands, like the people of the United Kingdom, are an island race" (Barnett 1982: 18). Also common among U.K. citizens of the twenty-first century is the notion that "each race is best suited to its own territorial space" (Lay citizen).

9. Many tourist places and big stores already accept the euro in their everyday dealings, particularly big stores that have many international outlets, such as Harrods, Dixon, Marks and Spencer, Virgin, and Selfridges. The Chamber of Commerce of the United Kingdom estimated in 2002 that about half of the large stores in London were accepting euros. British Telecom has already adapted the public telephones so that they can function with euros.

10. In 1998 some irregularities were discovered in one directorate of the European Union's Commission. Although no commissioners were directly involved, this issue received ample coverage in the United Kingdom's media.

11. Linda Colley (1992) argues that the monarchy became a symbol of the United Kingdom during the reign of George III. Before it was only a symbol for England.

12. A survey of leaders done on behalf of the Commission by EOS Gallup Europe in 1996 found that in general business and political leaders in the United Kingdom tended to support European Union, but this study did not really measure what kind of European Union they were supporting or rejecting.

13. This is perhaps due to historical memory and how the continent is represented in history and text books in schools. Manzo (1996: 114) suggests, "Britain has long been constructed in opposition to Europe, even as the peoples of the British nation have been taught to identify with other civilized peoples. National identity has been forged out of a sense of geographic isolation from the European continent," and, as it was the case for most other countries of Europe, from the threat of foreign powers, which were, usually, the neighboring nations. In fact, England forged its national identity in opposition to the Vatican and against the Catholic powers of the continent, such as France and Spain (Colley 1992). For an

analysis of the historical process of national identity formation in England from the fifteenth to the nineteenth century see Manzo (1996). For a more recent historical account, after World War II, see Williamson (1990, 1998).

14. The victory parades at the end of the two wars, annual Remembrance Day celebrations, and other national celebrations "have shaped popular memories of the war as well as reinvented the character and spirit of Britain." This notion "of British nation joined in war and ready to act in times of danger has been continually revived" (Manzo 1996: 122). More recent examples glorifying the U.K. nation, its people, and its armed forces can be found in the speeches of Margaret Thatcher during the Malvinas/Falkland war, and Blair's speeches during and after the war in Afghanistan.

15. Indeed, it is striking that Blair has espoused two very different U.S. policies with the same fervor. The aggressive stand and unilateral doctrine of the George W. Bush administration is very different from Clinton's government policy of cooperation with the international institutions. Whether the unilateral approach of Bush or the more multilateral approach of Clinton, it does not matter, he follows both with the same passion. In the name of national sovereignty Blair does not want to be a prisoner of the Brussels bureaucracy, but is he independent from the U.S. government?

16. Blair articulated better than George Bush the reasons for the war in Afghanistan, for example, especially in attempting to explain to his constituency and abroad how the war was not a fight against Muslims. However, his efforts were undermined by Bush's refusal to shake hands with Arafat during a UN-sponsored meeting in Washington in 2002, his unqualified support for Ariel Sharon, and most importantly, by including two major Muslim countries, Iran and Iraq, in the so-called "axis of evil." In fact, as the analysis of Fontaine (2002) suggests, it does not seem that Bush has been taking any of Blair's advice into consideration.

17. Galileo is a European project of radio navigation by satellite. Many applications are expected from this project, from rail transport and sailing safety to the orientation of cars. Here again, as in many technological projects, the United States was pressuring Europeans not to do it because, they argued, Europeans could use the U.S. system (called GPS) that has been developed, and the European system might interfere with the frequency of the U.S. military satellite version of their GPS. The French and Germans have expressed that they do not want to become the vassals of the United States. A German diplomat argued that if they do not develop Galileo, "the USA will be in a situation of monopoly that we will not be able to crack, because their technological advance would be too strong" (Zecchini and Jospin 2002: 5).

18. According to Stroobants (2002), the National Security Agency (NSA) of the United States manages the system that intercepts all electronic communications (by fax, telephone, or computer). The NSA has a budget of about 2 billion dollars a year. The network Echelon is capable of intercepting all satellite communications and filtering them with the help of a very powerful computer, by using keywords and by vocal recognition. According to Stroobants (2002) and other studies, Echelon can systematically gather economic information that is transmitted to the U.S. government, which may in turn pass that information on to U.S. companies in order to help them to get international contracts.

CHAPTER 5

Enlargement

In 1992 the heads of state of the then 12 member countries resolved that the countries of Central and Eastern Europe could become members of the EU if such was their will, and provided that they met the criteria for accession. These criteria were spelled out in the European Council meeting in Copenhagen on June 22, 1993. The country aspiring to become a member should: (1) have stable institutions guaranteeing democracy, the primacy of law, and respect for human rights, (2) have a viable market economy and the ability to face up to the pressure of competition and the market forces within the union, and (3) have the ability to assume the obligations stemming from membership, and particularly to take on the aims of political, economic, and monetary union (Europa 2002a). In addition, to participate in the common currency, the countries needed an inflation rate no more than 1.5 percent higher than the three lowest national rates in the EU and long-term interest rates not above 2 percent of the average of the three lowest EU rates, the individual state budget deficit (including central, regional, and local governments) should not exceed 3 percent of the Gross Domestic Product (GDP), and the public debt ratio of the member states should not exceed 60 percent of the GDP.

In 1998 negotiations began with 12 countries aspiring to become members, and finally, in the intergovernmental meeting, held in Copenhagen, on December 12–13, 2002, the European Council decided to accept 10 new countries from Eastern and Central Europe as members of the European Union. The Nice Treaty (drafted at the Nice European Council in December 7–9, 2000) paved the way for this new enlargement.[1] This treaty amended the Treaty on European Union, the treaties establishing the European Communities, and the Protocol on Enlargement of the European Union.

This enlargement would be the largest in the European Union history in terms of number of countries (10) and population (75 million). The countries that were admitted to join by May 1, 2004 are Cyprus (more precisely half of the country; the other half is under Turkey's control, with a population of 0.8 million), Czech Republic (pop. 10 million), Estonia (pop. 1 million), Hungary (pop. 10 million), Latvia (pop. 2 million), Lithuania (pop. 1 million), Malta (pop. 0.4 million), Poland (pop. 39 million), Slovakia (pop. 5 million), and Slovenia (pop. 2 million).[2] Romania and Bulgaria might join in 2007. Turkey is also aspiring to become a member of the EU, but negotiations to consider this country's membership will only start in 2004. This last enlargement differs substantially from previous ones, not only in size, but also in terms of the budget available to the new members.

PERCEPTIONS ON ENLARGEMENT

Until the Copenhagen summit of December 2002 the enlargement process has not encountered much opposition, and with the exception of Ireland, there has not been much public debate on this issue in the member countries. In particular in France and Spain not even in the parliaments has there been much debate. In the United Kingdom there had been some discussion in the parliament, but that was rather limited. In fact, there was almost a consensus on enlargement among political leaders. Most interviewees from all political tendencies, including many leaders who opposed further European integration, seemed to agree on enlargement. The exceptions were eight French political leaders (one from the Socialist Party, one from the Communist Party, one from the UMP, and six from the National Front), two Spanish leaders (one from United Left and one union leader from the UGT), and two U.K. leaders from the Conservative Party. Several arguments were articulated to oppose enlargement. On one side there were a few people supportive of further political integration who saw in this enlargement a danger of undermining a deepening of the union. They feared that it would not be possible to reach further political integration in the near future: "With all the problems that we have to solve with the new enlargement I am very concerned about other important EU policies that need to be reinforced. The new enlargement might undermine the political Europe, which has been advancing in very small steps"(Socialist Party leader, Strasbourg), and that the enlargement could bring to a standstill the already limited international role of the EU: "Would the EU be able to play even a major role in the international commercial negotiations and in all the international crises after enlargement? I doubt that this will be possible" (UMP leader, Paris). On the other hand, enlargement would imply more immigrants, and more problems for the national governments[3] (the latter ideas were mainly expressed by leaders form the Front National and two leaders from the U.K. Conservative Party): "How would we be able to control our borders? You see already all the prostitution, for example, that is already coming from these countries to France. Also immigrants will come not only from Eastern Europe, but also from other countries that can easily pass throughout their borders. It would be a disaster and a lot of jobs would be lost" (Front National leader, Toulouse).

Among business leaders there seems to be a wide acceptance of this enlargement. All the representatives of the large business organizations interviewed were very much in support of enlargement. In the population at large there are more variations regarding support for enlargement. The Eurobarometers 55 and 56 (2001, 2002) reveal that in general there are more people who support enlargement than are against. However, in the three countries analyzed here there appear to be considerable differences in their support for enlargement (61 percent in Spain, 39 percent in France, and 41 percent in the United Kingdom, while 18 percent, 46 percent, and 33 percent, respectively, oppose enlargement). In fact, in the survey, only France has fewer people in favor of enlargement than against.[4] However, in my in-depth interviews the answers that people gave were subtler and less supportive of enlargement than it might appear in the Eurobarometers results. Most importantly, the in-depth interviews indicated that very few lay citizens knew which countries would be included. They did not know how many and could not name more than two or three. Some even thought that enlargement included Switzerland, Norway, and Finland (ignoring that Finland was already a member of the EU). After I had explained which countries were close to be admitted as members of the EU, most of the interviewees in the three countries thought that there were too many countries to be admitted simultaneously. The majority of respondents were more in favor of a progressive incorporation. Furthermore, contrary to what the Eurobarometer results suggest, in my in-depth interviews I did not find such big differences between France, Spain, and the United Kingdom in terms of their views on enlargement. The following is a typical statement reflecting the ideas expressed by the majority of the interviewees, although the number of countries that should be included differed from one person to another: "we could accept three or four countries and a few years later two or three more and so on. I read in the newspaper that there were problems with the economic support the EU can provide for these countries, this then should be the way to go" (Schoolteacher, Toulouse). In sum, most people do not seem to be radically against the idea of enlargement at this point, but the large majority thought that too many countries could create a problem of coordination and also with resource allocation to the poorer regions by the EU. In short,

6 out of 10 people interviewed in France and in the United Kingdom, and 5 out of 10 people in Spain tended to be against the present plan of admitting 10 new countries, and many did not know for sure which position to adopt.[5] In other words, as it happened with some of the questions that the Eurobarometer has employed throughout the years, this particular question does not seem to be very useful to understand people's support for enlargement.[6] In fact, the same Eurobarometer 56 demonstrated that most people did not feel informed about enlargement. On average only 22 percent felt they were very well, or well informed. Most remarkably, according to the same survey, the populations from many of the member countries who support further enlargement in high numbers, such as Spain, Italy, Portugal, and Sweden are even below average in terms of feeling informed on this issue.[7]

Another question asked in the Eurobarometer, which is more revealing than the ones about general support for enlargement, deals with attitudes towards enlargement. This question attempts to reveal the perceptions of the consequences of enlargement. Respondents indicated that they tended to agree with the following statements: "The more member countries within the EU, the more important it would be in the world" (68 percent); "with more member countries, Europe will be culturally richer" (64 percent); and "the more countries there are in the European Union, the more peace and security will be guaranteed in Europe" (59 percent). However, people interviewed also consider that with more countries it would be much more difficult to make decisions on a European scale (66 percent) that once the new countries have joined the European Union, their country would receive less financial aid from the EU (48 percent), and only 32 percent agreed with the statement "the European Union should help future member countries financially, even before they join."[8] The Eurobarometer did not sort the data by country, but the ambiguity in the views expressed was very much reflected as well in my interviews in the three countries studied: "We already have serious problems agreeing on anything with a Europe of 15, I do not see how we will be able to work with so many countries and particularly with countries that will be requiring so many resources" (Bank employee, London).

Regarding the views of the population from the candidate countries there are some indications from press reports and recent studies that there is widespread support among leaders for membership in the union. It seems that most political, union, and business leaders consider membership in the EU as unavoidable and necessary because of the perceived benefits. The public at large does not appear as supportive in all countries. To be exact, a recent survey (Candidate Countries Eurobarometer 2002) shows that most candidate countries' populations support membership in the EU; an average 6 out of 10 people felt that the EU membership would be a good thing.[9] However, in some countries populations are not very enthusiastic about membership in the EU, as is the case in Estonia (only 33 percent thought that membership was a good thing), Latvia (33 percent), and Malta (39 percent). The most negative of all is Malta, since 31 percent of the respondents considered membership in the EU a bad thing. When asked how they would vote in a possible referendum about EU membership, all the countries had a majority of people saying they would vote positively. The answers to these questions, which seek to reveal the level of support for European union in general more than predict the outcome of a future referendum, do not reveal overwhelming support. Estonia's population appears as the least supportive of European Union membership: Only 38 percent of respondents from Estonia indicated they would vote in favor of membership, while a considerable 27 percent would vote against. The population of Malta also appears rather divided about this question of membership in the European Union: 40 percent of Maltese would vote for and 36 percent would vote against.

The same Eurobarometer also examined the attachment to nationality and identification with Europe in the candidate countries. On this question the majority felt both nationality and European identification. Only in Lithuania did more of the population expect to continue to identify themselves with their nationality only (nationality only 44 percent, nationality and European 34 percent, European and nationality 7 percent, European only 3 percent), although, as we can see, even in this country there is a considerable proportion that identifies with Europe.[10] This question does not necessarily measure identification with the European Union but with Europe in general. These results contrast with the findings in the member countries. In the member countries those who say that they feel identified with nationality only are in the majority in 6 out of 15 (Eurobarometer 54 2000). This might confirm the idea put forward by some scholars that "there is often a greater motivation for those on the far periphery to assimilate into the norms of the center than is the case for the population close to the center" (Laitin 2002: 56). Other indications of feelings for Europe that the Eurobarometer attempted to measure were the "things coming to people's minds when thinking of EU." In general, the first thoughts about the European Union were largely positive in most countries, and the most salient response was a positive economic outlook. Latvia (35 percent of positive views versus 32 percent negative) and Estonia (32 percent positive versus 31 percent negative) were the least cheerful about the European Union. In sum, the data from the Candidate Countries Eurobarometer 56 (2002) suggest that Estonia, and to a lesser extent Malta, are reluctant candidates for EU membership.[11] In addition, not all social institutions in all candidate countries seem to be supporting integration. For instance, Osa (1992) and Anio et al. (1997) suggest that the Polish Catholic Church will most likely be on the side of the opposition rather than in support of joining a West European culture that they perceive as too secular and laic.[12] Furthermore, there are also indications that, as it happens in most countries of Western Europe, urbanites and the most educated citizens tend to support membership in the European Union and people living in rural areas, farmers, and manual workers who will be more directly bearing the constraints imposed by the requirements for membership would tend to oppose it. In the following section we address the economic aspects of integration.

SOCIOECONOMIC COHESION

In terms of economic cohesion within the present 15 member countries of the EU, there has been considerable progress. Particularly, during the last decade of the twentieth century the economic disparities between member states have diminished substantially. The case of Ireland was the most remarkable; from 1988 to 2001 the per capita GDP of this country went from 64 percent of the EU average to 119 percent. The per capita GDP of the poorer countries such as Greece (69 percent of EU average), Spain (82 percent) and Portugal (74 percent) have moved from 68 percent of the EU average to 79 percent from 1988 to 2001. Similarly, the socioeconomic situation of the weakest regions has also improved considerably. The ratio between the richest 10 percent of the EU regions and the least developed 10 percent was 2.6 in 2000 (Commission of the European Communities 2002: 8). Furthermore, income inequality, measured as the ratio of the richest 20 percent of households to poorest 20 percent of households, varies from 3.8 in Sweden to 7.0 in the United Kingdom. That is an average of 5.5 in the European Union of 15.[13] In terms of income inequality the poorer countries have also closed the gap.

With the planned enlargement of 10 more countries, the new Europe of 25 would be a far more unequal Europe (it would be even more unequal with 27). Indeed, the most developed 10 percent of regions would have a per capita GDP of 170 percent of the European Union average while the least prosperous 10 percent would be at about 38 percent. The ratio of inequality between the two groups would therefore be 4.5 (Commission of the European Communities, 2002). The income inequality within the EU in average will also go from 5.5 to about 6.4. The data produced by Wagstyl (2002) shows that the average per capita income of all the candidate countries is only 45 percent of the current EU average. Only Greek Cyprus has a per capita average income of $20,780, relatively close to the present EU average.

This implies that in a Union of 25 there would be an extensive geographical rearrangement of disparities, which in turn would change dramatically the assignment of cohesion and structural funds. The regions with a per capita GDP of less than 75 percent of the community average would mostly be in the newcomers. As the commission report indicates

(2002:15), "the threshold under the present *acquis* for eligibility for Objective 1, will have a population of 115 million people, 25 percent of the total population of the EU."[14] Consequently, 4 out of 10 people that would be eligible to receive structural funds under Objective 1 would be in the current 15 member states and 6 would reside in the candidate countries.

The regions currently eligible under Objective 1, which, after enlargement, would be above the 75 percent threshold, contain 37 million people. Hence, about two-thirds of the population of these regions would automatically cease to be eligible because of the fall in the community average of about 13 percent. The regions, which account for the bulk of the least prosperous after enlargement, would be located principally in Poland and Hungary (Commission 2002). Therefore, "the least developed region in the present Union (Ipeiros, in Greece) would not remain on the list of the least prosperous 10 percent of regions in a union of 25" (Commission 2002: 16). Consequently, the Mediterranean countries mentioned above (Greece, Spain, and Portugal) would receive less regional aid and, thus, limit their ability to close the gap with the richest countries of the union. Although these Mediterranean countries have improved their economic performance, proving that there has been a continuous trend towards convergence within a Europe of 15, the new enlargement would most likely prevent them from catching up with the richest countries in the near future. Even Spain, which has a relatively large economy, was still at 82 percent per capita GDP of the EU average in 2001.[15] In a European Union of 25, Spain would be very close to the EU average, and above the EU average in a Union of 27.[16]

Other economic data presented in the Commission report suggest a marked improvement in the current member countries in recent years and a worsening in the candidate countries. Such is the case of unemployment rates: "The union of 15 experienced a net gain of about 3 million jobs in the year 2000 while the candidate countries lost some 600 000 jobs" (Commission 2002: 8). In fact, unemployment continued to rise in most candidate countries in recent years, ranging from 6.9 percent in Slovenia to over 19 percent in Slovakia. In 2000, the largest increases in unemployment among the 10 candidate countries were recorded in Poland and Slovakia.[17] The same report also points out that the wide disparities in the candidate countries in levels of income or employment "are unlikely to be reduced appreciably before the long-term" (2002: 10). Other major differences related to the welfare of the population between present members and candidate countries include the levels of "air pollution, frequency of work accidents, number of abandoned children, street beggars" (Kovács 2002: 177).[18] Unless there is a major change in the international economy that would produce very high growth rates, in the medium term the national and regional income disparities as well as inequalities and the levels of unemployment will increase as consequence of enlargement.[19]

Therefore, with so many countries and so many disparities the challenges for reaching cohesion would be enormous. Considering past experiences one could estimate that in order to reach even the limited cohesion of the European Union of today it would take at least half a century. Perhaps with this new Europe of 25 (and 27 before the end of the decade) the word *cohesion* should be replaced by *limiting inequalities* to make this policy more credible.[20]

Indeed, because disparities will increase as a result of enlargement, it would have been logical to boost cohesion efforts, as leaders interviewed recognize. But the same leaders are quick to point out that in the present economic environment there would be no substantial increase in funds available to help the new member countries. Most states have been rather reluctant to increase the allocation of resources not only for cohesion and structural funds but also for the Common Agricultural Policy.[21] Furthermore, there are substantial divergences among the 15 present member countries on the question of financing enlargement.[22] Although in the Copenhagen meeting of 2002 an agreement was reached regarding some aspects of the budget for enlargement, it is clear that the redistribution of resources for structural and cohesion funds and the question of farm subsidies (CAP) have not been solved yet.[23] The most vocal in asking for a reduction of its participation to the EU budget has traditionally been the United Kingdom, but other countries, such as Germany, are starting to push for a revision of the CAP.[24] The German chancellor, Gerhard Schroeder, is quoted as saying that "unless Europe's agricultural policy is reformed, his country cannot afford to pay farm subsidies that would be due to new, poorer members when they join" (*Le Monde* 2002:6). Some political leaders from the United Kingdom have proposed not only to limit substantially the agricultural aid for new members but also to phase out subsidies for current members.[25] The following statement reflects ideas expressed by most of the U.K. political leaders I interviewed from different political parties on the question of the agricultural aid: "With the enlargement we will have to deconstruct the Common Agricultural Policy. We, as tax payers in the richer nations of Europe will revolt if we have to extend the current agricultural policy in its present form to Poland, Hungary, and the Czech Republic, because we can't afford it. They would take half the budget and make no contributions" (Conservative Party leader, London). Another interviewee from Spain also expressed concern over a too large support for agriculture: "We are already helping with the structural funds, we are already committed to making payments to these countries in order to bring them up to speed. But we can't extend the same level of the Common Agricultural Policy to them as well, it is impossible" (Popular Party leader, Barcelona). The Common Agricultural Policy (CAP) is a subsidy system that benefits about 5 percent of the present European Union population who are farmers. The 10 candidate countries will more than double the number of farmers and increase the amount of land under cultivation by 42 percent. As the above quotes reflect, most political leaders from current member countries want to keep new members from getting full benefits immediately after membership becomes official in May 2004. A measure that seemed to have the support of most of the current member countries was that the new members enter with only 25 percent of the agricultural subsidies they would normally receive and wait for full benefits to be phased in over 10 years, but substantial debate on this remains, and every indication seems to suggest that the contribution to the CAP will most likely be substantially reduced after 2007. Furthermore, there are other problems that are still unsolved. For instance, some of the countries that would like to become members of the EU, such as Hungary or Poland, have kept hardly any economic statistics, or even a basic infrastructure to check on the origin and direction of their agricultural products. That means it would be difficult to check where the help from the EU to agriculture goes.

Regarding cohesion policy, most leaders interviewed are aware that cohesion funds benefit not only assisted regions, but also the EU as a whole, particularly since it stimulates demand for goods and services in the poorer regions. According to a Spanish MEP, it is estimated that between 60 and 70 percent of the financial aid that the richest countries such as Germany, France, Belgium, or the Netherlands contribute to the cohesion and structural funds comes back to them as a result of goods (equipment and technology) and services that they provide to the net receivers of these funds. Some officials would also argue that these resources increase the overall competitiveness of the Union, and therefore provide opportunities for sustainable growth. However, this aspect is not as visible and easily quantifiable and easily explained to the population at large to justify an increase of funds for this facet of the EU policy. Furthermore, given the economic situation of Germany and France (which have been running relatively large public deficits for the last three years) no substantial additional funds will be made available in the near future, beyond what was established in the Copenhagen agreement in 2002. It is one thing to make general statements about solidarity, however sincere these statements might be, and another thing to commit more financial resources to a situation of limited economic development.[26] As part of the agreement on enlargement, the European Union allocated about 0.15 percent of the Gross Domestic Product in aid to the new members, that is, a total amount of 40.4 billion over three years (2004–2006).[27] This amount, though rather limited, was still considered too generous by some member states (Leparmentier 2003a), and too low by the leaders of the candidate countries, which even demanded increased aid for agriculture and rural development, as well as for environment and transportation. Two-thirds of the approved 40.4 billion would be directed to the structural and cohesion funds, one-fourth would be allocated to the Common Agricultural Policy, and the rest would be reserved for the modernization and improvement of the safety of nuclear plants.

Given the limited amount of structural funds available to the candidate countries, the chances for these countries to change substantially in the near future and to respond to the expectations that membership in the European Union would create are very limited. In addition, because of the requirements and the differential ability to compete with the current member countries in an open market there is a chance that many small companies and particularly many small farmers would have to abandon agriculture. Since the welfare system is rather problematic in most candidate countries, many people could end up in a rather difficult situation as a consequence of membership in the EU. Indeed, during the 1990s the governments of these countries have dismantled the old socialist welfare system, which, although it had limitations, provided basic support for poor people, in order to replace it with a less costly system, more welfare-capitalist oriented, that is not responding yet to needs of the population.

As I write these pages there are reports in the media of people from the candidate countries concerned about their economic standing after enlargement. Indeed, in order to fulfill the economic requirements for accession, the governments of the candidate countries would have to apply policies that would impose considerable sacrifices on the population. These harsh policies would not be compensated by the resources made available to them from the EU in farm and regional aid, because, as we have seen, they would be relatively limited. The funds for these items are well below the level the representatives of Poland and the Czech Republic have argued that they need. The financial concessions that the candidate countries obtained in the Copenhagen summit in December 2002 are still considered insufficient to adjust their economies to the requirements of membership. Some politicians and intellectuals in the candidate countries are already expressing apprehension with what they consider unequal treatment. Former Czech Prime Minister Vaclau Klaus is quoted by Agence Press (Brand 2002) as saying: "we hope that we will not get the status of second-class citizens which could bring us lower benefits." The same concern was expressed by Polish conservative Janus Wojciechowski: "Poles do not want a union of two-class citizens . . . Public opinion is worried by the proposals on EU farm handouts . . . In Poland this could lead to a 'no' in the national referendum" (Brand 2002). Some studies, in particular Spohn (2000), suggest that there are already significant defensive reactions vis-à-vis the European Union among the populations of the candidate countries. In fact, not everything has been solved at Copenhagen; there are many important and controversial details still in the working. The accession of the candidate countries would require ratification by national parliaments or referendums that would most likely produce struggles within the countries and ongoing demands from these countries' governments for more concessions in subsidies, compensation, and aid from the EU.

This situation might not be limited to the candidate countries only. Indeed, as the conditions in which the poorer member countries of the present union deteriorate, there will most likely be a resurgence of nationalism and discontent. The Spanish and Portuguese representatives have already expressed their concerns in Copenhagen in December 2002 about the possible drastic reduction of structural and cohesion funds for their countries.

The cohesion funds are certainly means for the European Union to express solidarity and to show that it is not just a large market but also the guardian of a particular model of society as the Commission report (2002) suggests. However, the problem faced here is that with so many poor countries entering the EU simultaneously and needing help, there would not be enough for all of them in the quantity needed. There is a limit to what the member countries are able or willing to allocate to this cause. Therefore, because of the enormous demand, and the lack of available funds to fulfill those demands, the enlargement process might cause frustration in both the candidate and the member countries, which can end up generating public unrest and anti-European Union feelings.

But economic convergence is not the only issue that this enlargement involves. Questions of democracy, language, immigration, criminal law, and so on are some of the other important implications of enlargement that need to be addressed in this intricate and complicated process of European integration.

DEMOCRATIC AND SOCIOCULTURAL INTEGRATION

A major aspect debated on the question of enlargement revolved around how well the candidate countries really would integrate into a club of democratic nations. A recent study by Fuchs and Klingermann (2002) suggests that in terms of levels of democracy there are still considerable differences between the candidate countries and the member countries. In analyzing the extent to which the candidate countries can become part of a democratic community similar to that of the member countries, which they define in terms of political culture, political structure, and political process,[28] these authors did uncover some clear indications of differences in the predominance of a democratic community between member countries and candidate countries, although their overall results are ambiguous. On the one hand the authors suggests that "there is little difference in the political values and behaviors that are essential to a democracy" between candidate and member countries (2002: 24); on the other hand, it reveals that in the candidate countries law-abidingness is well below average when compared with member countries, and that civil engagement and trust in others are also weaker than in the member countries. Fuchs and Klingermann conclude that the present differences are not abysmal and insurmountable, and that there is potential for understanding and for creating a democratic community, but in the near future eastward enlargement does pose integration problems and increases the difficulty of constituting a European democratic community.

Another study of the cultural identity of eastern European countries suggests more optimistic outcomes regarding the possibility of these countries' integration into the EU cultural arrangements. Laitin analyzes and compares aspects of popular culture, religion, and language with western Europe, and concludes, "the incorporation of East European states into the EU, from a cultural point of view, has greater potential for the deepening of European integration than for its erosion"(2002: 57). He claims that eastern candidates and western European members of the EU share the same level of cosmopolitanism and secularism, use the same supplementary languages (English, French, and German), listen to the same music, and watch the same movies. A common measure of cultural integration is indeed the sharing of languages. In the particular context of the EU, this includes all the languages spoken and understood by the populations of the different member countries. Eighty-two percent of the population in the 10 candidate countries that are scheduled to become members in 2004 can participate in a conversation in a language other than their mother tongue.[29] This high percentage is due to several factors: many of these nations have common Slavic roots in their maternal languages and can understand and speak other Slavic languages. That is the case of Slovenia, Slovakia, the Czech Republic, and Poland. Also there are large minorities in these countries who speak the language of their home country as a second language (Russian in Latvia, Lithuania, and Estonia for example). However, there is also a considerable percentage that speaks at least one of the most widely spoken languages in the European Union. English tops the list with an average of 20 percent. According to Candidate Countries Eurobarometer (2002) English is the most spoken foreign language in all but 2 (Czech Republic and Slovakia) of the 10 candidate countries scheduled to become full members of the EU by May 2004.[30] The second language spoken by the candidate countries is German with an average of 13.5 percent, which is the most spoken foreign language in Czech Republic and in Slovakia. A very distant third is French, with an average of 2.7 percent, which is most spoken in Malta (the least populated country).[31] As part of the expansion the EU will adopt 10 new official languages. Thus would bring the total number of languages spoken in the union to 21. Certainly, it would too ponderous and costly to translate into all 21 languages. The practical solution that is been considered by the Commission is to translate them into English first and then into the other languages. English will become de facto the lingua franca of the European union.

Another argument advanced by Laitin that suggests a smooth cultural integration of the candidate countries is that "the pressures of peripheralisation will induce East Europeans self consciously to promote a deepening of a European culture that West Europeans themselves have less motivation to foster" (2002: 78).

Other scholars on the contrary assert that political cultures between east and west are too dissimilar and that this new enlargement would create much chaos and certainly not contribute to deepening. For instance, Ralf Darendorf claims that "there is in the heart of Western Europe a common element or value, one that respects the rule of law, carries with it a desire for social democracy and reflects a combination of a desire to be a successful part of the global economy, but to also conduct policies that favor cohesion and justice. This value is not shared in the East" (quoted in Laitin 2002: 76). Darendorf joins here the few political leaders from France and Spain that have expressed in interviews the concern over diluting the core values of the EU, which, as one Spanish interviewee said, "are still in the making."

The process of social integration after enlargement would also require dealing with the burning issue of immigration, particularly in what pertains to the growing anti-immigrant sentiment in all the countries of the EU. Once the enlargement is official there is a good chance that, at least for the first years after enlargement, many people from the east would go to the more developed countries of the west. This could exacerbate the already existing anti-immigrant feelings, which in turn would give certain right-wing populist, xenophobic, and anti-European integration parties more support.[32] Some countries, such as Germany and France, have introduced a provision into the Copenhagen agreement on the free movement of workers that would prevent nationals of the new member countries from working in their territory for the first seven years after 2004. But this provision would not prevent the flow of illegal immigrants.

With the enlargement to the south in 1986, immigration was not such a big factor because in the case of Spain and Portugal, immediately after their accession there was an economic boom in both countries (we have seen the specific data for Spain in chapter 3). Also, the number of poor people living with less than $5000 per capita was less than would be the case with the new enlargement. Furthermore, most of the people inclined to emigrate in these two countries had already done so in the 1950s, 1960s, and 1970s (a proportion of these immigrants were in fact returning to their country of origin by the 1980s). Countries such as Belgium, France, Germany, the Netherlands, and Switzerland were among the recipients of the larger contingent of these immigrants.

Officials of the European Union and many political leaders (particularly from the left) tend to underestimate questions of xenophobia and the negative feelings that lay citizens have against the outsiders, who "come into our country and work for half our salary," those who come from different religious backgrounds and "require special accommodations," those who "do not even bother to learn our language or to adopt to our culture," those "foreigners many of whom commit crimes," those foreigners that "come here and trick the system for their advantage," and so on. I hear the above statements in my interviews but also in informal conversations with people from all socioeconomic backgrounds in France, Spain, Germany, the United Kingdom, the Netherlands, Belgium, and Italy.

Certainly, these statements do not imply that there is a consensus on this issue and that everybody in Europe is a xenophobe and anti-immigrant (far from it), but they reflect a sentiment that is more widespread in all the European Union than one might believe. People do not always express in public these feelings, but they are widespread enough that they could severely affect the process of European integration. In the three countries studied here, the issue of immigration is associated by most workers and employees interviewed with loss of jobs, devaluation of the job market, and a perception of rising crime.

The fact is that immigration has become a major election issue in most countries of the Union and has already provided votes for right-wing anti-European Union politicians, changing the face of democracy in Europe (recent examples were Austria, the Netherlands, France, and Germany). In short, immigration is already an important factor in political issues, but the new enlargement might exacerbate the anti-immigrant sentiment and could contribute, over time, more power to anti-immigrant and anti-European Union political parties. If this issue is not properly addressed it might produce not only a turn to the right in most countries, but also, the anti-Europe parties could become powerful enough to stall the process of European integration.

The 2002 presidential elections in France have seen the leader of the right-wing Front National party, Jean Marie Le Pen, win a relative success. This success was based mostly on two interrelated major issues of his party program: immigration and crime. The reason Jean Marie Le Pen is not more successful is because the majority of French people are somehow still afraid of him; he and his party are associated with fascism and Nazism, and Le Pen is not media savvy enough to dispel that traditional image. My hypothesis is that the problem here is not with the xenophobic and anti-immigrant content of his party's program but with the messenger. If another person or party takes on this message, this program could become policy. Certainly, this problem is not only limited to France. These views are also promoted with relative success by right-wing parties in many other countries, such as in the Netherlands and Austria, and the same ideas are also very much present in more mainstream parties in other countries of the union, even though they do not have the so-called extremist parties to convey them openly. For instance, the Conservative Party in the United Kingdom is widely considered mainstream, but, along with some rather centrist and progressive individuals and elected officials, this party also comprises several groups that are relatively right-wing. Particularly the sector of this party close to the former Prime Minister, Margaret Thatcher, is not so far, in my opinion, from the views of LePen on European issues and foreigners. The form might be different but the content is strikingly similar.[33] The same can be said of certain sectors within the party in power in Italy (Forza Italia), or the Conservative Party in Denmark, for example. The fact is that in most countries of the European Union, including in the three countries analyzed here (France, Spain, and the United Kingdom), but also in Germany, Belgium, the Netherlands, Italy, and Denmark, people perceive the issue of immigration as not properly addressed by those in power.

One of the pillars of the EU identified in the Treaty on European Union (Maastricht) is Justice and Home Affairs, which seeks to coordinate European laws in many areas related to justice and crime. Since the Treaty on the Union was ratified at the beginning of the 1990s, European Law has grown progressively in scope. In every member country judges and lawyers have to accept and deal with European law. Although the Treaty on European Union seeks harmonization of the law in the member countries, this specific process of creating a European law has not been something imposed by a particular institution or directive. It has come out of everyday practices. In fact, European law is not something foreign and separate from the member states; rather it is the law of the member states and develops in all the states simultaneously. Law professionals, judges, and lawyers have been cooperating in trying to find similar standards. Lately we have seen considerable advances in attempting to harmonize criminal law, as Prowse (2002: 11) suggests. However, by integrating so many countries at the same time this process might be affected as well and might prolong for many years a real harmonization of European law. It would be impossible for most lawyers to master all the laws from the 25 countries. Thus, either there would be a big mess in years to come or a process devised, perhaps at the level of the Convention on the Future of Europe, that might end up accelerating the legal integration.

CONCLUSION: ENLARGING VERSUS DEEPENING

This enlargement is perhaps the most problematic so far. Even its most enthusiastic supporters recognize the existence of many problems that the EU must address, most of which have been laid out by the Commission. One might ask: Why then such a big enlargement now? The most evident benefit of enlargement is the widening of the market, mostly for goods and services produced in the west. Indeed, especially large and medium companies from member countries in the west would be in a better shape to compete for the market than their eastern counterparts. Furthermore, these companies would have access to a rather inexpensive labor market compared to their home countries. This will most likely fortify the euro as well. Finally, this enlargement would increase the population, and especially the proportion of the younger population. Current member countries are at or below population replacement.

The officials of the European Union foresee "the strengthening of the unions' role in world affairs—in foreign and security policy, trade policy, and the other fields of global governance" (European Union 2002)—as a consequence of enlargement, but this remains to be seen. Officials and some politicians interviewed (particularly members of the European Parliament) defended the idea that enlargement would not hamper deepening, on the contrary they see that Europe at present is going through an interrelated process of deepening and enlarging simultaneously. The Commission expects that in order for the EU to work suitably with this new enlargement there is no choice but to modify the workings of the institutions, as was established in the Nice Treaty. This treaty proposed structural and procedural changes in the EU institutions' cumbersome procedures in order to make the EU both more efficient and more democratic, as most critics are demanding; one of the major tenets of these suggestions is to make decisions in the Council by a qualified majority in all but a few core areas. Indeed, most officials and political leaders agree (those in favor of further integration as well as those against) that it would be impossible to reach any agreement with 25 member countries with the current system of national veto in most relevant areas of EU action. This enlargement could provoke as well the reform of the current structure of the European Central Bank, which is perceived by specialists as rather heavy with a governing council of 18 members. When new countries are added to the Council, reaching decisions on monetary policy would be rather difficult. That means that there should be also here adaptations to keep the number of members at an acceptable working size. In sum, this enlargement would require addressing the extent to which "the competencies to make binding decisions are to be transferred from the nation states to the supranational regime of the EU"(Fuchs and Klingemann 2002: 49).

The Commission and those leaders supporting further political integration are hoping that, given the necessity to modify its working structures, the EU will end up adopting a more federal-oriented decision-making procedure and thus deepening the ties among the member countries. In this view, enlargement, rather than slowing down the deepening process, would accelerate it.

Those opposing further integration see a chance in the enlargement process to dilute Europe. That is in part why many who are otherwise euroskeptics and pro-intergovernmentalist leaders are also supportive of enlargement. They think that beyond certain economic advantages that some argue, an enlarged Europe would have to abandon at least for now the idea of deepening. Perhaps it is not a coincidence that the U.K. government, which is in favor of a loose organization for the EU, and has been rather consistent throughout the years in attempting to keep Europe from deepening, has been very supportive of enlargement, pushing even to include Turkey in the short term.[34] For the opponents to further European integration, this enlargement is an opportunity to diffuse as much as possible the European Union in order to avoid cohesion among its member countries and thus to dissolve the political power of the union. They hope that with 25 countries in 2004 and 27 in 2007 this enlargement would produce a slowdown, if not a halt, to the process of European integration. Indeed, several factors could apparently contribute to undermining further integration. The more countries there are in the Council, the more diverse the national interests, and this, coupled with more cultural heterogeneity, would make it more difficult to reach agreements on important issues such as a common foreign policy,[35] a common tax system, justice and home affairs, or social welfare. Indeed, the process of enlargement has reactivated the debate on such practical issues as EU income,[36] toll taxes, and the proportion of the Value Added Tax. Moreover, the need to address the most immediate issues of enlargement such as the budget for the CAP and structural and cohesion funds, for example, and to deal with the many aspects that the adjustment of the new countries would require, might well put the question of deepening on hold for a few years.

In sum, by its magnitude and the characteristics of the countries involved together with limited resources available, this enlargement might instigate and/or reinforce feelings of relative deprivation beyond what has been seen so far in both new and old member countries. This sentiment could in turn contribute to people seeking refuge in the traditional nationalistic thought and resisting further integration on the basis of defending national sovereignty and/or national identity. A French socialist leader, Michel Rocard (2002), predicts in a rather pessimistic tone that the most likely outcome of this enlargement would be a vast market for goods and capital and no more than that because of the nationalist views of many political leaders, and particularly the U.K. opposition to further integration.[37] Indeed, Blair's government, as with the previous U.K. governments, is clearly working "to shape Europe to its image, steering it away from more radical, overtly federal proposals" as Tsatsas (2002: 20) writes.

However, as important as enlargement is for the future of the EU in terms of political integration is the Convention on the Future of Europe. In fact, enlargement depends on adjustments that would be made in the Convention. Although propositions for deep structural changes were made during the debate on enlargement in the Nice Treaty in 2001, the modifications needed were not concluded then. The Convention on the Future of the European Union, which started to work in Brussels on February 28, 2002, is charged with writing a document that could become the Constitution of the European Union.[38] The success of the Convention would be fundamental to determine which Europe to build. As a member of the European Parliament puts it:

We cannot enlarge under our present system. Going to 25 from 15 would halt the workings of the EU if we do not deepen in our relationship. If the Convention does not go far enough it could mean the end of the EU as we aspire right now, and it would be even less integration than we even have right now. We need to have the mechanisms to be able to work together, and therefore we will have to accept that we have to give up some national control. (MEP U.K.)

The Convention objective is to create some type of confederation of nation-states and to improve the legitimacy of European institutions in the eyes of the citizens while making the decision making more efficient. It would produce a document with concrete recommendations that is supposed to solve at least the problems of decision making and the structural changes in general, expanding on the process initiated in the Treaty of Nice regarding the voting process and the weight of the votes (qualified-majority voting). Because the ambitions for Europe are very diverse, it would be fundamental for the future of Europe that qualified-majority voting is applied to areas related to further integration where there is still unanimity vote required, such as in common foreign and security policies, judicial cooperation, immigration, and economic and social cohesion policy and taxation. However, it is not certain that everything proposed by the convention would be accepted by the national states, and thus further negotiations might continue after the Convention ends its work. In other words, the Convention might come up with a system of governance of the EU that will facilitate the decision-making process but there is no guarantee that it would end up producing what the more pro-European integration forces would like to see, and that it would generate a mechanism that would prevent the states from going in separate ways.

Although the Commission and its representatives in the Convention are pushing for a more federal European Union, most of the 105 delegates do not seem to be inclined to follow its lead to create a more supranational form of decision making on key issues.[39] One of the first public presentations on the advances of the workings of the Convention on October 28, 2002, already showed a tendency to keep the nation-states in control. This presentation revealed also a concentration on rules and institutional mechanisms, and little was said on defining the European Union project in general. As the commissioner, Pascal Lamy, deplored, the Convention does not seem to be addressing the project that ties Europeans together (Leparmentier 2003b). But most fundamentally, if the Convention does not produce a clear-cut supranational decision-making process in key issues, and the enlargement goes ahead as scheduled, the anti-European integration forces will be winning. A timid and vague report of the Convention would not be enough to keep the European Union advancing towards further unity.

The position of the candidate countries on the question of further integration and the shape of the organization of the EU (federalism/inter-governmentalism) is not very clear. Are they "anxious to safeguard their newfound sovereignty" or are they "Atlanticists in orientation" as Tsatsas (2002: 20), Achcar (2003), and Cassen (2003) suggest, and therefore allies of those who oppose further integration beyond a single market? In that case, what would become of the Common Security and Defense Policy, or the plan to integrate the Western European Union (the European Army) into the EU?[40] There is nothing cogent at this point, but most likely there would be differences among the candidate countries regarding commitment to a more united Europe. The Candidate Countries Eurobarometer 2001 does suggest some tendencies in this respect. In particular, two countries (Estonia and Malta) have a population that seems less enthusiastic than the other applicants to become members of the EU, and in certain questions regarding identification with Europe, Lithuania's population appears very much attached to the nation-state. As the debate on the Constitution of the European Union will intensify during 2003 and 2004 we might be able to know more about the position of the new members on this issue.

In summary, because this enlargement is more difficult than any before, it might end up inciting the EU actors to give some more power to the supranational institutions. However, the most likely scenario would be the establishment of some intermediate mechanism that would still keep the nation-states in control of the most important policies.

NOTES

1. The heads of state and government of the 15 member states concluded the Intergovernmental Conference on Institutional Reform by reaching agreement on the draft of a new treaty at the Nice European Council of December 7–9, 2000. All the member states in accordance with their respective constitutional arrangements have ratified the new treaty. Ireland was the latest to ratify it by referendum in November 2002 (Irish voters had originally voted against the treaty in the referendum of June 7, 2001).

2. The total GDP of all the candidate countries is $782 billion, the equivalent of the Netherlands' GDP. Poland accounts for 44 percent of the total GDP for these countries. The GDP is based on 2000 figures of Purchasing Power Parity (Source: Wagstyl 2002).

3. The European Commission estimates that about half a million illegal im-migrants, and 680,000 legal immigrants enter each year in the European Union member countries.

4. The Eurobarometer 56 (2002) suggests that support for enlargement in the 15 current members of the EU is on average 51 percent. The support in each specific country varies considerably but is positive in all the countries with the exception of France: Greece 74 percent, Sweden 69 percent, Denmark 69 percent, Spain 61 percent, Italy 61 percent, Ireland 60 percent, the Netherlands 58 percent, Portugal 57 percent, Finland 54 percent, Luxembourg 37 percent, Belgium 49 percent, Germany 47 percent, Austria 46 percent, United Kingdom 41 percent, and France 39 percent.

5. Given the qualitative nature of my interviews I cannot claim that the results are representative in the same way as a survey research (using scientific random sample) but as an orientation I present some numbers to reflect the tendencies expressed by the respondents. I asked the questions in an open manner, such as what they thought about enlargement, and when necessary I asked follow-up questions. Considering all the lay citizens interviewed from the three countries the results were as follows: 56 percent were against enlargement to all the countries from East and Central Europe that were considered, and 26 percent did not know what to answer. Only 18 percent of interviewees favored a big enlargement such as the one that was planned during the period of the study.

6. In certain questions asked in the Eurobarometer, the lack of knowledge of the population on the issues under consideration makes the data gathered irrele-vant. In fact, the same Eurobarometer also suggests that only 22 percent of citizens from the member countries felt that they were well informed about enlargement in the spring of 2002 (Eurobarometer 56 2002).

7. The Eurobarometers 55 and 56 measured the extent to which people felt informed about enlargement. Following are the results corresponding to the latest survey, Eurobarometer 56, starting from less informed to better informed: United Kingdom 10 percent, Italy 15 percent, Spain 17 percent, Belgium 21 percent, Por-tugal 21 percent, Sweden 21 percent, Ireland 22 percent, Netherlands 23 percent, France 24 percent, Greece 24 percent, Germany 30 percent, Denmark 35 percent, Luxembourg 39 percent, Austria 45 percent, and Finland 51 percent.

8. The Eurobarometer 56 (2002: 85) results also highlight that 48 percent of the population believed that the European Union must reform the way its institutions work before welcoming new members. Furthermore, the Eurobarometer also mea-sured the perceived effect of enlargement for the member countries. Thirty-eight percent agreed with the following statements: "After enlargement to include new members, our country will become less important in Europe" and "the more coun-tries there are, the more unemployment there would be in our country," while a majority of respondents (48 percent) disagreed with the subsequent statement: "enlargement will not cost more for existing member countries like our country" (only 31 percent agreed).

9. In this survey were included Bulgaria, Romania, and Turkey (countries that were also engaged in negotiations for EU membership), but in my analysis I focus only on the 10 countries that are supposed to become members in 2004.

10. The identification with Europe was measured by asking the population from the candidate countries how they see themselves in the near future, and the survey

offered a choice of four answers: nationality only, nationality and European, European and nationality, European only. The net percentages of feeling European (sum of answers to nationality and European, European and nationality, European only) minus nationality only are the following: Slovakia 35, Poland 28, Cyprus 28, Czech Republic 16, Estonia 13, Slovenia 16, Latvia 12, Malta 6, Hungary 1, and Lithuania 1.

11. The results of other measurements such as personal benefits from European Union membership, European pride, meaning of Europe, and others, consistently show that of all the candidate countries the Estonian population is the least interested in the European Union.

12. Based on a historical analysis of the Polish Catholic Church, Anio et al. assert that the leaders of the Polish Church have authoritarian tendencies and therefore would be concerned about losing influence as a result of the integration of Poland into a Western Europe that they see as rather tainted by individual secularism and agnosticism. The authors compare the Polish Church in the 1990s with the Spanish Catholic Church in the post-Franco period (late 1970s) and suggest that there are deep differences between the two as the Catholic Church in Spain aligned itself with the changes in that society and accepted the European vocation of Spain, while the Polish Church does not seem to be ready to accept the challenge of Europe. I would add that in the case of Spain, the church was widely perceived as supportive of the Franco regime, so when change came it could not play much of a role in defining the new constitution and the direction that the country took. Furthermore, after the change of regime the church had lost much of its influence on society. In today's Spain the church is very much limited to the private sphere, and, as in most of the EU member countries (with the exception of Ireland and perhaps Greece) religion's role in political affairs is very insignificant. Such is not the recent history of the church in Poland, which played an active role in the political debate and was perceived as an agent of change during the socialist regime.

13. By comparison the ratio on income inequality is 4.1 in Japan, 11 in the United States, and 10 in Australia. With very few exceptions Anglo-Saxon societies tend to be the most unequal of the advanced capitalist societies.

14. Regions classified as Objective 1 receive in priority most resources to improve infrastructure and their economic situation in general. Most of these regions are at present in Greece, Spain, and Portugal.

15. These three countries (Greece, Portugal, and Spain) moved up about 10 percentage points in average from 1990 to 2001. Assuming they would be receiving equivalent resources in cohesion and structural funds from the EU and their economies would grow at the same rate or greater in the near future as it did in the previous 11 years, Spain would need 10–15 more years to reach the current EU average, Portugal 20–25 years, and Greece 25–30 years. However, since the newcomers have a very low GDP, in comparison these three countries would be at or close to the EU average. Most likely, cohesion funds would be directed towards those countries and regions that need it the most after enlargement and essentially divert the largest proportion of the cohesion funds from these countries to the newcomers.

16. The union of 25 countries may be broken down into three groups of states according to their per capita GDP. Using data from 2001, the first group, compris-

ing six of the candidate countries (Estonia, Hungary, Latvia, Lithuania, Poland, and Slovakia), with an average GDP of about $9200, and a population of 61 million (13.6 percent of the total population of a union of 25, which would be 450.6 million). The average per capita GDP of these countries is about 46 percent of that of a Community of 25. The second group, which includes two existing member states (Greece and Portugal) and three applicant countries (Czech Republic, Malta, Slovenia) have a per capita GDP of about 82 percent of the future union average and with a population of 33.4 million (7.4 percent of the total population). The third group includes all the other existing member states plus an applicant country (Cyprus), with an average per capita GDP at and above that of the future Union of 25, with a population of 356.2 million (79 percent of the total population). Spain, with a per capita GDP of $19,260, would be at about 96 percent of an enlarged EU of 25 (Source: author's calculation with data provided by Wagstyl 2002).

17. Regional disparities in unemployment in the candidate countries also continued to rise from 1999 to 2001. In the top 10 percent of regions in terms of population, the unemployment rate averaged 4.9 percent, whereas it stood at 23.4 percent in the bottom 10 percent of regions (Commission of the European Communities 2002).

18. The question of pollution also affects directly the neighboring member countries. For instance, Austria has expressed strong concerns over the use of nuclear reactors in some of the candidate countries.

19. The report also identified the scale of regional imbalances in the labor market and economic development following enlargement, the polarization of the labor market and society, the persistent gender inequality, and the growing pressures from migration and mobility as challenges for cohesion.

20. With the expected inclusion of Bulgaria and Romania in 2007 the disparities would increase even more. For instance, "within the enlarged union of 27, the ratio between the richest 10 percent of regions and the least developed 10 would rise to 5.8, compared with only 2.6 in the present union" (Commission 2002: 14).

21. The principal objectives of the Common Agricultural Policy (CAP) are the growth of the productivity of farming and insuring a market for the products. It undertakes two types of actions: the establishment of common organizations for the market, implying fixing and sustaining an acceptable level of the agricultural products' prices; and actions on the agricultural structures, in order to improve productivity. The CAP is financed by the European Funds of Orientation and of Agricultural Guarantee-EFOAG (obligatory contributions, rights of customs, fraction of the TVA), and represents close to 45 percent of the community budget. This policy is the most contested and the most costly of the union. The power of the EU is, in this domain, more definite than in all other aspects of EU action. The redistribution of the funds is favorable to the countries having a strong agricultural sector. The two principal problems in the near future for the PAC are the enlargement of the Union, which creates a problem of financing the larger agricultural sector that the EU of 25 would have, and the imposition of more constraining norms, notably in the matter of environment and of food security after the crisis of the mad cow disease.

22. The different views on how to finance enlargement were obvious in several European Union meetings in the last two years (for instance, in Caceres in 2001,

and Barcelona in 2002), and they have not waned after the Copenhagen summit of 2002.

23. There have been several alternatives debated on the question of financing enlargement. One of them, proposed by a group of EU experts from the accession countries and the current EU member states, called the Villa Faber Group (2001), suggested that the structural funds support should focus on the less developed member states in order to better target EU assistance (this seems to be the solution most widely accepted), and the ceiling on structural funds inflows increased if a state has a higher absorption capacity. This group also suggested that those rural development expenditures "currently part of the Common Agricultural Policy should be integrated into the structural funds."

24. The question of the Common Agricultural Policy is rather problematic because a change in this policy would also have to include a negotiation with the United States on a bilateral basis, or through the World Trade Organization, and probably with other countries as well. For instance, if there were a reduction of subsidies for agriculture in the EU, the farmers would be at a disadvantage with the U.S. farmers, who already receive in proportion even higher subsidies. Indeed, the United States has the same amount of money for subvention of their two million farmers as the EU has for six million. This means that a downscale of the CAP would need to be matched by a downscale of the U.S. subsidies to their own farmers.

25. The United Kingdom is the only one of the richest countries that is a net receiver of EU funds. This happens because in the mid-1980s when this country was relatively poor, it was granted a reduction of its participation to the EU budget. In 2001 the United Kingdom contributed 7 percent to the European budget and ended up with a balance of 700 million euros net income. It contributed less than Spain, even though the United Kingdom's per capita GDP is about 4000 dollars more than Spain. In contrast, France contributed 19.6 percent to the EU budget, and even though France is one of the big beneficiaries of the CAP, it still ended up with a negative balance of 2 billion euros, behind Germany, which was a net contributor to the EU with 7 billion euros (data provided by Leparmentier 2003a).

26. The Commission report (2002: 16) summarizes some of the proposals produced in the Cohesion Forum that took place in Brussels in May 2001, which was attended by 1,800 delegates. Two of the main competing suggestions debated were: (1) a demand by some political leaders of the member countries for a substantial increase in resources for cohesion beyond the figure of 0.45 percent so that the policy can be extended to regions other than those that are defined as least developed (the target of an amount equivalent to 0.45 percent of GDP for cohesion and structural policies in 2006 was suggested in the European Council in Berlin in 2000), and (2) the other suggestion contemplated "to cut cohesion policy expenditures sharply, mainly by removing Community support for areas other than the least developed regions and through applying, without exception, the ceiling of 4 percent of national GDP to transfers from the Structural Funds and the Cohesion Fund."

27. During the Copenhagen summit of 2002, the member states were able to obtain a redistribution of the package aid, but not an overall increase in the total amount, which remained at 40.4. Poland will receive an additional 1 billion euros

for its government budget for 2004–2006 taken from its overall structural funds allocation and the other candidate countries about 300 million euros (Wagstyl 2002). Basically this formula would allow these countries to have access to cash, which otherwise would have been invested in projects that might take years to finish.

28. In determining the properties of a democratic community Fuchs and Klingemann (2002: 22–23) use an analytical model that divides democracy into three hierarchical structured levels: "The topmost level is that of political culture, whose constitutive elements are the fundamental values of a democracy, the next level is that of political structure, which consists of the democratic system of government of a country, generally laid down by the constitution, and the lowest level in the hierarchy is that of the political process. The political process is concerned with the realization of the collective goals of a community by the actors. Their action is controlled by the political structure, and this means, among other things, that normative expectations about the behavior of political actors are associated with the constituted systems of government in a given country. The three levels thus form a control hierarchy that begins with culture and ends with the process of actual activity on the part of actors." This includes, then, support for democratic values, respect for rules and democratic institutions, and political action.

29. My own calculations based on data provided by the Candidate Countries Eurobarometer 2001 (2002).

30. In Malta, a former British colony, English is the official language along with Maltese.

31. Among the ten candidate countries listed to become members by 2004 there are a total of about 15 million people who can conduct conversation in English, 10 million in German, and 2 million in French. Following are listed the candidate countries with the percent of their population's proficiency in these three major languages of the EU. English: Malta 84 percent, Cyprus 57 percent, Slovenia 46 percent, Estonia 29 percent, Czech Republic 24 percent, Latvia 23 percent, Poland 21 percent, Lithuania 20 percent, Hungary 14 percent, Slovakia 13 percent; German: Slovenia 38 percent, Czech Republic 27 percent, Slovakia 20 percent, Poland 16 percent, Latvia 14 percent, Hungary 13 percent, Lithuania 13 percent, Estonia 13 percent, Cyprus 2 percent, Malta 2 percent; French: Malta 9 percent, Cyprus 6 percent, Slovenia 4 percent, Czech Republic 3 percent, Poland 3 percent, Slovakia 2 percent, Hungary 2 percent, Lithuania 2 percent, Latvia 1 percent, Estonia 1 percent (Source: Candidate Countries Eurobarometer 2002).

32. However, it seems from my interviews and from informal conversation, that this sentiment is not as strong against eastern Europeans as it is against Arabs and Africans in general.

33. There is no need to develop more on this subject here, but I encourage the interested reader to compare the writings and/or declarations of Margaret Thatcher (for instance, her latest publication [*Statecraft,* 2002]) and some of her close allies in the Conservative Party with the program of the Front National, and declarations of LePen on Europe and immigration.

34. As we have seen in chapter 4, the U.K. government has traditionally strived to restrain European integration. With a few cosmetic differences both parties (Labor and Tories) that have dominated British politics since the United Kingdom became a member of the EU have had a very similar approach to Europe. The

leaders of these parties have generally agreed on creating a large market for goods and capital with no strong coordinating body. Blair's government has been a strong supporter of the latest enlargement and has strongly lobbied to include even Turkey, a country of 75 million people, with a per capita income of $7030. At the same time the U.K. government is aggressively seeking to limit aid for new members. This apparent contradictory policy (of supporting enlargement and pushing for reduction of financial support for the new countries) is part of the traditional larger U.K. government strategy of diluting Europe as much as possible to prevent a strong politically united Europe.

35. The Common Foreign and Security Policy (CFSP) is one of the pillars of the European Union, but under the form of an intergovernmental cooperation. Set up by the Treaty of Maastricht, its ultimate objective is to create a common defense policy. It does not include in its mission the collective defense of the European countries, guaranteed by North Atlantic Treaty Organization, but the management of internal crises, by operations or keeping or restoring peace and humanitarian missions grouped together under the name of missions of Petersberg. The European Council defines the principles and orientations of this policy and the Council of Ministers on the positions and common actions. The decisions are taken by the Council ruling unanimously. Since 1999, the CFSP has endowed itself with a top representative, Javier Solana, who is assisted by a unit for planning the policy of rapid alert, which provides evaluations of situations. Two instruments contribute to the application of this policy: the Western European Union, the Cooperation for the Defense Organization, and the political European Policy for Security and Defense (EPSD), created in Nice in 2000. In 2003, it would have an autonomous capacity, allowing swift operations with an intervention force of 60,000 men.

36. According to the Edinburgh agreement the member countries must participate with 1.27 percent of their GDP to the EU budget, but, as indicated by Leparmentier (2003a), the actual percent of the expenditure for this concept is only 1 percent.

37. He writes that by accepting the United Kingdom as a member in the 1970s, the European Community had already renounced the idea of a united Europe. Although it is true that historically the United Kingdom has been a reluctant member of the EU, and has contributed to holding back the integration process, it has not always been successful in preventing Europe from deciding on further unity.

38. In June 2003, the Convention presented the proposal that is now being discussed and reworked by different instances of the member countries and the institutions of the European Union. The Convention is made up of 105 people from both the government and the national parliament of the member states and the countries applying for membership in the union as well as from members of the European Parliament and the European Commission. The convention also receives input from a forum that has been set up with nongovernmental organizations representing the diversity of the civil society. In addition, the Convention holds regular public meetings and has also consultation meetings with the European Council. There is a marked desire to encourage participation of all sectors of the society in the debate on the creation of a constitution for the EU.

39. The constitution proposed by the Commission includes seven main policies that would be led at the level of the European Union: freedom, security and justice, internal market, economic competition, economic and monetary policy, agriculture

and fishing, transport, and pacific use of atomic energy. It includes also seven policies in which the union would support and coordinate the action of the member states: economic and social cohesion; employment and social policy; environment, research, and technological development; consumers' protection; trans-European networks; and health (Leparmentier 2003b).

40. Cassen (2003: 9) cites a German official as saying: "the entrance into the EU of the countries of Eastern and Central Europe, fundamentally pro-United States, means the end of any attempt for the EU to define itself, and the end of its foreign and security policy independently from the United States." Furthermore, the economic orientation of the parties in power in these countries, with the exception perhaps of Poland (but this remains to be seen), is strongly neoliberal, which might incline the balance even further on the side of those who want Europe to remain only a zone of free exchange of goods and capital, in opposition to a more politically united Europe.

CHAPTER 6

Conclusion: The Enduring Myth of National Sovereignty

"In the state, man is the imaginary member of an imaginary sovereignty, divested of his real, individual life, and infused with an unreal universality."
Karl Marx

The European Union, and particularly a more politically united Europe, constitutes a challenge to established thinking, to what has been done in terms of social organization, and to what traditionally has happened in the relationships between states. Indeed, no nation-state has ever willingly consented to give up sovereignty to a supranational organization. The unification of Europe is a totally new process, which implies a transition from an intense and celebrated nationalism (including old images and rivalries that have historically divided Europeans) to a more international and cosmopolitan view, which requires Europeans to redefine their symbolic boundaries.[1] There is no textbook model of what Europeans are trying to create. It is different from all the other federal models such as the United States, Switzerland, Canada, India, Australia, or South Africa. Those are all nations with federal models as building blocks. In Europe there are a number of states that have been independent for a long time and are very much attached to their independence, and proud of their sovereignty and their national identity.[2] The development of the European Union has occasioned the questioning of those widespread sentiments.

The results of this research highlight the importance of identification in defining the European Union and the multidimensional and diverse origins of social representations of the EU in France, Spain, and the United Kingdom. Because these views of the EU are diverse, the reasons for opposing or supporting further European integration are also manifold and multifaceted. I tried to identify the most salient representations of the EU and have attempted to catalogue some of the determining factors in the EU–member states relations that are contributing to the reproduction of particular views on Europe. Various events, policies, and structural arrangements were identified as examples of mechanisms that were activating negative feelings against the European Union in the member countries. The book also attempts to explain the role that the media and other actors play in shaping those representations. However, the results of this research are by no means explanatory of all the complexities of this process.

In this concluding chapter are analyzed and explained the main findings common to the three countries studied. First examined is the issue of economic integration, then the question of national identity versus European identity, followed by an explanation of the issue of sovereignty, including the preferences for the organization of the EU with the intergovernmental/supranational models as background, and then how the predominant views on national identity and national sovereignty affect a development of a united foreign policy and defense. Finally, the immediate future of the European Union is assessed.

THE BIG MARKET

The EU has advanced in creating an appropriate environment for the development of market and industry, including a free movement of capital and labor in the 15 member countries, a common currency, and the European Central Bank. In addition it has also produced a certain number of standards in many areas (work safety, sanitary regulations, medical and pharmaceutical issues, civil laws, etc.) that are making commercial exchange as well as many other aspects of life easier for all citizens. Also, planning and cooperation at the European level in certain areas has given the members of the EU a comparative advantage through the resulting common utilization of resources. Through the years reports have revealed the savings from the abolition of borders, increasing the scale of production of manufactured goods, the creation of the common currency, the abolition of administrative formalities, and opening up public procurement markets. In short, it has responded rather efficiently to the needs of capitalist development.

At the same time, the EU has kept a certain equilibrium between the forces of the market and a relatively efficient social protection and redistribution, which has limited the inequalities between the haves and have-nots. As the work of Sobish and Immerfall (2000) explains, there are a number of political-structural commonalities among the EU member states that have distinguished them from the other democratic societies of the Western world, such as the United States and Australia for example: a parliamentary system of government, a party system that plays a major role in deciding which individuals would be elected, a very strong laic society, a quasi-corporatist industrial relations, a considerable level of intervention of the state in the economy, and a strong social safety net. This traditional path of the EU (robust welfare state policies and preoccupation with reducing inequalities), has wide support among the population of the member countries, including in the United Kingdom. An overwhelming majority of Europeans support in all member states the social aspects of the Treaty on European Union.

However, this model of society is at present questioned by the evolution of the world economy. The now predominant neoliberal policies, inspired by the monetarist school of Milton Friedman, developed rapidly in the 1980s and 1990s all over the world. These policies, which imply prevailing laissez-faire practices, lowering barriers for free trade, unrestricted competition among companies, privatization of state enterprises, and no restriction on foreign investments, are now taking hold in the EU.

Within the European Union institutions there is far from being a consensus regarding these neoliberal perspectives, even among the officials of the Commission. However, it seems that voices of dissent, including the uneasiness that this alternative provokes among the EU social democrats (a predominant political force in the EU), are not enough to prevent the implementation all over Europe of measures based on the premises of neoliberalism.

Leaders from leftist parties and some union leaders accuse the EU of being basically an organization at the service of large corporations. Although this criticism is not without fundament, it seems clear that the nation-state does not offer a better alternative, far from it. To equate European integration with economic liberalism and to assume that the nation-state is the defense against the dictatorship of the market, as the leaders from the French Communist Party and United Left in Spain, for example, suggest, is a fallacy that will end up undermining the interests of the working class. Indeed, the pressures of economic globalization are so strong that neoliberalism imposes itself even in countries where the government is not in favor of the model. The big regulations that aim at stabilizing societies, based on ideas of Keynes and Beveridge, have been abandoned by the majority of the nation-states themselves.[3] Furthermore, economic globalization has not been imposed by the European Union independently from the member states. The acceptance of the rules of the market and the relative weakening of the welfare state have been done with the direct participation of every state, through the decisions taken in the Council.[4]

In other words, to oppose European integration in the name of the working class is illogical. Defending the nation-state will not favor the working class because no small country (be it France, Spain, or the United Kingdom) could resist by itself the forces of world economics, nor could any be effective in addressing the precariousness of the workers, the global domination of a ruthless capitalism, pollution, unemployment, safety at work, and so on. Those opposing European unification end up, by default, supporting a nation-state that cannot do anything for the workers because the structures of the economy escape, if not completely, mostly, its control. The state has a very limited authority over transnational companies or general organization of the world market and most areas of the national economy, even including resources for public service. Indeed, the extent and quality of social security and health coverage in France, Spain, the United Kingdom, or any other country in Europe depend to a large extent on happenings outside the borders of the nation-state. Corporations are already not only pan-European but also global, and many of these companies have more power than any European government.[5] Certainly, the economic integration reached in the EU by the beginning of the twenty-first century has eroded considerably the ability of the member states to control economic policies (chiefly in the euro group). Its economic function is shifting from the formulation of national policies to the management of policies devised by the European institutions. The most visible of these institutions is the European Central Bank, which establishes largely monetary policies that affect the other areas of the economy directly. Other economic arrangements that transcend somehow the nation-state include external commercial policies, harmonization policies, competition policies and regulations, and an overseeing by the Commission of major orientations of the member countries' budgets.[6]

In sum, the nation-state is only a player within this international consortium, a partner, but no state in Europe has any longer the power to significantly influence by itself economic or social models that could benefit the majority of the population. In fact, the consequences of the neoliberal policies might have been worse for the working class if the country were not a member of the EU. Most of the dramatic restructurings that were made in the last 50 years or so, and that ended up costing the jobs of many people, would have been made by the nation-states with or without Europe, and they would not have had the economic resources put forward by the EU for reconverting and training of the work force. In this context, even to preserve social protection, health, and public services a strategy at the European level is necessary. Only within the European structures would it be possible to work on limiting the inequalities, influencing the general path of the world, and defending the workers' interests.

While the labor unions are just beginning to organize and to act at the European level (the Trade Union Council of the United Kingdom is the best organized at the EU level of all the labor unions studied), the businesses have been organized already for years at the European level with the Union of Industrial and Employers' Confederations of Europe (UNICE) and the European Roundtable of Industrialists (ERT), among others who are actively lobbying the European institutions.[7] In fact, economic leaders in the decision-making networks of banks and corporations have not only overwhelmingly supported the common market and the common currency but have actively participated in their conception. According to many of the political and business leaders interviewed, the business community played a major role in the framing of the treaties, particularly the Treaty on European Union, and strongly supported the latest enlargement to 10 countries of Eastern and Central Europe.

Supporters of further European integration tend to expect that as a result of the economic interdependence there would be a spillover leading to broader supranational identities and unite even further in the political arena.[8] However, economic interdependence—as my research and other studies (Brewer 2000) also show—does not necessarily lead to further integration. As we have seen, national interests and nationalist ideologies have prevented so far this expected effect.[9] This interdependence could even promote antagonism and conflict.[10] The European Union remains a collage in which assertions of national sovereignty based upon diversity of interests are the order of the day. Indeed, in the Council of Ministers, the predominant decision-making institution of the EU, each minister mainly looks after the interests of his or her country, and confrontations on economic policies are common. There are also confrontations between the supporters of neoliberal policies and those seeking to keep strong social policies.[11] These divisions on occasions are so deep that some countries opt out of applying a given directive, for instance, a 2002 initiative of the Commission (approved by the EU Parliament and the Council) for improving workers' information on the firms has been rejected by the United Kingdom and the Irish government, which opted out of their obligations until 2005.[12] In fact, a major role of the EU as a transnational power has been to manage conflicts between countries.

The increased globalization of the world economies in the twenty-first century is causing questioning of this traditional role of the EU as mediator between nation-states. The members of the Union are faced with the dilemma of uniting further to generate convergent economic policies (which seems the best alternative to keep a stable and strong economy), or defending the nation-state against the erosion of economic sovereignty, with all the confrontations, due to national egoisms, that this alternative implies. It seems evident that the continuing defense of European Union common interests relies on a sound organization that would be able to coordinate the most important policies.

Despite gigantic advances in the path to economic integration, there is not yet a common budget policy decided by the Council, or any other EU institution, similar to the unified monetary policy of the European Central

Bank. The monetary federalism has no corresponding budgetary federalism. The logical response to the monetary union would be a use of the national budgets such that the economic growth of the member countries converges. This would be a necessary condition to avoid a penalization of some countries when the ECB decides on a particular interest rate. The lack of a common economic policy would explain why the euro, although it accounts for a little more than 30 percent of the international exchanges (the U.S. dollar accounts for about 43 percent) is not yet a currency of international reserve. Only about 15 percent of worldwide monetary reserves are in euros, while about 67 percent are in U.S. dollars.

All indications suggest that if there is not more unity, the economies of the EU member countries would be reduced to large supermarkets, and subcontractors for the large corporations, which will dominate not only the economy but also social policies. In other words, a more united European Union is needed not only to stand up to other external economic powers such as the United States or China, but also to be able to defend the interest of the citizens and their social well-being from the increasing neoliberal influence of the transnational corporations, which would contribute to eroding the European cultural economy, and particularly the deep-seated European ideology of the welfare society. However, this project of further unity has to deal with a widespread attachment to national identities in the member countries.

IDENTITIES

In the three countries studied, there is a strong identification with national symbols, with their own history and institutions. However, the use of these symbols and institutions in opposition to the EU is far greater in the United Kingdom than in France and in Spain. And the concerns over a possible loss of national identity as a result of further European integration are stronger in the United Kingdom than in France, and more in France than in Spain. Furthermore, in Spain there is not a social belief in the exceptional status of the Spanish society as marked as in France and the United Kingdom.[13] However, while French exceptionalism comes mostly in European colors, the U.K. exceptionalism is more isolationist and profoundly marked by its alliance with the United States, and its special relation with the Commonwealth countries.

The idea of national identity has no clearly defined meaning in the population.[14] Concepts such as nation, commonwealth, ethnic group, culture, language, and geopolitical space overlap in lay citizens' thoughts and also in the practice and discourse of politicians. Moreover, identity, citizenship, and nationality are mixed in people's minds, as well as political belonging and national boundaries. Many people also use the concept of nationality as synonymous with race, particularly in the United

Kingdom (where several people referred to the "glorious British race"). In this view, race is more linked to fixed genetic cultural characteristics than to particular physical features, as if the people from a particular descent were to develop a specific culture. Race is conceived as a natural difference that influences a given behavior and the development of a given society and civilization.

But whatever the understanding, national identity remains a strong feeling linked to the nation-state and often used to oppose further integration in the three countries studied. The process of European integration has not lessened the claims to national identity and has not yet produced an emotional attachment with the European Union. Although there is some consciousness about generally shared values,[15] this feeling is rather vague and distant. It is easier to feel French, Spanish, or British than European because people have a sense of knowing what their nationality is, or at least they have a positive representation that they learned in school, through the media, and in their everyday relationships. Only in European Union documents and interviews with officials have I found some attempts at defining European identity. European identity would imply, in these versions, attachment to political democracy, respect for human rights and the rule of law, acceptance of different national and regional cultures, everyday shared lifestyles, common heritage (Christianity, roots in ancient Greek civilization, concordance of myths and folklore, etc.) and reference to some political and technological landmarks in history (industrialization, attachment to technological progress, etc.). The speech of Vaclav Havel (1994) in the European Parliament reflects well these ideas: "The European Union is based on a large set of values, with roots in antiquity and in Christianity which over 2,000 years evolved into what we recognize today as the foundations of modern democracy, the rule of law and civil society. This set of values has its own clear moral foundation and its obvious metaphysical roots, regardless of whether modern man admits it or not." Indeed, most lay citizens and many leaders do not recognize these shared historical roots as important enough to feel symbolically attached to the European Union, and many citizens (particularly farmers, working class people, and older people) even perceived European identity in opposition to the national identity, and cultural differences among member countries are viewed as alien and threatening. This results from years of socialization in which ethnocentrism was a predominant ideology. Children's stories, schoolbooks, films, newspapers, and magazines (in addition to the traditional rituals such as military parades, annual remembrance days, national holidays, and so on) are constantly reproducing the idea of the nation-state as the overarching attachment of any human being. Most interviewees still believe in the inherent psychological characteristics of a particular nation.

In the European Union there is not a widespread belief in the idea of *God's People* as in the United States and other religious quasi-fundamentalist societies such as many Middle East countries, but the nation-state is still viewed by the majority of the population as the principal object of individual loyalty.[16] In sum, in the three countries "the system of ideas and signs and associations and ways of behaving and communicating" (Gellner 1983: 67) that constitute a collective identity, as well as the wants for protection (economic and legal) still have overwhelmingly as main references the nation (by opposition to the EU).[17] These findings support Rex's argument (1991) that feelings of national identity include not only abstract and emotional attachment to a particular nation but also the belief that individual and social rights are guaranteed and protected by the state, and that national sovereignty remains a pre-eminent rhetorical tool in attempting to demarcate political communities.

These views are based on a deep-rooted and widespread tendency to conceive of identity as something fixed, as fundamental essence of the nation that does not change. Thus, most people ignore the historical evidence, which suggests continuous and dynamic cultural change, and see the EU "as a collection of fixed identities, each with inherent prejudices, stereotypes, and misunderstandings of the others" (Menéndez Alarcón 1995: 555).[18] Most people do not recognize that in reality, every member country's identity contains certain aspects of European identity, and that the differences between the national culture of one particular member country and the other is more a question of degree than of binary nature. That is to say, one could find among European member countries as many similarities as differences.

Furthermore, people would not identify with the European Union in the same way they identify with the nation-state; the concept of a united Europe is relatively new. For most of the interviewees the European Union started to be perceived as something more or less palpable only in the early 1990s, when the debate over the future Treaty on the Union spurred frequent media reports. The European Union is perceived either as a good thing or a bad thing. That is to say that European Union identity is more evaluative and perceived in terms of cost/benefit, advantages/disadvantages than is the national identity, which is much more intense, intuitive, and affective.[19] Therefore, the lack of strong cultural attachment to the European Union does not mean that the population ignores it. Indeed, the European Union is starting to be perceived as part of the political order in all the countries. Whether perceived as a negative or as a positive organization, the EU is now part of the political institutions recognized by the population as affecting them. In other words, one could say that the EU is already institutionalized in the sense that the population at large is now aware that they have to deal with European-wide issues, and that their leaders have to deal with specific rules and procedures proper to this supranational organization. The introduction of the euro in 2002 constitutes a vivid example of this process. In fact, the euro, which was embraced by the population with much more enthusiasm than expected, might end up, with time, making Europe more real in people's minds.[20] As Romano Prodi, President of the Commission, put it, the euro is a "little piece of Europe" that everyone carries with them everyday, and indeed it is the most concrete and direct connection that the population of the member countries has with the European Union. The euro, more than any other European directive, simplifies things for many who can now cross borders without the need to change money. This might even produce some changes in the sense of a more positive attitude towards further European integration; if not an emotional attachment, identification with a civic identity, or with a political identity at the European level could develop.

This research also reveals that national identity, in addition to the initial process of socialization, is reconstituted, maintained, and reproduced in the process of European integration because of confrontations and competing interests among country members.[21] Indeed, although the process of European integration has produced considerable economic integration and has brought many people from different countries to understand the importance of unification, it has also had, as we have extensively demonstrated, the effect of highlighting the importance of national sovereignty and identity. The traditional theory that suggest that nationalist thinking implies identification with a particular nation-state, but also in opposition to other nation-states, also applies to the context of the EU. As a result of the historical cultural perceptions, people living in the EU countries tend to favor old nationalistic stereotypes unless the everyday experiences suggests other alternatives. However, their acceptance of (and/or identification with) the European Union depends on people's experiences with the manifestations of the integration process, but also on the representations they develop in their everyday interactions, including interactions with the media and leaders.[22] As we saw, the media have a tendency to focus on grievances when covering EU issues and tend to present news on the EU as *them* versus *us,* reproducing thereby a deep-rooted feeling that has long constituted one of the main ideological pillars of the nation-state. Another important aspect that we can imply from the analysis of the press coverage is that even when the content of the articles is relatively positive, the EU is always presented as the outside. With the exceptions of some special editorials, the three newspapers studied usually portray the EU as "that external institution" to which the different countries adhere.

Most political leaders also contribute to reproducing the competing dichotomy of nation-state/European Union. Those opposed to further integration are certainly more explicit and aggressive in depicting the European Union and its member countries as competitors and not as partners, but many of those supporting the EU also characterize the EU as an external force. Indeed, political leaders rely very much on their domestic agenda to be elected; thus, they have to present themselves as the defenders of the national interest. This system in turn promotes nationalism among the respective domestic populations.[23] Indeed, those politicians pro-European Union attempt to promote the EU by explaining that outside of the EU there is no future for their country, but they have a hard time convincing the population to give more power to the supranational institutions when they are themselves running for a position in the national government. For instance, in arguing how important the EU is for their country's greatness, political leaders typically present the EU as a means for its particular nation-state having more say in the international scene, a better economic outlook, and so on. In short, the EU is presented in terms of advantages for the country, not for all, thereby reinforcing the importance and role of the nation-state within the Union. In addition, EU policies often require changes in the country, which are not perceived as positive by many voters. Thus, political leaders have to take this element into consideration when talking about Europe, and, more often than not, they end up undermining the image of the European Union in the population.

The results of this study also show that the fear of losing national identity as a result of European integration is unfounded. The persisting attachment to the national culture in every country will prevent in the foreseeable future homogenizing national cultures. Not even the most federalist of the EU leaders would even imagine such a development, and such is not the aim of the integration process. In fact, as De Witte (1993) suggests, national identities may be better protected by closer formal interactions at the European level than by separate policies enacted in each member state. All agreements and treaties produced at the EU level clearly stipulate the value of each member country's national identity, and there is a great effort in the European Union to promote the different cultures of the union even from the smaller countries.[24] The EU policies show an explicit attempt to preserve the cultural diversity that characterizes the European Union, at the same time that they aspire to creating some type of identification of the citizens with the European Union (by promoting the values that Europeans have in common).

Nevertheless, the EU is a very complex system of governance based on continuing multilateral relations and negotiations at the transnational level. The growing importance of the supranational arrangement in this multilevel system is instigating discomfort among many national leaders and lay people and has provoked the reaffirmation of national identity (as we have seen), but also in the familiar national state. In the next section are analyzed the main findings regarding issues of sovereignty, nationalism, and the preferences for the type of European Union organization.

THE EUROPE OF NATIONS

The research shows an overwhelming support for the idea of an organization at the European level in the three countries studied. Indeed, with few exceptions (most notably sympathizers and political leaders of the far right and far left of the political spectrum), citizens and political leaders interviewed support some form of European organization in which their country participates. Most people interviewed recognized the need to unite in order to continue enjoying a relative prosperity and for security and peace concerns. However, the range of opinions regarding the preferred type of organization and the degree of unity is very diverse. It goes from a simple agreement of association in certain aspects, to aspirations for a Federal Europe. The most common wishes expressed regarding the level of EU integration include: (1) to limit Europe to a certain number of agreements between independent countries, (2) that Europe is fine as it is now, with a common currency and a relatively integrated market—there is no need for further integration, (3) more unity in certain aspects such as foreign relations, and more intervention at the European level on immigration, and/or environment, and (4) that Europe should strive to become a federal model similar to Switzerland or the United States.

Within this diversity of opinions, some generalizations could be made. In the three member countries studied, the characteristics of people that tend to be less defensive regarding further European integration are similar: The younger, the upper-middle class, and the university graduates are the social categories most open to the process of integration, and it is among these categories that I found less fear of losing sovereignty and national identity. Within the political spectrum the clearer cleavages occur at the extremes. The far-right and far-left parties oppose the EU, while the so-called mainstream conservative parties, the centrist, and the social-democratic parties tend to be rather divided. But on the whole in the center right and center left is where were found more support for further European integration and less concern for loss of national identity or sovereignty.

In the three countries studied, the major debate on European integration is not at the present as much between those who defend a federal Europe and those who do not want at all an organization at the European level, but between those who want more integration and those who want less European integration. The true debate then revolves around the level of integration, and about questions of subsidiarity; which aspects should be decided in common at the European Union level and which aspects should be left to the national states, particularly concerning a united foreign policy and defense, a united security and home affairs policy (including immigration) and a common tax system. The disagreements about how far Europe should go in terms of integration and which institutions of the EU should have more power exist among both categories studied, leaders and lay citizens, in the three countries, but also between countries. There are several propositions that seek to reinforce the power of the Parliament and other plans to concentrate even more power in the Council. For instance, Jack Straw, secretary of the U.K. foreign office, expressed the desire of the U.K. government to reinforce the power of the European Council to build a Europe that "would be better understood, more democratic, and that would function better" (Langellier 2002: 5).

The major treaties are a result of the interaction of a considerable number of actors, which are the Commission and the Parliament (as the most supranational actors), the Council of Ministers, the Council of Europe, and the lobbying of national and transnational business as well as some other social actors.[25] In this process no one actor imposes absolutely its views, but the empirical evidence suggest that in this puzzle the Council plays a major role and controls to a large extent the path that the EU follows, and particularly regarding fundamental issues such as further integration in economics, in the areas of foreign relations and defense, as well as in security, and on further political unity. The Council is already the most important decision maker of the three major EU institutions. It concentrates the legislative and executive function—anything that pertains to surrendering of sovereignty. What we have had so far has been a "European policy of the nation-states" (Schild 2001: 333).

The partisans of this type of loose organization for Europe argue that the Europe of Nations is more democratic because a democracy can better be developed within historico-cultural units, to which people are committed, and strengthening the supranational decision making can weaken national democracies and provide a fake legitimacy for the institutions of the European Union. In this view, democratic accountability can only be achieved at the national level, emphasizing the primordial role that the Council should be playing in the governance of the EU. Many have even suggested making the Council accountable to the national parliaments.

Certainly, by reinforcing the Council even further without changing the voting procedures, the EU would end up undermining the possibility of a supranational Europe. However, if the mechanisms of voting change from consensus to qualified majority in most key issues, then even the Council could make the European Union more supranational than it is at the present. In external trade, monetary policy, and agriculture, the decision-making process has already been accelerated because the majority and the qualified vote in the Council have been used much more extensively in recent years.

The Convention on the Future of the European Union, which would end by mid-2003, is reflecting the debate on these issues.[26] The Convention has to find the way to manage the nationalist objectives of the member countries and simultaneously advance a European agenda, expanding also on the European-wide arrangements that already exist, such as European citizenship (which includes the right to vote in municipal elections in other countries of the EU, the homogenization of passports, and the elimination of border controls between most members states), the European-wide arrest caution, the structural funds, and the common currency. It would also have to define more precisely some federal-like institutions such as the Commission itself, the Parliament, and the European Central Bank. Contrary to the European summits, which seem always trying to solve the most urgent problems and issues, the Convention is an attempt to offer a clear direction on the future of Europe.

Given my findings and judging by the declarations of its different members, including its president Valery Giscard d'Estaing, the Convention would most likely produce some charter of fundamental rights that would be accepted by everyone. But there would be far less agreement on the question of power and the re-funding of the constitutional triangle made up of Council, Commission, and Parliament, as well as in the questions of market regulation and the configuration of a social Europe.[27] There are delegates in the Convention pushing for further integration; for instance, Pierre Moscovici, French Socialist (former Minister for European Affairs in Jospin's government), called for the reform efforts to "go beyond a strict adherence to a nation and seek what is in the interest of Europe as a whole. We need to move towards a United States of Europe" (Zecchini 2002a: 4). However, on the other hand, delegates are resisting the creation of an all-embracing constitution, most particularly delegates from the United Kingdom, but also many from the other 15 member countries and the candidate countries. In short, with the present ideological configurations and power relations, the new organizational arrangement would not respond to any already established system, but it would still have mostly intergovernmental characteristics that would reflect the prevailing attachment to the nation-state.[28]

Although the specific characteristics of this attachment to the nation-state vary from one member country to another, and vary in intensity among the different segments of the population, there is a widespread concern over the possible formation of a new centralized foreign organization that will decide everything from Brussels and will impose unilateral views on the nation-states. Moreover, the specificity of the EU member countries' nationalism is that many grievances are directed against the institutions that represent this supranational organization. In other words, this nationalism still has all the classical ingredients of nationalism with an additional institutional framework to blame.

In sum, the development of the EU has thus far not contributed to superseding the subjective prominence of the nation-state and nationalism, corresponding with the changes in the objective role—to use the Peterson et al. (1999) concept—of the state, as some postnational theorists suggested (Bauman 1992; McNeill 1986; Miller 1993), and has not yet engaged the countries' members, and particularly the populations of France, Spain, and the U.K. to support a federal Europe, as the neofunctionalists (Cameron 1992; Haas 1968) predicted. An erosion of the subjective attachment to the nation-state has not accompanied the relative erosion of the objective power of the nation-state.

Indeed, the postnational theorist judgment regarding the objective superseding of the state is certainly corroborated in the EU. For instance, the major directions of the economy are more and more established at the supranational level; one of the main agents is the ECB, but there is also a predominant influence of transnational corporations in the economy of the EU. Indeed, the weakening of the nation-state and of its ability to exercise autonomy within its geographical borders is as much the result of regulations established in Brussels as of the increasing power of private multinational companies in controlling the economy and communications. Therefore, the opposition of state sovereignty to European Union sovereignty is an absurd proposition, because even without European Union, the nation-states would have less and less sovereignty. In fact, the timid resurgence of the EU in the 1990s was to a large extent due to some leaders' perceptions and understanding of this loss of sovereignty and the need to face this problem. European leaders (such as Mittterrand, Kohl, Gonzalez, and others) proposed more unity at the European level to be more effective in their own country and more influential on a worldwide scale.

National sovereignty implies ability to negotiate on equal terms with other nations, the power to decide on economic policies at least within the borders of the sovereign state, the power to control borders, the military power to defend the country against external threats, the power to control education of the citizens, and flow of culture. A brief analysis suggests that in this increasingly globalized world even medium-sized states such as the France, Spain, or the United Kingdom are not able to control most of the above functions. The economy of the EU member countries is controlled mostly by large transnational companies as well as by some international agreements, such as the World Trade Organization (in which the governments are merely agents of large multinational companies), and the European Central Bank (not to mention the influence of the U.S. federal bank). As is well known, the neoliberalism now predominating in the world has forced even the most reticent social-democratic governments to reduce the welfare programs all over Europe.

Furthermore, most European Union member countries in isolation do not have a voice that counts in world politics and neither have they the military power to defend themselves against external threats. Formal education is still somehow controlled by the state but cultural flows from abroad are escaping state control. National sovereignty is challenged by the forces of globalization well beyond the EU.

In sum, because sovereignty implies above all the control over one's destiny through political association, it is in reality more sovereignty and not less that is achieved through further European integration. This alternative is new and there are many uncertainties, but it is still better than the lack of sovereignty that the national states are now experiencing.

Thus, as we advance into the twenty-first century, what would be left of national sovereignty? Mostly a myth. Those who oppose further European integration in the name of national sovereignty are defending something that does not exist anymore. The political elites opposed to further integration have a choice of governing over nothing, an illusion, and the possibility of making their voice really count. This is what a united Europe has to offer. The difference would be that instead of exerting a sovereignty over 60, 50, or 40 million people, political leaders will be exerting sovereignty over 375 million, and in a few years over 450 million.

THE EU AND THE WORLD

A united foreign policy has been contemplated since the Treaty on the European Union, but until now little progress has been made to accomplish this objective. There has been a renewed debate on the need for a united foreign policy after the government of George W. Bush started to develop what was widely considered by European leaders a unilateral policy. EU leaders consider that the United States treats them as junior partners, and they judge this treatment unacceptable: "There is a power divide between the United States, on the one hand, and any other country in Europe, because the United States is the world's sole superpower and the only power in a position to act on its own . . . one can occasionally feel a bit of a junior partner in dealing with the United States, in political and also in economic terms, and then the answer or remedy is easy: a more integrated and enlarged Europe" (Schroeder, cited in Friedman 2002: 1). Michel Rocard, a French socialist leader, writes: "whether it is about war and peace, development or financial stability, fight against inequality or criminality, or a fair regulation of the world economy, the world confronts today a dominant problem, from which all the others are dependent: the determined unilateralism that the U.S. Republicans impose on the rest of the world" (2002: 21).

The challenge in economics and politics of the United States is not a question of clash of civilizations but still a reality that every politician and business leader I interviewed felt they had to deal with. For example, commenting on the crisis with Iraq, the foreign minister of France, Hubert Védrine, declared that the United States has in foreign affairs a "unilateral approach, does not consult the others, and considers only its own interests. It does so in a utilitarian manner, since it could need the help from one or another country at a given moment, and refusing any international agreement or multilateral negotiation which could limit their decision-making process, their sovereignty, or their freedom of action" (Corine Lesnas 2002: 3). French prime minister Jospin warned the United States "to refrain from unilateralism and work with the Europeans on finding solutions" (Zecchini 2002a: 4), and German foreign minister Joschta Fischer stated that Washington should distinguish between "allied countries and satellite countries" (Tertsch 2002: 5). Even U.K. leaders, closest allies of the United States, such as Peter Hain, the number two of the foreign office, criticized the U.S. government diplomacy of being "absolutist and simplistic" (Zecchini 2002 b: 4). The Spanish prime minister, Aznar, usually very cautious regarding criticism of Washington, also said that "attacking Bagdad was not antiterrorism" and that Europeans "do not have to agree with everything the United States said" (El País 2002: 6).

The fact is that Europeans talk a lot but do not act much. They are not even able to agree on basic common declarations, and many political leaders often act with no regard for their partners in the EU.[29] Even during the spring 2002 period, in which it seemed that every European country (including the United Kingdom) was unhappy with the unilateralism of the United States, they were unable to produce something meaningful regarding the Bush government, while the U.S. government is generally very explicit about rejecting European propositions whenever it likes.

With some variation, the United States has tended to act as they wanted in the international scene for the last decade, even during the period of Bill Clinton, who seemed more oriented towards a soft cooperation than Bush. Indeed, several of the international agreements that Clinton accepted in principle were rejected by the U.S. Congress. In any case, states act in what they perceive to be their own interests, which include at the core international strategic security, economics, and internal politics. If we look at the relations (as they are reported in the news) between the EU and the United States only within the last four years, we find disagreements on many issues. France has been traditionally the most vocal to express discomfort with given U.S. policies, but most countries' politicians have expressed displeasure with the international behavior of the United States, including leaders from Germany, the Netherlands, Belgium, Spain, Italy, and even the most unconditional ally of the United States, the United Kingdom.[30] The United States, however, has continued to act as it pleases. In fact, it will probably continue to act unilaterally because it can. This is related to the relative weight that a country has on international affairs. Independently, even the biggest country of the EU has very limited power in international affairs.

The difference in approaching world affairs between the EU and the United States is also present in the media coverage. Newspapers and TV news from any country of the EU usually report on all the meetings, visits to the Middle East, China, Africa, or elsewhere of their president (be it Aznar, Blair, or Chirac). The same news outlets will also report on President Bush or other U.S. officials' activities and visits mostly anywhere in the world. In contrast, the U.S. newspapers, including a serious one like the *New York Times*, rarely even mention the activities of the European presidents (unless these activities concern the United States), and none of the U.S. TV networks do so. The U.S. media position responds to two interrelated reasons: (1) most U.S. citizens do not care about what is happening in other parts of the world unless that affects them directly, and (2) what most countries of the EU do is not really important to them.

In short, if Europeans do not want the United States to continue to act unilaterally, they do not have other choice but to unite further, and to give up some semblance of sovereignty to obtain a real one, one that really counts. As Lord Robertson, the General Secretary of NATO, warned, "Europe could not expect to have political influence on Washington if they had no effective power to bring to the coalition," and he added that the European countries "must be more united on military and foreign policy"(Fitchett 2002: 3). But, this is easier said than done. The fact remains that few political leaders in the EU have a sense of destiny for Europe. They seem to act according to circumstances. For example, José Maria Aznar, head of the Spanish government, stated in 2003, referring to the EU: "we should now decide if we want to assume responsibility for our security and how far we want to go" and added that "if the EU wanted to have a major role at the world level, it has to create the necessary political, technological, and economic conditions" (*El País* 2002: 6). But then the same Aznar, a year later, drafted a letter, which was signed by Italy, Portugal, the United Kingdom, and some candidate countries (Czech Republic, Hungary, and Poland), siding with the United States in opposition to the stance of France, Germany, and the EU Parliament. In fact, repeated confrontations and divergences on foreign policy among all member countries and the lack of coordination on important issues are made evident every time there is an international crisis. Such was the case during the conflict in the former Yugoslavia in the 1990s, the Iraq war in 1991, and the Iraq war in 2002–2003. The U.K. government in particular has been very explicit in supporting the U.S. government foreign policy over the years, even against the interest of the European Union.

In any case, to avoid Europe's submission to the variations and moods and particular orientations of the political leaders from each country, only a common foreign policy subordinated to the policy making at the level of the European Union would be real and efficient. Until then, European Union leaders can complain all they want, but the U.S. government when it consider it necessary will continue to act as it pleases.[31] As Fontaine (2002) writes, the United States has been saying since the time Kissinger was secretary for foreign affairs that Europe would exist for them when someone would be able to speak in the name of the whole continent (he reports that Kissinger said once: "If I call Europe, what number should I dial?") The relative unity that Europeans have shown in international trade constitutes an example at point. When the United States resorted to using economic sanctions because of divergences over level of hormones in the meat, or over subsidies and other issues, the EU was able to retaliate. Thus, the confrontations in the World Trade Organization between the EU and the United States are more between two equal partners.

For Europeans to reach the objective of having more weight in the world they have to articulate the European interest, not the national interest. In international relations, Europe should come first. Therefore, a surrender of sovereignty is absolutely necessary in international affairs and on matters of national defense.[32] The political power of the EU countries can only be exerted if they are all united with a single voice. In that sense the commission has proposed to the Convention on the Future of Europe that foreign policy should come under the community method. This means that the right of initiative as concerns foreign relations would be transferred to the European level. Moreover, the commission has also proposed to weave the job of Javier Solana, the European Union's senior representative for international relations, now under the Council control, into the European Commission.[33] But there are many leaders reticent to give up more power to the Commission.

International issues, and how the EU reacts to them, are also important elements that contribute to positive or negative social representations. In other words, a strong EU and a single voice in international affairs could in turn create more support for integration among the member countries' populations, and could contribute to developing a sense of European uniqueness and unity; while a weak EU, as it is today, tends to activate negative feelings among the same citizens.

The enlargement that is supposed to happen in 2004 represents another challenge for a united foreign policy. The commission's officials argue that the enlargement would not be done at the expenses of deepening, but this would really depend on the results of the Convention. If the Convention were able to produce a constitution, which would clearly and without ambiguity force stronger unity on key issues, then the enlargement would not in itself pose major problems for the future of the European Union foreign policy. However, as this book goes to print, there are not yet indications that this is the course that the Convention is taking. The Convention seems to be oriented to merely produce a framework for coordinating relations among separate nation-states. In short, if the convention fails to produce an appropriate supranational constitution, this enlargement could slow down even more, if not stopping completely, the road toward, not only a united foreign policy, but also further political unity. With the present structure of the EU, this large enlargement implies more conflict and more difficulties in reaching agreements, and above all, the diluting of any possible common identity.

The applicant countries have just managed to separate from the Soviet Union; therefore they would most likely be reluctant to give up their sovereignty. These countries entering the EU have even more disparate interests than those from western Europe and have shown so far a marked Atlanticist orientation in their foreign policy. One could witness in the debate around the invasion of Iraq in the winter/spring 2003 where the foreign allegiances of most of these countries were.[34] One can expect that they would most likely side with the U.K. government independentist stance in most issues pertaining to a united foreign policy. In this context, I do not see how a Common European Foreign and Security Policy could become a reality. The European Union would be even more than it is today based on the lowest common denominator.

In other words, the big risk with the new enlargement is that the European Union would only accomplish becoming a larger free-market area open to the power of the finance and the multinational companies, with little power over the path of world: a Europe with no sovereignty, and this in the name of a widespread myth, national sovereignty.[35] The imagery of Guillebaud (2002) calling the EU the "ventre mou," the "soft belly," of the occidental world, describes very well what the European Union would continue to be if there is not further political integration and further unity in foreign affairs.

FUTURE OF THE EUROPEAN UNION

The Treaties of Paris and Rome, which above all emphasized cooperation in the economy, have finally produced the single market envisioned. There are now solid ties of economic interdependence among the European Union member countries that cannot be undone without a big risk for most countries involved. The euro is one of the most recent achievements of this economic interdependence. However, as recognized in the treaty on European Union, the twenty-first century needs a different response; Europeans cannot continue to be dispersed into "a multiplicity of self-enclosed petty nationalisms" (Derrida 1992: 39). The European Union has either to integrate further or fail to respond to the challenges of this new millennium; particularly, there should be some shifting in the sharing of sovereignty from the nation-states to the EU, at least in those areas that are of vital importance for European survival as a democratic and progressive area.

As long as the states continue to have so much power in the decision-making process and in the establishment of policies at the European level, it would be unlikely that citizens develop a significant attachment to the

European Union. Indeed, the status quo of an intergovernmental Europe (equivalent to a Europe of Nations) will continue to privilege the negotiation between countries according to circumstances and issues. Besides, the issues would be addressed differently every time that a government changes in a particular member country. In short, an intergovernmental Europe will continue to be the Europe of dealings, and basically a "polygamous" (Langellier 2002) Europe, in which each government changes partners according to its interests at a particular moment. Nation-states will continue competing against each other, and from these power struggles the strongest ones will continue to be the definite leaders, imposing their views on the weaker states. The story of Europe has been that bigger nations have tended to dominate smaller ones. This is a reality today even within the European Union. The largest and most powerful (economically and politically) countries such as France, Germany, and the United Kingdom, have by far more weight than the other countries. So, with few exceptions, bargaining converges on their minimum common ground. Intergovernmentalism would also prevent the EU from acquiring power in world politics and would continue to reproduce negative social representations of the European Union among the population.

Only the establishment of a supranational organization with fair rules of power sharing, voting procedure, and so on, could give the smallest and less powerful nations of Europe a say in the evolution of the world, which is to say to have some control over their own destiny. This does not mean that powerhouses of the European Union, such as Germany, France, or the United Kingdom will cease to be, but their power of action would be more subdued in a supranational Europe than in an intergovernmental Europe.

The subsidiarity principle introduced in the Treaty on European Union should be the guiding principle in the process of further integration.[36] That is, the central institutions of the European Union (the triangle Council-Commission-Parliament) should deal with those matters that are not handled as well by individual member states. As my research and the experiences of the last 10 years have demonstrated, there are several aspects that should be handled at the European Union level. These include foreign relations, common defense, single market (which needs to be even more integrated by equating the law and financial systems), and energy policy (some form of deliberate mechanism across Europe should be developed so they can make better use of their resources). Accordingly, the EU could legislate in these areas and leave other aspects open for negotiation with some major directives coordinating education and some cultural policies, and "leaving the questions of languages, religion, relations to minorities and the like to the nations, and to the internal politics of citizenship and local government," as Delgado-Moreira (1997) suggests.

Those who defend the prominence of the nation-state argue that people need their national values to strive, and to feel identified with a collective identity that can only be the national state—the European Union being only a distant idea removed from the reality of people's lives. This is to a large extent true (we have seen in previous chapters people's strong attachment to the nation-state), but the desire for authenticity, and a symbolic reaffirmation of history and traditional values attached to the nation-state should not prevent more European unity.

At any rate, the present configuration of the national sentiment has to be taken into consideration as a strong variable in the development of a more integrated Europe: uniting Europeans on the basis of common cultural grounds is not yet an alternative. However, in the same way that Europe has developed a single market together with a single currency, a form of political unity could also develop. A loyalty of the citizens towards the European Union as a political institution is more possible, and easier to reach than a cultural identification. It seems that most citizens would go along with a basic project of unification around specific overarching policies in economics, foreign affairs, and defense, or a common European law (with a collection of citizens' rights and duties). There is already a body of universal human rights, and statutes regulating citizens' rights, which could be expanded and institutionalized at the EU territorial level. Even a limited European law would instigate a strong bond among Europeans, stronger than most would even realize. As Prowse points out, "when peoples agree to be bound by the same law they are unifying in the most fundamental way imaginable" (2002: 11).

In this process, a European citizenship could develop along the lines of the "constitutional patriotism" suggested by Habermas (1992: 643–51). The issue at stake is to develop a political union without threatening the population of the EU with homogenization and loss of national identity. The idea of European citizenship implies cultivation of a sense of membership based on loyalty to institutions first, with the expectation that later on, a "sense of a common possession" might develop as well (Marshall 1964: 92). Furthermore, civic identity at the European level is not an "all encompassing identity." Underneath the European level, it "allows the individual to bear as many other identities as he or she wishes"(Delgado-Moreira 1997: 8). That is, European citizenship is mostly linked to participation of the population in the polity of the European Union.

This scheme would require as well having a Parliament with increased power of decision. A European Parliament with more legislative power will strengthen democratic control over the Commission and the Council, resulting in more power to the citizens of the member countries. This does not necessarily means that the Parliament will replace the Council in everything but that it would play a major role in more issues than it actually does. By giving more power to the Parliament, the member states become constituent parts of the EU and not simply some aggregates of countries that legislate in the Council on the basis of the lowest common denominator. Furthermore, citizens would most likely participate with more interest in electing the members of the European Parliament, and this will also give the EU more political presence in citizens' lives. As Laffan (1996) envisages, the citizens of the member countries would vote on the basis of political programs and policies for the European Union as a whole rather than on "the second-hand basis of national interest, as in the current situation." The idea here is to embed the civic dimension of nationhood in a European-wide political process.

In sum, the European Union cannot really offer yet a unique sense of common history as the nation-state does, but it is possible for the EU to offer a sense of common destiny. By creating the type of European citizenship proposed above (which includes the creation of a civil, political, and social citizenship), it has the potential to provide a political and economic solidarity that could elicit popular assent and support, which in turn would most likely attract many citizens to the idea of a more united Europe, and perhaps even further cultural identification in the long term.

In addition, the dissemination of the European idea should operate in social institutions and organizations, particularly in education. Indeed, the teaching of history, in elementary and high schools, by the beginning of the twenty-first century, even when addressing recent history, is still plagued with constructs and interpretations that present the other member countries of the EU in a rather negative light. A fundamental rupture in ways of thinking about nation and sense of community should be brought to school; for example, focusing on the EU as a network of communities linked to each other in the same fate and with mostly the same interests, and also emphasizing what has been achieved together.

By the same token, the EU must be represented more positively in the media. To that end, some type of EU agency should be in charge of providing the information to the media on an everyday basis; for instance, through development of several forms of common communication (such as an EU news agency, and mass media programs that cross national borders).[37] In order to win the hearts and minds of the population the EU institutions must be able to respond to the overtly negative and biased content in the popular media (electronic and printed media). Additionally, the EU should provide directly further information to the population about their policies and explain them to the people, not rely only on the nation-states to provide this information. We have seen how national politicians use the EU as a buffer against unpopular policies and take credit for popular policies. There are some fundamental shared values (such as the EU Charter of Fundamental Rights, and support for the European social model and the welfare system), which are not enough promoted by the institutions and political leaders. Furthermore, to reaffirm the European Union's significance for people's lives, the diversity of Europe should be celebrated as the core of the European Union culture. To educate people about the meaning of Europe is not as much to explain what the different populations have in common as to make clear that the local culture is Europe. The devotion that people have for their country or region has to be celebrated as European: national and regional identities are not different from European identity; they are the essence. People possess more than one identity and can identify with all of them without necessarily opposing one against the other. European Union culture can only be conceived as a constellation of supranational, national, and regional cultures in a complementary rather than adversarial form.[38] In fact, the model of the European Union as a mosaic of diversity is very much expressed already in the makeup of the different EU institutions.

Finally, and most importantly for the future of Europe, the enhanced cooperation that was proposed in the Nice Treaty[39] should be the guiding principle in the years ahead. Indeed, it would be pointless to expect that every member country would be ready to accept further integration. My research shows that there is more desire to go ahead with, for example, further political integration among the political leaders of Spain and France than among the leaders from the United Kingdom.[40] Those countries so inclined (for example the 12 Eurogroup countries or even a smaller group) could establish a common foreign and defense policy and designate a foreign minister and its cabinet that will have a strong voice on their behalf in the world. This group could also, as Moscovici (2002) proposes, develop a more integrated economic policy and some specific coordination of these integrated policies. If not, 20 years from now Europe will still be discussing whether such or such little directive would be undermining the sovereignty of the nation-state.

As many European leaders have said often: no country in Europe can stand up alone to the challenges ahead.[41] The history of the twentieth century has demonstrated that only united could the European countries live not only in peace but be prosperous and somehow be heard, as well as gain access to speak for the world. By keeping a predominant intergovernmental system in which the major policies are decided by the nation-states, the European countries will be expressing many voices and competing among themselves, thereby limiting themselves to be political dwarfs and futile followers of other powers. Nationalism has proved to be an obstacle to the development of an enlightened Europe; it should now be dismissed so that a new Europe will come to be. Reinforcing Europe is reinforcing every country and every citizen.

NOTES

1. On national holidays, all member nations of the EU celebrate the heroes from World War I and World War II and from previous wars. Even though "the

myth of the fallen soldier" has undergone a weakening among younger generations (Mosse 1990: 224), politicians still use martial imagery and heroic discourse
to appeal to older generations.

2. Europeans grew up experiencing the nation-state as a natural entity. The
school, the discourse of politicians, and the media in general present the idea of
nation as a given, and patriotism as a basic value that has a hierarchy of taboo.
This is no different from the other nations of the world. In fact, nationalism is the
only ideology shared and respected internationally, from the richest to the poorest
nations around the globe.

3. Of course, there are differences in the application of those economic models.
The United Kingdom is at an extreme of the most neoliberal orientation in the EU,
and the Nordic countries, such as Sweden and Finland, are on the other extreme,
embracing a more moderate application of these policies.

4. There are several institutions at the European level involved with social
issues, but these institutions do not generate binding policies. These institutions
include the Employment and Social Policy Council, Social Protection Committee,
Directorate General for Employment and Social Affairs, Economic and Financial
Committee, Economic Policy Committee, and to a certain extent the Economic and
Financial Council (ECOFIN), which plays a major role in setting broad economic
policy guidelines.

5. The power of the companies does not lie only in their enormous economic
capacity, which in certain cases is even greater than the states themselves, but in
their ability to move their productive facilities from one place to another—creating
or eliminating jobs, to which any European government is extremely sensitive—
as well as supporting economically certain political parties closer to their ideology,
and the power of lobbying both the national governments and the institutions of
the EU.

6. Even those political leaders opposed to further integration recognize that
the EU member countries have benefited a great deal by negotiating in the World
Trade Organization as a united block.

7. The workers' organizations that want to be effective in the defense of their
interests would have to work at the European Union level, for example, by revi-
talizing the European Trade Union Confederation (ETUC), or perhaps by creating
a new labor union that will widen its activity to the European Union area. The
ETUC includes in its membership National Trade Union Confederations of 34
European countries from Western, Central, and Eastern Europe. The most important labor unions of France, Spain, and the United Kingdom participate in this
organization. The ETUC contemplates in its constitution to direct its activities
towards the EU, and it has often made suggestions on the EU agreements and
treaties (the latest on the Treaty of Nice), but so far the effects of ETUC actions for
EU workers have been rather limited.

8. The idea of spillover was suggested in the 1960s by Haas (1964) and Mitrany
(1966), and later by Gellner (1983), who suggested that the united market would
contribute to the construction of a common identity.

9. In reality, member states are often confronted, and these confrontations can
be very damaging for reaching further integration. For example, in 2002, leaders
like Berlusconi from Italy and Chirac from France blocked the creation of important agencies, such as Food Authority and Eurojust, because they could not obtain

the seats they wanted for representatives of their respective countries and the dozen of agents that accompany those seats.

10. Many leaders and most of the media in every country have presented the EU as the instigator of the economic policies that have restructured the industries of the member countries during the 1990s, and affected the job stability of thousands of workers.

11. The government of the United Kingdom has been traditionally a strong supporter of neoliberal policies. When an agreement or a directive proposed by the Commission affects the perceived interests of the corporations or the dogma of the market by giving some rights to the workers, the U.K. government is often on the side of the opposition. However, the Blair government does not enjoy the full support of the Labor Party on this issue. About half of the Labor Party leaders seem to be closer to the socialist parties of France and Spain in support of some form of Keynesian economy at the European level and remain committed to some regulations of the labor market and to a social welfare system established under the European social model.

12. This directive seeks to keep the workers informed and consult with them on issues that directly impact their lives, such as the economic situation, the evolution of the company's activities, employment structure, and work organization. As approved by the European Parliament, after being modified and accepted by the Council, this law would require companies with more than 50 employees to keep them informed on the issues mentioned. But the United Kingdom and Ireland obtained special concessions. This law will only apply to them in 2005 and in companies that have more than 150 employees, then 100 in 2007, and only in 2008 would they be in the same situation as the other Europeans (Europa 2002b).

13. The three countries studied here are among the biggest in Europe, and all have had an imperial past that has contributed to creating a strong sense of national identity and civilizing mission among the leaders and citizens alike; particularly in the case of the United Kingdom and France, with recent roles as world powers. In Spain, although there is a desire among political leaders to play a more important role than it has played in the past century in world affairs, there are less widespread international ambitions than in the other two countries among its citizens. Most leaders interviewed in the three countries recognized that they needed Europe to be influential in the world. However, the government of the United Kingdom so far has made a clear choice; its main partner in the international arena is not Europe but the United States.

14. There is a widespread belief that the nation corresponds to a natural geographical and cultural division, and that a given country has clear identifiable characteristics different from other countries. Edwards (1985) notes that self-awareness and self-consciousness constitute the main factors of nationalist thinking, and these feelings are expressed by the use of markers. The national markers most often mentioned by the interviewees were religion, food, music, and above all language. Language constitutes an important marker for national consciousness because it is an unambiguous indicator of difference and uniqueness (Menéndez Alarcón 1998). In fact, almost all interviewees consider language as essential to the maintenance of a national identity. The notion of linking a particular language to a given population within a given territory, under the control of a given political power, has been part of the nationalist discourse since the sev-

enteenth century. Herder (2002) and Fichte (1968) were among the most influential thinkers of linguistic nationalism.

15. There are some broad values predominantly shared by the populations of the three countries studied here (and, I believe, by all the countries of the European Union), such as political democracy, aesthetics, egalitarian ideology, and peace ideology. Furthermore, the majority of people interviewed (54 percent), although strongly interested in keeping their identity alive, have also shown awareness of a possible new European identity (see also Eurobarometer 56 2002).

16. David Apter (1963) argues that historically the state has been promoted as a form of "political religion." Similarly, Slezkine (1994: 186) points out that "by the eighteenth century the rise of national states, national vernaculars, and national churches had resulted in the nationalizations of paradise (claims have been made that Adam and Eve spoke Flemish, French, and Swedish among others, and then in the appearance of multiple autonomous paradises (all nations/languages had their own excellent ancestors)." Sletzkine (1994) also explains that models of the nation originated in the idea of family with a common language and descent. This idea is also articulated by Greenfeld (1992: 38), who suggests "the use of the term nation in 'the Second Treasons Act of 1571 in England' meant a family of kin." In sum, not only have the nation-states been given a sacred status, but they have also been epitomized as natural social units.

17. Lay citizens still identify mostly with the state because it offers to them a familiar cognitive representation and a greater sense of control. It is also perceived as a basic support system, providing for the social needs of the lower social classes.

18. Historical evidence demonstrates that neither group identities nor national identities are static. Culture is always a result of the incessant process of change. In fact, even the nation itself exists only as a process, constantly building its identity (Menéndez Alarcón 1995).

19. There is not a European common language and there are not positive common memories and traditions that would challenge or replace national representations. As Smith asserts, "there is no European analogue to Bastille or Armistice day, no European ceremony for the fallen in battle, no European shrine of kings or saints. When it comes to the ritual and ceremony of collective identification there is no European equivalent of national or religious community, . . . above all it [European Union] lacks a pre-modern past which can provide it with emotional sustenance and historical depth" (1992: 62–63).

20. Support for the common currency has increased after it has reached people's pockets. According to a January 2002 survey on the euro, carried out on behalf of the Commission of the European Union (2002), 60 percent of euro-zone citizens feel that the euro will bring to them advantages, 67 percent declared themselves happy that the euro has become their currency, and 66 percent that it will facilitate growth.

21. In chapters 2, 3, and 4, I described and analyzed how competition among member countries for resources and power contribute to reproducing negative social representations of the other countries and reinforce nationalism and national identity; sentiments that have deep historical roots. Hobsbawm and Ranger (1983), Oriol (1979), and Schudson (1994: 63), among many others, have documented how given typologies of collective identity have been promoted by the state and its apparatus (the schools, the media, etc.). As Derrida writes, "national hegemony

justifies itself in memory of the universal, of the transcendental or ontological" (1992: 47); for instance, state-apparatuses organize and encourage rituals that celebrate the higher historical legacy and values of a given nationality. The education system also emphasizes the same nationalistic values. The school system in France, Spain, and the United Kingdom (and most likely in the other EU member countries) promotes a culture whose basic environment is always the nation. Geography is taught with the assumption that the national territory constitutes the fundamental space, while the European continent is presented as a vague environment. In other words, from elementary school on, the national entity is proposed as the legitimate frame of culture and knowledge, and as the principal model of cultural identification. Consequently, people have difficulties overcoming the idea that yesterday's enemies are today's friends (Menéndez Alarcón 1998).

22. Because the decision-making process in the EU is largely controlled by the Council of Ministers, citizens would inevitably see sometimes on their TV and/ or read in the newspapers that their country representative in the Council has been overruled. Indeed, alliances are formed according to the issues; therefore no one single country will always be on the side of the winners. This contributes to creating a sense of frustration and powerlessness in the population of a given country, and most likely prompts negative feelings against the European Union.

23. Most politicians are concerned primarily about their voters at home and about obtaining seemingly favorable treatment for their country. Indeed, their population will evaluate them on the perceived quality of the deals they obtain. This dynamic induces the politicians to be responsible to a considerable extent for diffusing negative images of the EU. As the examples mentioned in previous chapters illustrate, politicians rarely recognize the key role of the EU in those policies that benefited their constituents; their inclination is to promote themselves for the popular and successful policies, and to blame the EU for unpopular policies.

24. Many nationalists complain that their country is losing national identity, and point at the cinema, the music, and clothing styles as strongly influenced by the United States. The reality is that the European Union is not to blame for that. In the present configuration of intergovernmental dealings, with the national state in charge of deciding cultural policies, there is not much that the EU can do, and the nation-states themselves have not the power to do anything about it. For example, there is no way that a film produced in France with less than 60 million potential national consumers can compete with a film produced in the United States with its 350 million (just to compare national consumers). Certainly, it would be different if there were films produced systematically with resources from all European Union members and if there were projects at the European level to produce films that can reach the masses not only in Europe but worldwide. The same could be said of other areas of the cultural industry.

25. In the interactions between the Commission and the Council there are many debates and negotiations, but the Council has always the last word. The Commission launches some initiatives and sometimes suggests modifications of a given policy to the Council, but at the end, the major initiatives are only transformed into decisions by the representatives of the government acting in the Council of Ministers or the heads of the government in the European Council. Most often than not the decisions taken at this level are based on domestic politics and nation-

states' perceived interests. In this context there is always a question of limiting as much as possible transfer of sovereignty to the institutions of the EU.

26. The Convention on the Future of Europe has to produce a long-term project charting the future of the European Union after 2004, when the EU plans to start welcoming the new members from central and southeastern Europe. This effort to write a constitution includes a large number of issues, such as a bill of rights in all the EU territory, the possibility for the EU to receive tax revenues to finance operations, the equilibrium between big states versus little states, centralization versus local government, the separation of powers, accommodating future members, democracy and efficiency, foreign policy and defense, and forging a more concrete connection between the Brussels bureaucracy and the citizens.

27. Many proposals and suggestions have been presented to the Convention. The German government is pushing for a European Union modeled on Germany's own federal system, with some EU functions such as agriculture transferred back to the member states. The commission has also made a detailed proposal that includes a direct EU tax to finance operations, a greater Commission role in setting economic policy for countries adopting the euro currency (including representing the European countries in such bodies as the World Bank and International Monetary Fund), and a single EU foreign and immigration policy under the direct control of the Commission. Another relevant proposal has been presented by Javier Solana, the European Union's foreign policy chief, which suggests reducing the bureaucratic departments of the Council from 16 to 10, and increasing the term for the rotating presidency of the council from 6 months to 2½ years.

28. Regardless of the final draft, the constitution would most likely renew interest in European-wide issues and would certainly contribute to some clarification of what the European Union is for the citizens. The present treaties are not only unfinished but also difficult to understand by the population, including by many political leaders, who confessed to me that they often have to ask specialists to explain to them the specific implications of the different agreements. A unique constitutive text could also accomplish more simplicity and perhaps make the EU easier to understand by the population, which in turn could stimulate not only more interest in European affairs but also more political participation.

29. For instance, during the war against the Taliban in Afghanistan, the president of France, the chancellor of Germany, and the prime minister of the United Kingdom had several meetings among themselves to decide on strategy regarding the war. They did not invite the other 12 EU members and did not share with them the discussions or the conclusions of the meeting. The reason presented by the U.K. Prime Minister, Tony Blair, was that "it was normal that nations very closely involved in the military should be able to exchange information with each other" (Jones and Evans-Pritchard 2001:1). The leaders of the other countries were upset, and many interviewees from Spain considered this meeting as another example that they were second-class citizens of the EU. In other words, this kind of action is contributing as much—if not more—as historical attachments to the nation-state to reproducing nationalism among the member countries of the EU.

30. The U.K. prime minister is an articulate leader, who is able to deliver powerful and convincing speeches. His public presence is gigantic compared to George W. Bush, but Blair is the leader of a country of 60 million and Bush the leader of a country with 350 million, with a powerful economy and army. Therefore, the

United Kingdom has a status of junior partner in its association with the United States, and this will be as such no matter how hard the U.K. government tries to prove that they are equal partners. The fact is that the talents of Blair as well as many other European politicians are lost because they do not have enough power to give weight to their ideas.

31. This is especially so when the United States knows that it has a considerable influence in European actions. As Josep Piqué, foreign minister of Spain recognized: "Certain countries are sensitive to U.S. criticism" (Yárnoz 2002: 1). For instance, just after the strong expressions of outrage from all European member countries regarding the U.S. unilateral actions during and after the Afghan war, including a speech on the "axis of evil" of U.S. president George W. Bush in February of 2002, the European Plan for Peace in the Middle East was modified under the pressure of Germany, the United Kingdom, and the Netherlands, who were responding to the demands of the United States.

32. The Treaty on European Union already emphasized the importance of a common foreign policy and common military defense in order for the EU to be independent and to assert its identity on the international scene. The Declaration on the Western European Union (WEU) states that in order to build a "genuine European security and defense identity" it would be vital to include the Western European Union as the "defense component" of the European Union.

33. The European resources available to the Commission could then be combined with the resources that the Council has assigned to Javier Solana.

34. In February of 2003 the Czech Republic, Hungary, and Rumania signed a declaration on the side of the United Kingdom, Spain, Italy, and Portugal supporting the U.S. position in a clear rebuffing of the position adopted by France, Germany, and the European Parliament, which were confronted by the United States on how to proceed regarding Iraq. The leaders of the United Kingdom, Spain, Italy, and Portugal adopted a position that was contrary to the large majority of their own population and many leaders from their own party, who opposed attacking Iraq without the backing of the UN.

35. The EU is very involved in international affairs. It contributes to world stability with its large support for development (55 percent of global international aid and two-thirds of subventions to developing countries), but it has little weight in the major orientations of world politics because it does not have a single voice in foreign policy.

36. The application of subsidiarity has two main functions: relieving the member states of competencies they can not carry out properly, and releasing the centralizing activities of the union in favor of the states when the states can better address the problem. This implies as well the corollary principles of sufficiency and effectiveness.

37. Some ideas in this direction have already been contemplated by the Commission. For instance, in a communication to the European Parliament (Comisión de las Comunidades Europeas 1988) the commission mentioned the need to create a "European cultural space" and to promote a European audiovisual industry in order to develop a European consciousness among the people of the member countries.

38. The European Union would certainly not become a single overriding culture that will assimilate the old cultures of the diverse nations. With time, European

culture might become an expression of the convergence of several cultures as a result of increased exchanges.

39. The Treaty of Amsterdam already allowed for the possibility of closer cooperation, but the mechanism was hedged around with so many strict conditions (particularly the right to veto by any member state) that it limited its application. The Treaty of Nice removed the right of each member state to veto enhanced cooperation, although it requires a minimum of eight member states for establishing enhanced cooperation. This treaty also provides "for the possibility of enhanced cooperation in the field of common foreign and security policy (CFSP), except as regards defense. It ensures that enhanced cooperation occurs within the framework of the European Union, respects the role of the institutions and allows the member States that do not participate immediately to join in whenever they wish" (Europa 2000a: 1).

40. As we have seen, the U.K. government is not interested in a more united Europe (this position has been predominant in the last 20 years). In fact, the United Kingdom's government strategy seem to be oriented to keeping Europe as divided as possible to avoid any further political integration.

41. For instance, German chancellor Schroeder: "We should integrate and build a deeper and bigger Europe to have more clout" (cited in Friedman 2002: 1), or Jack Straw, the U.K. Foreign Office Secretary: "It is at the supranational level that we can reach our objectives." (Langellier 2002: 5).

Bibliography

ABC. 1985. Lead article (1–31), cited by J. Diéz Medrano, and P. Gutierrez. "Nested Identities: National and European Identity in Spain." *Ethnic and Racial Studies* 24, 5 (September): 753–78.

Achcar, G. 2003. "L' OTAN à la conquête de l' Est." *Le Monde Diplomatique* (January): 18.

Alvarez-Miranda, B. 1996. "El sur de Europa y la adhesión a la comunidad: los partidos políticos." Madrid: Centro de Investigaciones Sociologicas (CIS).

Amey, L. 1973. "Fewer Defences and More Competition in Bacon Market." *The Times* (3 January).

Amstrong, K. A., and S. J. Bulmer. 1998. *The Governance of the Single European Market.* Manchester, N.Y.: Manchester University Press.

Análisis Sociológicos, Económicos y Políticos-ASEP. 2000. Madrid: Encuesta Nacional.

Anderson, B. 1983. *Imagined Communities: Reflections on the Origin and Spread of Nationalism.* London: Verso.

Anderson, C. J., and K. C. Kaltenthaler. 1996. "The Dynamics of Public Opinion toward European Integration, 1973–1993." *European Journal of International Relations,* Vol. 2, no. 2: 175–99.

Anderson, J. J. 1995. "The State of the (European) Union: From the Single Market to Maastricht, from Singular Events to General Theories." World Politics 47 (April): 441–65.

Anio, W., et al. 1997. "Returning to Europe: Central Europe between Internationalization and Institutionalization." In *Taming Power: Germany in Europe,* ed. Peter J. Katzenstein, 200–204. Ithaca, N.Y.: Cornell University Press.

Apter, D. 1963. "Political Religion in the New Nations." In *Old Societies and New States,* ed. Clifford Geertz. New York: Free Press.

Axford, B. 1995. *The Global System: Economics, Politics and Culture*. New York: St. Martin's Press.

Barker, E. 1927. *National Character and the Factors in Its Formation*. London: Methuen.

Barnett, A. 1982. *Iron Britannia*. London: Allison & Busby.

Bauman, Z. 1991. *Modernity and Ambivalence*. Cambridge, U.K.: Polity Press.

———. 1992. "Soil, Blood, and Identity." *Sociological Review* 40, 675–701.

BBC Monitoring International Reports. 2002. (30 April): 5.

Bosch, A., and K. Newton. 1995. "Economic Calculus or Familiarity Breeds Content?" In *Public Opinion and International Governance*, ed. O. Niedermayer and R. Sinnot, 73–104. Oxford: Oxford University Press.

Boski, P. 1989. "Social Cognitive Methods in the Study of Immigrants' Psychological Acculturation: Reaction Time and Person Prototype Approaches to Retention and Acquisition of National Self-Identity." In *Heterogeneity in Cross-Cultural Psychology*, ed. Daphne M. Keats, Donald Munro, et al. Amsterdam: Swets & Zeitlinger.

Bourdieu, P. 1984. *Distinction: A Social Critique of the Judgment of Taste*. Cambridge, Mass.: Harvard University Press.

Brand, C. 2002. EU Parliament Holds Special Debate. Associated Press. http://www.thestate.com/mld/thestate/news/world/4554712.htm (retrieved on December 11, 2002, posted on November 19, 2002).

Breakwell, G. M. 1993. *Empirical Approaches to Social Representations*. Oxford: Clarendon Press.

Brewer, M. 2000. "Superordinate Goals Versus Superordinate Identities as Bases of Intergroup Cooperation." In *Social Identity Processes*, ed. D. Capozza and R. Brown, 117–32. London: Sage.

Bryant, C. G. A. 1991. "Europe and the European Community 1992." *Sociology* 25: 189-207.

Bulletin of the European Communities. 1983. European Commission: Luxembourg.

Cahoun, C. 1993. "Nationalism and Ethnicity." *Annual Review of Sociology* 19: 211–39.

Cameron, D. 1992. "The 1992 Initiative: Causes and Consequences." In *Euro-Politics: Institutions and Policymaking in the "New" European Community*, ed. Alberta Sbragia. Washington, D.C.: Brookings Institution.

Camilleri, J. A. 1990. "Rethinking Sovereignty in a Shrinking Fragmented World." In *Contending Sovereignties*, ed. R. B. J. Walker and S. H. Mendlovitz. Boulder, Colo.: Lynne Rienner.

Candidate Countries Eurobarometer. 2002. Directorate General Press and Communication. Brussels: European Commission. Released March 2002 (fieldwork October 2001). http://europa.eu.int/comm/public_opinion/archives/cceb/2001/cceb20011_en.pdf (retrieved December 15, 2002).

Cappellin, R. 1993. "Interregional Cooperation in Europe: An Introduction." In *Regional Networks, Border Regions and European Integration*, ed. R. Cappellin, and P. W. J. Batey. London: Pion Limited.

Cassen, B. 2003. "Une Europe de moins en moins européenne." *Le Monde Diplomatique* (Janvier): 8–9.

Cecchini P., M. Catinat, and A. Jacquemin. 1988. *The European Challenge 1992: The Benefits of a Single Market*. Aldershot, Brookfield, Vt.: Gower.

Centro de Investigaciones Sociológicas-CIS. 2000. "Frecuencias del Barómetro de Mayo 2000." http://www.cis.es/baros/mar2392.htm.

Centro de Investigaciones Sociológicas-CIS. 2002. "Resultados del Barómetro de Abril 2002." http://www.cis.es/baros/mar2454.htm.

Chryssochoou, X. "How Group Membership Is Formed: Self Categorisation or Group Beliefs? The Construction of a European Identity in France and Greece." In *Changing European Identities: Social Psychological Analysis of Social Change*, ed. Glynis M. Breakwell and Evanthia Lyons. London: Butterworth Heinemann.

Cinnirella, M. 1996. "A Social Identity Perspective on European Integration." In *Changing European Identities: Social Psychological Analysis of Social Change*, ed. G. M. BreakWell and E. Lyons. London: Butterworth Heinemann.

Colley, L. 1992. *Britons: Forging the Nation 1707–1837*. New Haven, Conn.: Yale University Press.

Comisión de las Comunidades Europeas. 1988. "Nuevo impulso de la política cultural de la Comunidad Europea." *Boletín de las Comunidades Europeas, suplemento 4/87*. Luxembourg: Oficina de Publicaciones Oficiales de las Comunidades Europeas.

Commission of the European Communities. Second Progress Report on Economic and Social Cohesion. Brussels 30.1.2002, COM (2002) 46 final. http://europa.eu.int/eur (retrieved on March 7, 2002).

Commission of the European Union. 2002. Survey on the Euro 21–31 January, http://europa.eu.int/comm/public_opinion (retrieved on August 2, 2002).

Connor, W. 1994a. "A Nation Is a Nation, Is a State, Is an Ethnic Group, Is a . . . ." In *Nationalism*, ed. J. Hutchinson and A. D. Smith. Oxford: Oxford University Press.

———. 1994b. *Ethnonationalism: The Quest for Understanding*. Princeton, N.J.: Princeton University Press.

Corine Lesnas, Hubert. 2002. "Védrine dénonce le "simplisme" et l' unilatéralisme 'utilitaire' des Américains." *Le Monde* (8 February): 3.

Coudenhove-Kalergi, R. N., Graf von. 1922. *Paneuropa*. Vienna: Munchen, Herold.

Cox, R. W. 1987. *Production, Power, and World Order: Social Forces in the Making of History*. New York: Columbia University Press.

Crawshaw, R. H. 2000. *Exploring French Text Analysis: Interpretations of National Identity*. London, New York: Routledge.

Daily Mail. 2002, April 30, 5. Cited in European Union Representation in the UK. 2001. *Press Watch*. http://www.cec.org.uk/press/pw/latest.htm (retrieved on July 6, 2002).

Daly, E. 2002. "Europeans Urge Morocco to Withdraw from Spanish Island." *Financial Times*, Monday (15 July) sec. A, p. 2, col. 3, Foreign Desk.

De Lange, R. 1995. "Paradoxes of European Citizenship." In *Nationalism, Racism, and the Rule of Law*, ed. P. Fitzpatrick. Aldershot, Brookfield: Darmouth.

De Rosa, A. S. 1996. "Reality Changes Faster than Research: National and Supranational Identity in Social Representations of the European Community in the Context of Changes in International Relations." In *Changing European Identities: Social Psychological Analysis of Social Change*, ed. G. M. Breakwell and E. Lyons. London: Butterworth Heinemann.

De Tocqueville, A. 1955. *The Old Régime and the French Revolution*. Garden City, N.Y.: Doubleday & Company.

De Witte, B. 1993. "Cultural Linkages." In *The Dynamics of European Integration*, ed. W. Wallace. London: Pinter Publishers, 1990.

Debray, R. 1990. "A demain de Gaulle." *Nouvel Observateur* (19–25 July): p. 6.

Deflem, M. and F. C. Pampel. 1996. "The Myth of Postnational Identity: Popular Support for European Unification." *Social Forces* 75 (1): 119–43.

Delgado-Moreira, J. M. European Politics of Citizenship. [60 paragraphs]. *The Qualitative Report* [On-line serial], 3(3), 1997. http://www.nova.edu/ssss/QR/QR3-3/delgado.ht (retrieved on April 4, 2002).

Derrida, J. 1992. *The Other Heading: Reflections on Today's Europe*. Bloomington: Indiana University Press.

Díez Medrano, J., and P. Gutierrez. 2001. "Nested Identities: National and European Identity in Spain." *Ethnic and Racial Studies* 24, 5 September, 753–78.

Douglas, M., and B. Isherwood. 1979. *The World of Goods*. New York: Basic Books.

Duchesne, S., and A. P. Frognier. 1995. "Is There a European Identity?" In *Public Opinion and International Governance*, ed. O. Niedermayer and R. Sinnott, 193–226. Oxford: Oxford University Press.

Duhamel, A. 2002. "Les français et la situation internationale." SOFRES. http://www.sofres.com/etudes/pol/110902_chron_n.htm.

Dunne, D. 1997. *Political Identity in the European Union*. Dissertation. University Dublin College, January.

Eastman, C., and T. Reese. 1981. "Associated Languages: How Language and Ethnic Identity Are Related." *General Linguistics* 21: 109–16.

Edwards, J. 1985. *Language, Society and Identity*. Oxford: Basic Blackwell.

Egan, K. 1997. *The Educated Mind: How Cognitive Tools Shape Our Understanding*. Chicago: University of Chicago Press.

El País. 1979. "La Bofetada Europea" (9–18), cited by J. Diéz Medrano, and P. Gutierrez. 2001. "Nested Identities: National and European Identity in Spain." *Ethnic and Racial Studies* 24,5 (September): 753–78.

El País. 1994a. "Coles de Bruselas." June 5, p. 5, section *Domingo*.

El País. 1994b. April 3.

El País. 1996. "Los Mercados visten de Euro a la peseta." December 15, pp. 1–3, (section negocios).

El País. 2002. "Aznar afirma que atacar a Bagdad 'no es antiterrorismo.' " No author, February 17, p. 6.

EOS Gallup. 1996. *Top Decision-Makers Survey*. Brussels: European Commission.

Esping-Andersen, G. 1990. *The Three Worlds of Welfare Capitalism*. Princeton, N.J.: Princeton University Press.

Eurobarometer 27. 1987. Directorate General Information, Culture, Audiovisual, European Commission, Spring.

Eurobarometer 30. 1988. Directorate General Information, Culture, Audiovisual, European Commission, Fall.

Eurobarometer 32. 1989. Directorate General Information, Culture, Audiovisual, European Commission, Fall.

Eurobarometer 34. 1990. Directorate General Information, Culture, Audiovisual, European Commission, Spring.

Eurobarometer 36. 1991. Directorate General Information, Culture, Audiovisual, European Commission, Spring.

Eurobarometer 38. 1992. Directorate General Information, Culture, Audiovisual, European Commission, Spring.

Eurobarometer 44. 1995. Directorate General Information Culture, Audiovisual, European Commission, Fall.

Eurobarometer 45. 1996. Directorate General Information Culture, Audiovisual, European Commission, June.

Eurobarometer 46. 1996. Directorate General Information Culture, Audiovisual, European Commission, December.

Eurobarometer 46. 1996. Directorate General Information Culture, Audiovisual, European Commission, Fall.

Eurobarometer 48. 1997. Directorate General Information, Culture, Audiovisual, European Commission, May.

Eurobarometer 49. 1998. Directorate General Information, Culture, Audiovisual, European Commission, May.

Eurobarometer 50. 1999. 25th Anniversary. Directorate General Information, Culture, Audiovisual, European Commission, March.

Eurobarometer 54. 2000. Directorate General Information, Culture, Audiovisual, European Commission. Released December 2000. Retrieved October 10, 2001. http://europa.eu.int/comm/public_opinion/archives/eb/eb54/en.pdf.

Eurobarometer 55. 2001. Public Opinion in the European Union. Directorate General Press and Communication. Brussels: European Commission, Release December 2000. Retrieved September 4, 2002. http://europa.eu.int/comm/public_opinion/archives/eb/eb54/en.pdf.

Eurobarometer 56. 2002. Public Opinion in the European Union. Directorate General Press and Communication. Brussels: European Commission, Release April 2002 (fieldwork Oct.–Nov. 2001). Retrieved December 14, 2002. http://europa.eu.int/comm/public_opinion/archives/eb/eb56_en.pdf.

Eurobarometer. 1994. *Trends 1974–1993.* Directorate General Information Culture, Audiovisual, European Commission, April.

Eurocom. 1996. *Monthly Bulletin,* vol. 8, no. 1 (January). New York: European Commission.

Eurocom. 1996. *Monthly Bulletin,* vol. 8, no. 9 (October). New York: European Commission.

Eurocom. 1998. *Monthly Bulletin,* vol. 10, no. 4 (April). New York: European Commission.

Eurocom. 1999. *Monthly Bulletin,* vol. 11, no. 11 (December). New York: European Commission.

Euro-OP News. 1995. "More Democracy Is Needed!" Vol. 4, no. 2 (Summer), Luxembourg.

Euro-OP News. 2002. "Unemployment Is Down." Vol. 11, no. 1 (January), Luxembourg.

Euro-op News. 1996. *Commission Report on the Cultural Aspects of EU Policies,* Com 160, vol. 5, no. 2 (Summer).

Europa. 2002a. European Union. http://www.europa.eu.int/comm/igc2000/dialogue/info/.

Europa. 2002b. "Guide to Citoyen." European Union. http://www.europa.eu.int/comm/2002/info/offdoc/guidecitoyen_en.pdf.

Europa. 2002c. http://www.europa.eu.int./comm/enlargement/arguments/index.htm (retrieved on September 12, 2002).

European Commission. 2000. *Program Culture 2000–2004*. Brussels: Directorate General.

European Union Representation in the UK. 2002. *Press Watch*. www.cec.org.uk/press/pw/latest.htm (retrieved on September 20, 2002).

Featherstone M. 1995. *Undoing Culture: Globalisation, Posmodernism and Identity*. London: Sage.

Ferry, J. M. 1992. *Discussion sur l'Europe*. Paris: Calmann-Levy.

Fichte, J. 1968. *Addresses to the German Nation*. New York: Harper & Row.

Fiske, S., and S. Taylor. 1984. *Social Cognition*. New York: Random House

Fitchett, J. 2002. "Pentagon in a League of Its Own." *International Herald Tribune* (4 February): 3.

Fontaine, A. 2002. "L'Amérique trop forte, l'Europe trop faible." *Le Monde* (2 March): 17.

Fontaine, P. 2000. *A New Idea for Europe: The Schuman Declaration—1950–2000*. Luxembourg: Office for Official Publications of the European Communities.

Friedman, A. 2002. "Schroeder Assails EU Deficit Critics." *International Herald Tribune* (Saturday-Sunday, February 2–3): 1.

Fuchs D., and H. D. Klingemann. 2002. "Eastward Enlargement of the European Union and the Identity of Europe." *West European Politics*, Vol. 25, no. 2 (April): 19–54.

Gabel, M. 1998. "Public Support for European Integration: An Empirical Test of Five Theories." *The Journal of Politics* 60, no. 2 (May).

Garton Ash, T. 2002. "Tony Blair y Harry Potter." *El País* (17 February): 13.

Gellner, E. 1983. *Nations and Nationalism*. Ithaca, N.Y.: Cornell University Press, 1983.

Gilpin, G. S. 1992. "The Emerging World Order and European Change: The Political Economy of European Union." In *New World Order? Socialist Register 1992*, ed. R. Miliband and L. Panitch. London: The Merlin Press.

González, F. 1996. "Entrevista." *El País* (6 June): 8, Madrid.

———. 1997. "L' Espagne en Europe, l' Europe en Espagne." *Essais sur l' Union Européenne*. Paris.

Greenfeld, L. 1992. *Nationalism: Five Roads to Modernity*. Cambridge, Mass.: Harvard University Press.

Guillebaud, J. C. 2002. "L'euro sans l'Europe." *Le Monde Diplomatique*, (February): 2.

Haas, E. 1964. *Beyond the Nation-State: Functionalism and International Organization*. Stanford: Stanford University Press.

———. 1968. *The Uniting of Europe: Political, Social and Economic Forces, 1950–1957*. Stanford: Stanford University Press.

Habermas, J. 1992. "Citizenship and National Identity: Some Reflections on the Future of Europe." *Praxis International* 12(1): 1–19.

Hall, J. R., and Mary Jo Neitz. 1993. *Culture: Sociological Perspectives*. Englewood Cliffs, N.J.: Prentice Hall.

Hannerz, U. 1990. "Cosmopolitans and Locals in World Culture." In *Global Culture: Nationalism, Globalization and Modernity*, ed. M. Featherstone. London: Sage.

Haseler, S. 2001. "The Case for a Federal Europe." In *Federal Britain in Federal Europe?*, ed. I. Taylor. London: Federal Trust.

Havel, V. (1994). "A Charter for European Identity." *Speech to European Parliament.* 8/3/1994. http://www.europa.ed.int/Parliament/1994.

Held, D. 1992. "The Development of the Modern State." In *Formations of Modernity*, ed. S. Hall and B. Gieben. Cambridge: Polity Press.

Heller, Agnes. 1992. "Europe: An Epilogue?" In *The Idea of Europe*, ed. Brian Nelson, David Roberts, and Walter Veit, 12–25. New York: Berg, 12–25.

Herder, J. G. 2002. *Philosophical Writings*. Cambridge, U.K.: Cambridge University Press.

Hobsbawm, E. J. 1990. *Nations and Nationalism since 1780*. Cambridge, U.K.: Cambridge University Press.

Hobsbawm, E., and T. Ranger. 1983. *The Invention of Tradition*. Cambridge, U.K.: Cambridge University Press.

Hodgson, G. 1993. "Grand Illusion: The Failure of European Consciousness." *World Policy Journal* 10: 13–24.

Honko, L. 1996. "Changing National Identities: Finland." *Anthropological Journal on European Cultures* 5 (2): 35–63.

Hooper, J. 1987. *The Spaniards: A Portrait of the New Spain*. London: Penguin.

IFOP-Le Point. 1992. "Le Referendum sur Maastricht: Sondage IFOP," *Le Point*, 4 September.

Inglehart, R. 1977. "Long Term Trends in Mass Support for European Unification." *Government and Opposition* 12: 150–57.

Janssen, J. I. H. 1991. "Postmaterialism, Cognitive Mobilization, and Support for European Integration." *British Journal of Political Science* 21: 443–68.

Jareau, P. 2002. "Tension entre Paris et Washington." *Le Monde* (18 February): 5.

Jessel, Stephen. 1973. "Lord Bowden Says EEC Civil Servants Are Trying to Wreck English Education." *The Times* (6 January).

Jodelet, D. 1991. *Représentations sociales.* Paris: Presses Universitaires de France.

Jones, G., and A. Evans-Pritchard. 2001. "Summit Split as EU Leaders Snub Call to Overthrow Kabul Regime." *The Daily Telegraph* (19 October).

Kahler, M. 1987. "The Survival of the State in European International Relations." In *Changing Boundaries of the Political*, ed. Charles S. Maier, 287-319. Cambridge, U.K.: Cambridge University Press.

Kallenbach, M. 2001. "We Are Not Anti-Europe, Just Anti-integration, Say Tories." *The Daily Telegraph* (18 October).

Kaltenthaler, K. C., and C. Anderson. 2000. "The Changing Political Economy of Inflation." *Journal of Public Policy* 20, pt. 2 (May/August): 109–31.

Keating, M. 2000. "The Minority Nations of Spain and European Integration: A New Framework for Autonomy?" *Journal of Spanish Cultural Studies* 1, no. 1.

Keohane, R. O., ed. 1986. *Neorealism and Its Critics.* New York: Columbia University Press.

Keohane, R. O., and S. Hoffmann. 1991. *The New European Community: Decision-making and Institutional Change.* Boulder, Colo.: Westview Press.

Khon, H. 1948. *The Idea of Nationalism.* New York: Macmillan.

Kovács, J. M. 2002. "Approaching the EU and Reaching the US? Rival Narratives on Transforming Welfare Regimes in East-Central Europe." *West European Politics* 25, no. 2: 175–83.

Kramer, S. P. 1994. *Does France Still Count? The French Role in the New Europe.* Westport, Conn.: Praeger.

Laffan, B. 1996. "The Politics of Identity and Political Order in Europe." *Journal of Common Market Studies* 34, no. 1.

Laitin, D. 2002. "Culture and National Identity: 'The East' and European Integration." *West European Politics* 25, no. 2 (April): 55–80.

Langellier J. P. 2002. "Londres est contre l'election du président de la Commission." *Le Monde* (22 February): 5.

Le Monde. 1992. "Le référendum sur l'Union Européenne." 25 September.

Le Monde. 1998. "Les perspectives de Lionel Jospin avant l' euro" (25 April): 1, 8, and 10.

———. 2002. November 25, p. 5. Retrieved on November 29, 2002. *Le Monde.* http://www.lemonde.fr.

Leparmentier, A. 2003a. "Une opération budgétaire limitée." *Le Monde: Dossiers et Documents* (January): 6.

Leparmentier, A. 2003b. "La Commission bataille pour avoir plus de pouvoir." *Le Monde: Dossiers et Documents* (January): 4.

Limberg, L. N., and S. A. Scheingold. 1971. "Introduction." In *Regional Integration: Theory and Research,* ed. L. N. Limberg and S. A. Scheingold. Cambridge, Mass.: Harvard University.

Lipiansky, E. M. 1986. "L'identité nationale comme représentation." In *Identités sociales et changements sociaux,* ed. P. Tap. Toulouse: Privat.

Lyotard, J. F. 1984. *The Postmodern Condition: A Report on Knowledge.* Minneapolis: University of Minnesota Press.

Lyotard, J. F. 1988. "Interview." *Theory, Culture, and Society* 5: 2–3.

Mann, M. 1990. "The Emergence of European Nationalism." *Theory , Culture, and Society* 7: 2–3.

Manzo, K. A. 1996. *Creating Boundaries: The Politics of Race and Nation.* Boulder, Colo.: Lynne Rienner Publishers.

Marcussen, M., T. Risse, D. Engelman-Martin, H. J. Knopf, and K. Roscher. 1999. *Constructing Europe? The Evolution of French, British and German Nation State Identities. Journal of European Public Policy* 6:4 (Special issue): 614–33.

Marion, G. 2002. "Paris et Berlin: l' élargissement doit respecter le cadre budgétaire fixé." *Le Monde* (6 February): 5.

Marshall, T. H. 1964. "Citizenship and Social Class." In *Class, Citizenship and Social Development,* ed. T. H. Marshall, 65–123. New York: Doubleday & Co.

Martinotti, G., and S. Stefanizzi. 1995. "Europeans and the Nation State." In *Public Opinion and Internationalized Governance,* ed. O. Niedermayer and R. Sinnott. Oxford: Oxford University Press.

Massard, F. 1993. *L'Européen dans tous ses Etats. Entre mythe et contrainte communautaire?* Brussels: Bruylant.

Maxwell, R. 1995. *The Spectacle of Democracy: Spanish Television, Nationalism, and Political Transition.* Minneapolis: University of Minnesota Press.

McNeill, W. 1986. *Polyethnicity and National Unity in World History.* Toronto: University of Toronto Press.

McCoy, D. 2002. "Get a Move On!" *Financial Times Information* (20 May).

Méchet, P. 2002. "En France, l'anti-américanisme structuré apparaît minoritaire et politique." *Le Monde,* January 7. http://www.sofres.com/etudes/pol/.

Menéndez Alarcón, A. 1995. "National Identities Confronting European Integration." *International Journal of Politics, Culture and Society* 8, no. 4.

——— 1998. "National Identity, Nationalism, and the Organization of the European Union." *International Journal of Contemporary Sociology* 35, no. 1 (April).

Miller, T. 1993. "National Policy and the Traded Image." In *National Identity and Europe,* ed. Phillip Drummond, Richard Paterson, and Janet Willis. London: BFI Publishing.

Milner, H. 1992. "International Theories of Cooperation among Nations: Strengths and Weaknesses." *World Politics* 44 (April): 482–93.

Minogue, K. R. 1970. *Nationalism.* Baltimore, Md.: Basic Books.

Mitrany, D. 1966. *A Working Peace System.* Chicago: Quadrangle Books.

Monnet, J. 1976. *Memoirs.* London: William Collins & Son Ltd.

Moravcsik, A. 1994. "Preferences and Power in the European Community: A Liberal Intergovernmentalist Approach." In *Global Context,* ed. S. Bulmer and A. Scott. Oxford, Cambridge: Blackwell Publishers.

Moreno, J. A. 1990. "Algunos aspectos sobre la unidad europea en la bibliografía española de 1945 a 1962." *Hispania,* No. 176: 1453–73.

Morley, D., and K. Roberts. 1996. *Spaces of Identity: Global Media, Electronic Landscapes and Cultural Boundaries.* London: Routledge.

Moscovici, P. 2002. *L'Europe, une puissance dans la mondialisation.* Paris: Seuil.

Mosse, G. L. 1990. *Fallen Soldiers: Reshaping the Memory of the World Wars.* New York: Oxford University Press.

Munch, R. (1995). *Das Projekt Europa: zwischen Nationalstaat, regionaler Autonomie und Weltgesellschaft.* Frankfurt am Main: Suhrkamp (1993). Cited by Helmut K. Anheier, *Society,* 368–69.

Murray, I. 1973. "No Fear of a Two-Way Wholesale Invasion across the Channel." *The Times* (3 January).

Mutimer, D. 1989. "1992 and the Political Integration of Europe: Neofunctionalism Reconsidered." *Journal of European Integration* 13 (Fall): 75–101.

Neuman, W. L. 2000. *Social Research Methods: Qualitative and Quantitative Approaches.* Boston: Allyn & Bacon.

Oficina Nacional de Estadística. 1996. http://www.ine.es/ (retrieved on August 23, 2002).

Oficina Nacional de Estadística. 2002. http://www.ine.es/tempus/ (retrieved on August 24, 2002).

Oriol, M. 1979. "Identité produite, identité instituée, identité exprimée." *Cahiers Internationaux de Sociologie* 66 (June).

Ortega y Gasset, J. 1989. *Ensayos sobre la generación del 98.* Madrid: Alianza Eitorial.

Orwell, G. 1953. *England Your England and Other Essays.* London: Secker & Warburg.

Osa, M. 1992. "Pastoral Mobilization and Symbolic Politics: The Catholic Church in Poland 1918–1966." Ph.D. diss., Department of Sociology, University of Chicago.

Parlamento Europeo. 1983. Oficina de Publicación de las Comunidades Europeas: Luxembourg.

Peterson, J., and E. Bomberg. 1998. "Northern Enlargement and EU Decisionmaking." In *Deepening and Widening*, ed. P. H. Laurent and M. Maresceau. Boulder, Colo.: Lyenne Rienner Publisher.

Peterson, J. 1999. *Decision-Making in the European Union*. New York: St. Martin's Press.

Peterson, R., D. Wunder, and H. Mueller. 1999. *Social Problems: Globalization in the Twenty-First Century*. Upper Saddle River, N.J.: Prentice Hall.

Peyrefitte, A. 1994. *C'était de Gaulle*. Paris: Fayard.

Peyronnet, G. 1989. "De l'utilité de la psychology des peoples pour la realization de l'Union Européenne." *Cahiers de Sociologie Economique et Culturelle* 12.

Proudhon, P. J. (Pierre-Joseph). 1923. *Oeuvres complètes de P.-J. Proudhon*. Paris: M. Rivière.

Prowse, M. 2002. "Why a Common Law Remains at Europe's Core." *Financial Times Weekend* (14–15 December): 11.

Ragin, C. 2000. "The Place of the Case Study Research." *Comparative and Historical Sociology Newsletter* 13, no. 1 (Fall): 2.

Raymond, W. 1982. *The Sociology of Culture*. New York: Schocken Books.

Rex, J. 1991. "Ethnic Identity and Ethnic Mobilisation in Britain." *Monograph in Ethnic Relations* No 5. Coventry, U.K.: Centre for Research in Ethnic Relations, University of Warwick.

Riffe, D., C. Aust, and S. Lacy. 1993. "The Effectiveness of Random, Consecutive Day and Constructed Week Sampling in Newspaper Content Analysis." *Journalism Quarterly* 70 (1): 133–39.

Risse, T. 2000. "A European Identity? Europeanization and the Evolution of Nation-State Identities." In *Europeanization and Domestic Change*, ed. M. G. Cowles, J. Caporaso, and T. Risse. Forthcoming.

Rocard, M. 2002. "La France et son nombril." *Le Monde* (14 February): 21.

——— 2002. "Turquie: dire oui est vital." *Le Monde* 27 November. http://www.lemonde.fr/# (retrieved on November 27, 2002).

Romano, S. 1990. "Le poids de l'histoire." In *Six manières d'etre européen*, ed. Dominique Shnapper and Henri Mandras, 16–25. Paris: Gallimard.

Rosamond, B. 2000. *Theories of European Integration*. New York: St. Martin's Press.

Saint Pierre, C. I. C. de. 1761. *Extrait du projet de paix perpetuelle de monsieur l'abbé de Saint Pierre*. Paris: s.n.

Salmon, K. G. 1991. *The Modern Spanish Economy: Transformation and Integration into Europe*. London: Pinter Publishers.

Sands, D. R. 2002. "Special Report." *The Washington Times* (21 July): A01, (LexisNexis Internet delivery.)

Sbragia, A. 1992. *Euro-politics: Institutions and Policy Making in the "New" European Community*. Washington D.C.: Brooking Institution.

Schild, J. 2001. "National v. European Identities? French and Germans in the European Multi-Level System." *Journal of Common Market Studies* 39, no. 2: 331–51.

Schlesinger, P. 1991. "Collective Identities in a Changing Europe." *Innovation* 4 (1): 41–63.

———. 1994. "Europeanness: A New Cultural Battlefield?" In *Nationalism*, ed. John Hutchinson and Anthony D. Smith, 316–25. Oxford: Oxford University Press.

Schudson, M. 1994. "Culture and the Integration of Societies." *International Social Science Journal* 139, no. 1 (February): 63–82.

Schwarz, B. 1992. "England in Europe: Reflections on National Identity and Cultural Theory." *Cultural Studies* 6, 2 (May): 198–206.

Schwork, R. 1999. "La France et l' intégration européenne: une évaluation du paradigme identitariste." *French Politics and Society* 17, no. 1 (Winter): 56–69.

Seguin, P. 1998. "Discours à l'Assemblée Nationale." Rassemblement Pour la République. April 22. http://www.rpr.asso.fr.

Seidman, I. E. 1991. *Interviewing as Qualitative Research: A Guide for Researchers in Education and the Social Sciences*. New York: Teachers College Press.

Shore, C. 1993. "Inventing the 'People's Europe': Critical Approaches to European Community 'Cultural Policy.'" *Man* 28: 779–800.

Slezkine, Y. 1994. "Naturalists versus Nations: Eighteenth-Century Russian Scholars Confront Ethnic Diversity." *Representations* 47 (Summer): 170–95.

Smith, A. D. 1990. "Towards a Global Culture." *Theory, Culture, and Society* 7: 2–3.

———. 1991. *National Identity*. Harmondsworth, England: Penguin.

——— 1992. "National Identity and the Idea of European Unity." International Affairs 68, no. 1.

——— 1995. *Nations and Nationalism in a Global Era*. Cambridge, Mass.: Polity Press.

——— 1998. *Nationalism and Modernity*. London: Routledge.

Sobish, A., and S. Immerfall. 2000. "The Social Basis of European Citizenship." In *Developing European Citizens*, ed. Ian Davies and Andreas Sobish, 141–74. Manchester: Politics Association.

Sofres. 2001a.http://www.sofres.com/etudes/pol/070301_europe_r.htm

Sofres. 2001b.http://www.sofres.com/etudes/pol/030102_europe_r.htm

Sofres. 2002. http://www.sofres.com/etudes/dossiers/presi2002/

Soysal, Y. 1996. "Changing Citizenship in Europe: Remarks on Post-national Membership and the National State." In *Citizenship, Nationality and Migration in Europe*, ed. D. Cesarani and M. Fulbrook. London: Routledge.

Spohn, W. 2000. "Die Osterweiterung der Europaischen union und die Bedeutung Kollektiver Identitaten. Ein Vergleich west-und ostereuropaischer Staaten." *Berliner Journal fur Soziologie* 10, 2: 219–40.

Springer, B. 1995. *The European Union and Its Citizens: The Social Agenda*. Westport, Conn.: Greenwood Press.

——— 1992. *The Social Dimension of 1992*. New York: Greenwood Press.

Steinmo, S., K. Thelen, and F. Longstreth, eds. 1992. *Structuring Politics: Historical Institutionalism in Comparative Analysis*. New York: Cambridge University Press.

Stroobants, J. P. 2002. "Le système d'écoutes Echelon fâche la Belgique: La Grande Bretagne est accusée d'espionner ses partenaires européens." *Le Monde* (28 February): 6.

Sullivan, T. J. 1992. *Applied Sociology: Research and Critical Thinking*. New York: Macmillan.

Tajfel, H. 1981. *Human Groups and Social Categories*. Cambridge: Cambridge University Press.

Tamir, Y. 1993 *Liberal Nationalism*. Princeton, N.J.: Princeton University Press.

Tertsch, H. 2002. "La actitud beligerante de EE UU despierta el recelo de sus aliados." *El País* (17 February): 5.

Thatcher, M. 2002. *Statecraft: Strategies for a Changing World*. London: Routledge.

The Economist. 1993. "Raise Your Eyes, There Is a Land Beyond." 25 September–1 October 1993: 27, cited in Marcussen et al. 1999: 627.

———. 1993. "Constructing Europe? The Evolution of French, British and German Nation State Identities." *Journal of European Public Policy* 6, 4 (Special Issue): 614–33.

The New Statement and Society. 1989. "Tales of Thatcher." (8April): 8–11.

The Newcastle Journal. 2002. June 17, 4. Cited in European Union Representation in the UK. 2001. *Press Watch*. http://www.cec.org.uk/press/pw/latest.htm (retrieved on July 6, 2002).

The Times, 1971. "Towards a European Britain." (editorial) (8 July 8): p. 6.

The Times. 1971. "Text of Mr. Heath's Broadcast on EEC Entry." July 9, p. 5. Quoted in Manzo, Kathryn A. 1996. *Creating Boundaries: The Politics of Race and Nation*. Boulder, Colo.: Lynne Rienner Publishers, pp. 133 and 141.

Treaty on European Union. 1992. Title XII, art. 151. Luxembourg: European Commission.

Trade Union Congress. 2002. "John Mout Comments on the Prime Minister Speech." http://www.tuc.com (retrieved on May 2, 2002).

Tranholm-Mikkelsen, J. 1991. "Neo-functionalism: Obstinate or Obsolete? A Reappraisal in the Light of the New Dynamism of the EC." *Millennium: Journal of International Studies* 20 (Spring): 1–22.

Tremonti, G. 2002. "Le choix et les pièges." *Le Monde* (28 February).

Tsatsas, M. 2002. "Join the Club." *The World Today* (April): 19–20.

Turner, B. S. 1994. "Postmodern Culture/Modern Citizens." In *The Condition of Citizenship*, ed. B. van Steenbergen, 153–68. London: Sage.

Turner, J. C. 1981. "Towards a Cognitive Redefinition of the Social Group." *Cahiers de Psychologie Cognitive* 1: 93–118.

Vázquez Barbero, A., and M. Hebbert. 1985. "Spain Economy in Transition." In *Uneven Development in Southern Europe: Studies in Accumulation, Class, Migration and the State*, ed. R. Hudson and J. Lewis. London: Methuen.

Villa Faber Group on the Future of the EU. 2001. *Thinking Enlarged: The Accession Countries and the Future of the European Union a Strategy for Reform*. Published by Bertelsmann Foundation and Center for Applied Policy Research.

Wagstyl, S. 2002. "EU Entry Deal Secures Poland's Date with Destiny." *Financial Times* (14–15 December): 2.

Weber, E. 1976. *Peasants into Frenchmen: The Modernization of Rural France, 1870–1914*. Stanford, Calif.: Stanford University Press.

Williams, R. 1981. *Culture*. London: Fontana.

Williamson, B. 1990. *The Temper of the Times: British Society since World War II*. Oxford, U.K.: Basil Blackwell.

——— 1988. "Memories, Vision and Hope: Themes in an Historical Sociology of Britain since the Second World War." *Journal of Historical Sociology* 1, 2 (June): 161–83.

Wimmer R. D., and J. R. Dominick. 2000. *Mass Media Research*. Belmont, Calif.: Wadsworth Publishing Company.

Yárnoz, C. 2002. "Josep Piqué admite que las presiones de EEUU bloquearon su plan de paz para Oriente Próximo." *El País Digital*, February 20. http://www.elpais (retrieved on February 20, 2002).

Zavalloni, M., and C. Louis-Guerrin. 1984. *Identité sociale et conscience*. Toulouse: Privat and Montréal: Presses Universitaires de Montréal.

Zecchini, L. 2002a. "M. Jospin: S'attaquer ensemble aux problèmes de fond." *Le Monde* (12 February): 4.

———. 2002b. "Les quinze manifestent leur irritation face á l'unilateralisme des États Unis." *Le Monde* (18 February): 4.

Zolner, M. 1999. "National Images in French Discourse on Europe." Paper presented at the *ECSA Sixth Biennial International Conference*, Pittsburgh (2–5 June).

INDEX

About the Author

ANTONIO MENÉNDEZ-ALARCÓN is Chair of the Department of Sociology and Director of the International Studies Program at Butler University, where he teaches courses on the European Union, Globalization, Culture, Ethnic Relations, and Social Movements. He received his Ph.D. from the University of Notre Dame, Indiana. He has published several books and articles including *Power and Television in Latin America* (Praeger, 1992), which received the *Choice Magazine* 1994 outstanding academic book award.